P A R A C H U T I N G :
UNITED WE FALL

Flight
for the Joy
of Flying

RWunderground Publishing Co.
1656 Beechwood Avenue
Fullerton, Calif. 92635

ISBN 0-930438-02-7
Library of Congress Catalog Card Number: 77-84030

This book is dedicated to uniting relative work parachutists for the promotion of sport parachuting, with thanks to the many contributors who have shared their freefall joy with others through us.

"Relative Work": (from the French 'relatif'): *adj.* relative, relating; *n.* an art practiced by freefall parachutists performed with perfect body and mind control; the movement of the body in the air so that two or more relative workers may fly into various maneuvers such as "star", "snowflake", "wedge" or "bomb-burst funnel", *syn.* the practice of precision group skydiving, i.e. Skydancing and other mind-expanding flight activities.

INTRODUCTION

Parachuting shares much with ballet, bullfighting, motorcycle racing and mountain climbing. Each of these sports has as a common element mind's-eye perceptions of "perfect" motion.

Poetry-in-movement in each of these sports is performed and appreciated as art is, with the art form being movement perfectly orchestrated to the music of the participant's environment.

In parachuting, perfect freefall flight is the cognitive goal of relative workers. Perfect freefall flight, i.e. "skydancing" with the wind as performed by practitioners who enjoy the sport, is appreciated by all viewers. It is performed more perfectly by those who understand that the paths of fun and beauty lead to success and fulfillment.

Though a Western sport, the art of freefall relative work has a subtle Eastern character. This is the mystical element of linked mind and body movement, i.e. by mastering the mind, one's bodily movements are mastered. A skydance has a rhythm which you mesh to as you dance with the wind. You can easily fly anything you can imagine . . . imagining your flight to be perfect and then following your imagination with your body gives pleasant results. The perfect speed of flight is being there.

You already have the requisite skill for accomplished artful freefall flight if you can appreciate the beauty of skydivers flying together in bright rainbows of flightsuits in a landscape of clouds on a canvas of blue sky. Take this appreciation and paint your own fanciful sky capers.

The purpose of this book is to communicate to you the paths others who share your love for the sky have taken in their search for the secrets of relative work. It has been our primary concern in compiling this book to help you establish habits of mind through which thought impulses can be turned into fulfilling flight experiences.

The only laws of good skydiving are the laws of clear thought. At every stage of development freefallers look into themselves to discover their capacities and with what powers they may fly to make themselves successful and happy.

At its profoundest level, relative work transcends its own teachings and practices, yet at the same time there is no skydiving apart from these practices. The best way to communicate this doctrine, it seemed to us, was to compile a book of authentic doctrines and freefall flight methods from the mouths of the masters themselves -- other relative workers.

Additionally, we selected writings which would provide a fair view of the progress of freefall relative work. Share with us the wonderful store of recorded discoveries, experiences and reflections which parachuting has spawned.

We begin with articles on the technique of skydiving. The first chapter concentrates on the mechanics of freefall flight. Later on, Chapter Seven looks into the philosophy of relative work. Important elements of continuous good skydives are revealed by participants.

Everyone loves good jump stories. All of Chapter Eight concentrates on those special parachuting adventures we like to share and reshare. The middle chapters, Chapters Two through Four, cover competition, gear for relative work, and relative work with open canopies.

Interesting bits and pieces of information are tucked away into Chapter Five. Everything that doesn't easily classify fits here; it is an enjoyable potpourri.

The history of our progress in freefall is recorded in Chapter Six. Here we look back and see that "the way it was" has lessons to teach us so that we may continue to grow.

The last chapter, number Nine, wraps up with musings on sequential relative work, the skydance philosophy, ideas, wisdom and freefall dreams.

The book's original illustrations reflect the contents. On the cover, the little-freefaller stamp metamorphoses into skydivers, just as the skydives painstakingly stamped out on these pages turn into fun in the air. The illustrations mirror these images. Plaudits to non-skydivers designer Jim Bright and illustrator Hugh Dunnahoe for being able to see it through our eyes.

This book owes much to its contributors. Each author shares a special piece of knowledge so that we may all learn more quickly. By sharing, each author has provided sparks of creativity which encourage our sport's healthy growth.

We intended this book — this communication — to fan those sparks, building wildfires in our imaginations and giving reality to the flashes of thought that spill from our psyche and take shape in freefall.

Pure joy in flight — flying our fantasies to perfection — this is our collective freefall experience which we hope to communicate to you. Pass it on.

A few years back we communicated with fellow relative workers with the *RWunderground* newsletter — sharing ideas, news and information. When we quit printing, we promised to collect "the best" of the newsletter, add the best of the latest RW communications, and make them easily, widely and permanently available to others.

Friends we have jumped with, competed against, and partied with through the past few exciting years have shared their articles, poems, stories, etc. with us. Some of them have appeared in other parachuting magazines, and their editors are hereby invited to use this material as it is presented.

So this is our collective story. It is a story about skydiving, both past and present, by skydivers who love the sky. It is a collection of communications by those who fall united in the spirit of spreading the magic of freefall farther. Everything here provides food for thought on *your* flights of imagination into the bright blue skies we all claim as home.

Fly clean,
   land soft,
      love hard,
         give beautiful memories,

Pat & Jan Works

CONTENTS

Chapter 1   TECHNIQUE: The Boogie Mechanic's
Handbook   1

Part I: Sequential Input   2
Part II: Quality Skydives Versus Quantity of
Skydivers — Big Dives from Small Airplanes   36
Part III: Your Relative Work Technique —
Hints for Neophytes   60
Part IV: Exits — Better Exits for Better Skydives   89

Chapter 2   RW GEAR   97

Chapter 3   CANOPY RW   115

Chapter 4   COMPETITION   135

Chapter 5   SPECIALTIES   175

Chapter 6   TRADITION...LOOKING BACK   189

Chapter 7   HEAD TRIPS   227

Chapter 8   JUMP STORIES   269

Chapter 9   SEQUENTIAL   309

Part I: Musings on Sequential —
The Skydance Philosophy   309
Part II: What's What in Sequential —
Glossary of Ideas   317
Part III: Words of Wit and Wisdom on Skydancing —
Shared Sequential Dream Flakes   323
Part IV: Sequential History — Where We've Been   334

CONTRIBUTING AUTHORS

Bach, Richard .... .60, 230
Beckmann, Uwe .... .197
Bellak, Dave .... .175
Bishop, Dirty Billy ...... .290
Burrows, Greg .... .182
Chora .... .163
Cohen, Marc .... .84, 146
Cooper, Terry .... .247
Courbat, Tom .... .120, 122
Deluca, Rande .... .69, 316
DeRosa, Tony .... .364
Diamond, Neil .... .247
Farkle, Father .... .303
Farmer, Matt 3, 37, 274, 309, 365
Fulp, Estelena .... .150
Furlong, W.B. .... .254
Garrison, Skratch 1, 36, 61, 113, 135, 181, 183, 272, 329, 337, 347, 361
Godfrog, C.G. .... .108
Goethe .... .180
Gordon, R.W. .... .154
Gorman, Ken 2
Heaton, Norm .... .247
Hull, Roger .... .44, 81, 86, 97, 116, 230, 232, 260
Krueger, Al .... .95
Lao Tzu .... .164
Magee, John Gillespie .... .254
Mahler, Gustav .... .102
Morgan, Joe .... .192
Nelson, Carl .... .65, 89, 110, 112, 180
Nelson, Roger .... .64, 66, 67, 71, 111, 185, 186
Newell, Bill .... .202
Phillips, Tom .... .72, 144
Picciolo, Pete .... .222, 224
Poynter, Dan .... .125
Schultz, Michael .... .108
Shea, Kevin .... .74, 90, 124

Straightarrow, Charlie 132, 197, 273, 290
Taggart, Garth 190
Tolkien, J.R. 190
Tosi, Umberto 249
Tutko, Thomas A., Ph.D. . . .249
Unknown, Author 248
Vivekananda 181, 255
Wardean, Donna 269
Warsh, Weird Al 258
Weird, Capt. 158
Whitey 279
Works, Pat 60, 61, 80, 81, 90, 102, 104, 107, 112,
                                115, 136, 140, 143, 152, 164, 175,
                                185, 220, 223, 231, 244, 259, 269,
                                270, 271, 278, 280, 296, 313, 323, 328,
                                334
Works, Pat & Jan 35, 176, 209, 214, 227
Worth, B.J. 30, 189, 309,

I was blazing one day
in the energy of change
   When an agent from Chaos
   came swooping by
      "The answer," he mused, "is
      Boogie Mechanics."
      "The Skydance Approach to Boogie Mechanics.
      But what was the question?"
         And he was gone in the night.
         One day a long time ago.

Skratch Garrison

1

Technique

*The Boogie Mechanic's Handbook
–tips on using the Skydance Technique*

The Skydance approach to Boogie Mechanics means that
you view skydiving as a doorway into human experience.
And organizing dives means building Human Radios
trying to tune into that cosmic dance wavelength.
You create dive patterns by combining basic moves —
the swoop, the hop, the zoom, the lurk, the mesh, the weave…
to suit the situation purpose mood of the moment.
And you deal with wide ranges of experience by
varying the choice of moves from slot to slot.
Including students with nonessential slots.
Look at our dirt dives
with a whuffo's wide eyes.
And realize with finality
that a plan
is just a tangent vector on the manifold of reality.
How…?
You can't just say
"Let it be done."
You have to think
What it really is.
What it really is
is a state of mind
And the question now
is How…?
How do you create the consciousness for the Skydance dives?
Put your good where it will do the most?
Lead. Without leading?

–Skratch Garrison

PART I — Sequential Input — everything you wanted to know but were afraid to ask.

Steps to follow in learning sequential RW. While sequential maneuvers and large formations are unlimited in size and shape, they are related in the way they are put together. Here are some general steps and ideas that we have found helpful.

First, decide what maneuver to do. It helps to have a notebook with some ideas drawn out. Pick a maneuver that matches the ability of the people on the load.

The next step is to determine positions. There are usually three types of positions — basemen, middlemen, and floaters. The base must be built quickly and smoothly. If some of the more experienced people can be used to build a fast solid base, it will be easy for the middlemen to fly into position. While some flyer positions require the more experienced people, most positions need people who can fall slow.

Design an exit to best fit the jump. The sooner you can get everybody hooked up, the more maneuvers you can do on the way down. The exit should be as efficient as possible — as fast as possible. You can hang two and usually three people outside almost any airplane.

Gear up and walk through the jump on the ground from exit to breakoff at least two or three times. Make sure everybody knows exactly where to go and what to do. Practice an exit on the airplane before take-off. Make sure people can hang outside long enough to let the people just inside the door get stacked. With an efficient launch, the first six to eight people should leave the airplane in one lump.

It is handy to have a sketch of the maneuver that people can study during the climb to altitude.

Exit as fast and close as possible. The base must fall as fast as necessary to keep the maneuver from over-floating. Sometimes it is good to have the four or five base people wear fast-falling jumpsuits. As the maneuver builds, the people inside must absorb and dampen impact from bad approaches.

All docking should be done so that no momentum is transmitted into the formation. Occasionally a momentum approach is necessary to connect a section which is too wide to reach. During and after docking, do not add float to the maneuver. Fly with the base and tuck as necessary. Maneuvers fall slower as more people get on. Later approaches should be made from a slightly steeper angle. Anticipate how it will float and let it come up to you.

As soon as practical after landing, regroup and walk through the jump as it happened. Analyze and correct any mistakes.

Ken Gorman, Spotter, May-June 1975

Some mental attitudes and ideas helpful in sequential. Good sequential relative work requires the individual flyers involved to look at their roles a little differently than in round-star relative work. Basic to sequential relative work is the Zero Momentum entry. Don't use the formation to absorb any of your approach momentum. Fly into position and take that little extra time to "finger-tip it." Burning the man in front of you is meaningless in sequential relative work. Sequences build in order; if you burn the man in front of you, you probably won't have a slot when you get there.

Flyers must work as a group. The bases of most complete sequences take long enough to build that everyone is there by the time it is ready. Show discipline—set up in an orderly pattern around the base. Don't get tunnel vision—look around at the other flyers, watch the formation building as a whole, not just your slot. Try to mesh your approach with the flow of the dive. Try not to cut in front of other people to improve your position or make your approach easier. Work as a group—leave your personal ego trip on the ground.

Formations have been known to slide and float, especially when they're in trouble, so don't set up too close—cut yourself a little slack—but be there on time when your slot appears. There are no rules to sequential relative work. Do it with any number you like, out of any aircraft; use any technique you want to build anything you like. We are free to relate to each other in any way we choose.

General information on sequential relative work. Sequential Relative Work requires skills and techniques not used in star work. It also requires a basic understanding of certain formations and maneuvers and how they relate to each other. Like all relative work, sequential dives start with a hook-up. There are five possible hook-ups:

OPPOSED

COMPRESSED ACCORDIONS

CATS

SIDE-BODY

STAIRSTEPS

The bases for various sequential formations are built from these. Here are some possible base units using these hook-ups:

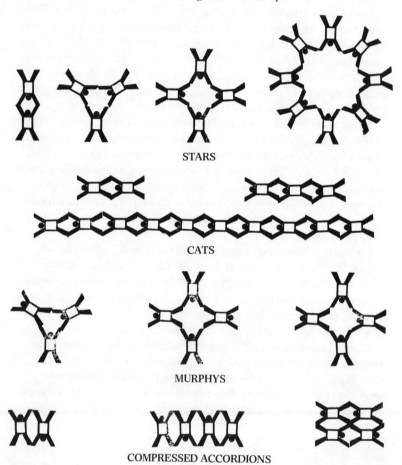

STARS

CATS

MURPHYS

COMPRESSED ACCORDIONS

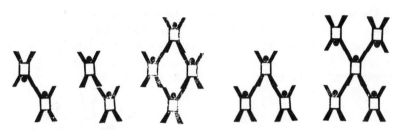

STAIRSTEPS/DIAMONDS/WEDGES

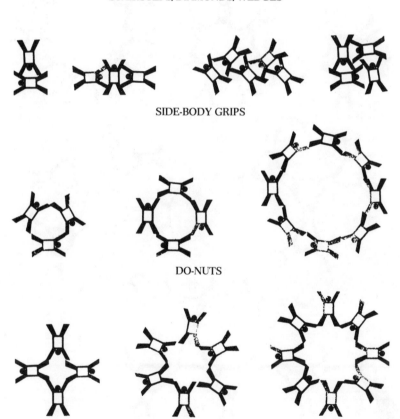

SIDE-BODY GRIPS

DO-NUTS

IN-OUTS

These base units, or combinations of them, make up all sequential dives. The ability to perform fast, stable, reliable bases is, of course, the first prerequisite to becoming a viable sequential group. A group beginning sequential relative work will usually build its first formations by repeating the same base unit in some logical pattern. Examples are:

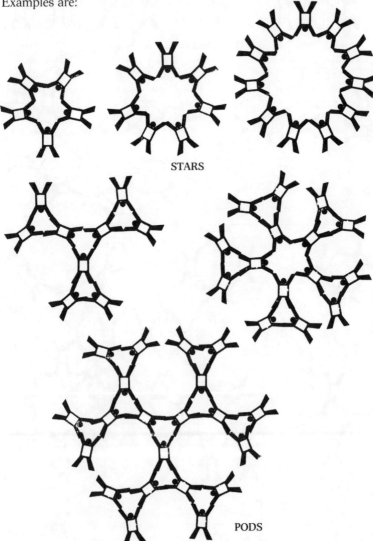

STARS

PODS

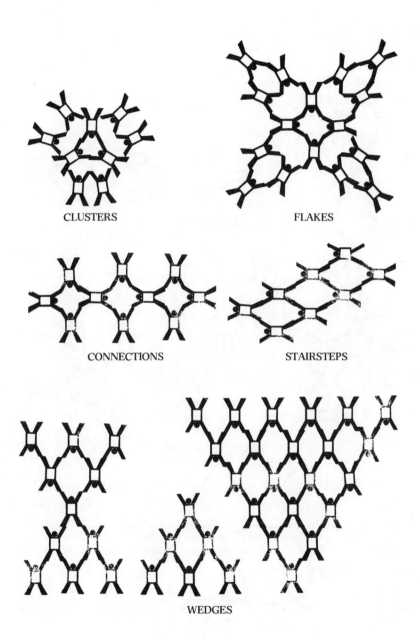

CLUSTERS

FLAKES

CONNECTIONS

STAIRSTEPS

WEDGES

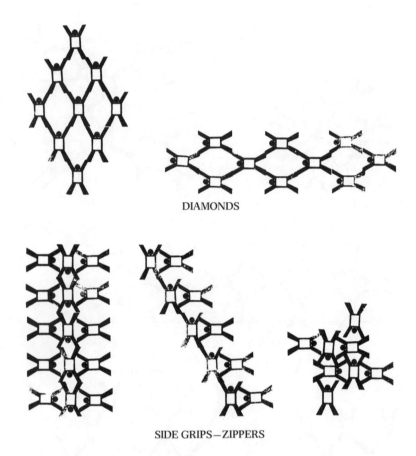

DIAMONDS

SIDE GRIPS—ZIPPERS

This type of formation can be made as large or small as desired. These are static formations, and require techniques and organization similar to stars. Once learned, they can serve as the base formations for the group's first dives that sequence. Such dives sequence by simple grip changes or partial break and secondary approaches. Here are some examples:

TRI-PODS TO 9—CLUSTER WITH A 3—WEDGE TRACK AWAY:

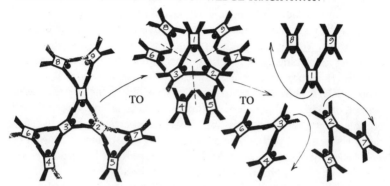

TRIPLE DIAMONDS TO A 10-WEDGE:

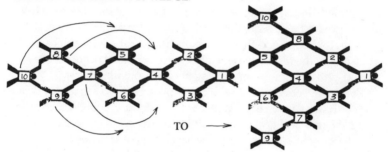

16-CLUSTER-FLAKE TO QUADRA-DIAMONDS:

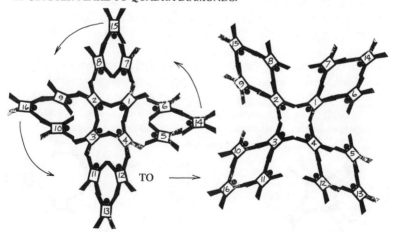

As a group moves from building static geometric formations to sequential routines, they must learn new skills and techniques. This can be a difficult time for experienced relative workers. Sophisticated sequences can easily turn to chaos. Sequences must progress smoothly with everyone doing his part or they cannot build at all. Formations are not always symmetrical while building, as stars are, and will spin more easily. It is frustrating to spend a whole dive watching the base funnel, or being in that spinning, funneling base, or not being able to complete a routine after many tries. But remember, learning to fly has never been easy. If you've been having an easy time flying, you haven't been learning. Sequential demands total group effort. The group must function as a unit within the framework of the sequence.

A group that is serious about learning sequential relative work must be able to build base units fast enough and reliably enough to make them viable initial maneuvers or bases for larger formations. They must acquire basic sequential techniques such as: grip changes, folding, fold-outs, odd-flying positions in formations, stability in transitions, the ability to remember a pre-arranged sequence, key breaks and transitions, and flying hooked-up with others.

Four-man sequences. As the group progresses to sequences that require bases such as bi-poles, accordions, donuts, or in-outs, and use complex keys and grip changes, it becomes necessary to work in smaller groups. It is not profitable for eight people to hang around for 40 seconds while four people fail to build a stable donut, or for sixteen people to fail over and over again to build a formation because of mental errors during changes or mis-communication in the keys. Working in groups of four is the most effective way to acquire the skills necessary for larger, more complex sequences.

The best way to use the advantages of small group relative work to learn sequential skills is to string together a fast-moving series of four-man bases. This way the group not only experiences building and flying each of the bases, but also learns transition skills, keys, timing, smoothness, and awareness of flying hooked-up with others.

The bases most used in complex sequences are

donuts (Fig. 1)

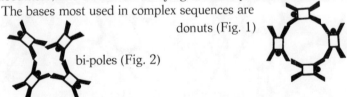

bi-poles (Fig. 2)

compressed accordions (Fig. 3),

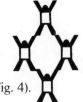

and diamonds (Fig. 4).

There are relationships between these bases that make a
fast-moving sequence possible. The series may be varied to emphasize
certain bases or grip changes or positions or transitions. It can be made
to repeat or change from base to base. Here are some possible series:

1. Full Sequence—

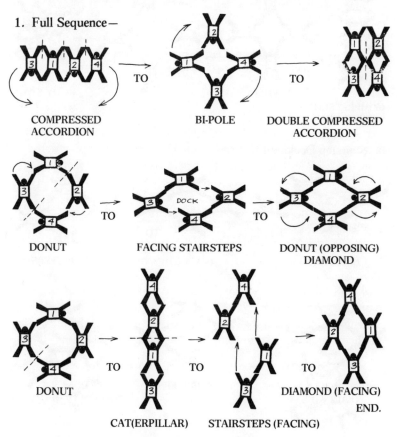

11

2. Bi-Pole Compressed Accordion Series:

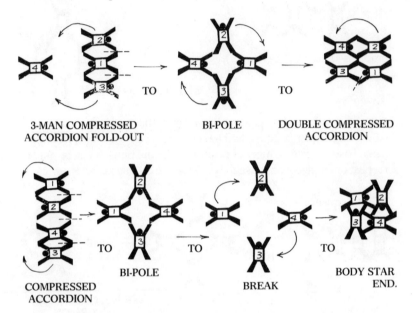

3-MAN COMPRESSED ACCORDION FOLD-OUT   **BI-POLE**   **DOUBLE COMPRESSED ACCORDION**

COMPRESSED ACCORDION   **BI-POLE**   **BREAK**   **BODY STAR END.**

3. Stairstep Docking Practice:

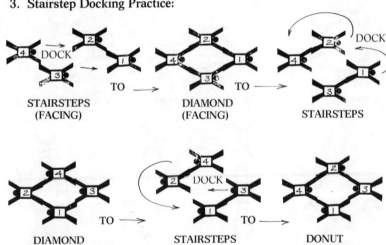

STAIRSTEPS (FACING)   **DIAMOND (FACING)**   **STAIRSTEPS**

DIAMOND (FACING)   **STAIRSTEPS**   **DONUT (OPPOSED) DIAMOND**

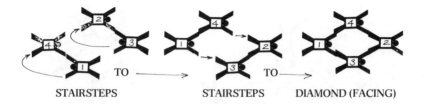

STAIRSTEPS STAIRSTEPS DIAMOND (FACING)

The particular order and parts of a four-man sequence are determined by what bases and skills the group needs to practice for more sophisticated routines. The four-man sequence is not an end, it is a means. Learn the relationships between the bases, know the transitions and make up your own sequence tailored to the needs of your group.

Repetitive four-man sequences are not a necessary prerequisite to every larger routine, but they are an excellent way for a group to quickly learn new skills and techniques. Here are some examples of larger sequences and four-man series that relate to the skills necessary to achieve them. Look at the transitions and watch the way various stages of the sequences relate. (Detailed explanation separate)

1. Dare To Be Great: (10-man)

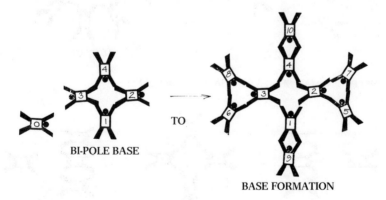

BI-POLE BASE

TO

BASE FORMATION

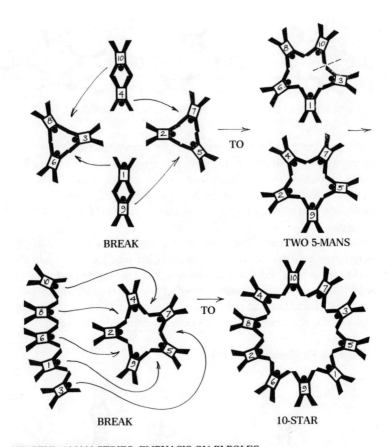

BREAK

TO

TWO 5-MANS

BREAK

TO

10-STAR

HELPFUL 4-MAN SERIES, EMPHASIS ON BI-POLES:

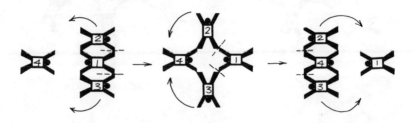

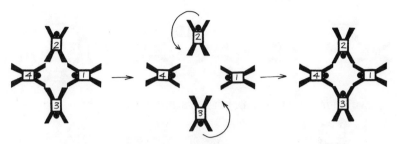

2. Donut Flake To Double Bi-Poles (8-man):

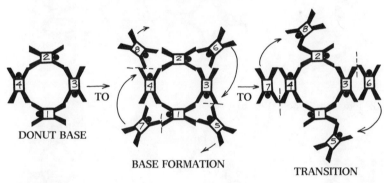

DONUT BASE   BASE FORMATION   TRANSITION

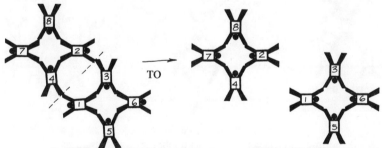

CONNECTED BI-POLES   DOUBLE BI-POLES

4-MAN SERIES, EMPHASIS ON DONUT, KEYED BREAKS:

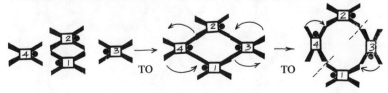

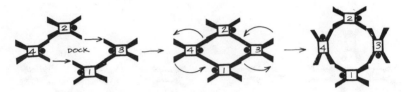

4-MAN SERIES, EMPHASIS ON FOLD-UPS, BI-POLE, KEYS.

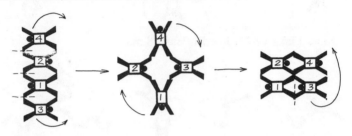

3. Diamond Dock (9-man):

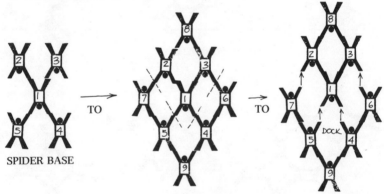

SPIDER BASE   BASE FORMATION   SPLIT & REDOCK

4-MAN SERIES, EMPHASIS ON DOCKING PIECES AND DIAMONDS:

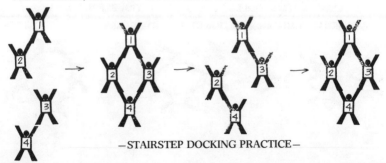

—STAIRSTEP DOCKING PRACTICE—

4. Triple Diamonds To Double Diamond Dock (10-man):

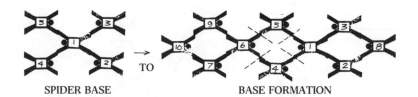

SPIDER BASE → TO → BASE FORMATION

TO → BREAK

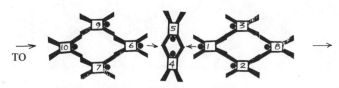

TO → DOCKING DIAMONDS

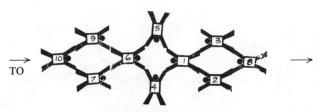

TO → COMPLETE FORMATION

4-MAN SERIES—STAIRSTEP DOCKING PRACTICE

Here are some more sequences—watch the progression of four-man skills as they build.

5. Quadra-Bi-Poles (12-man):

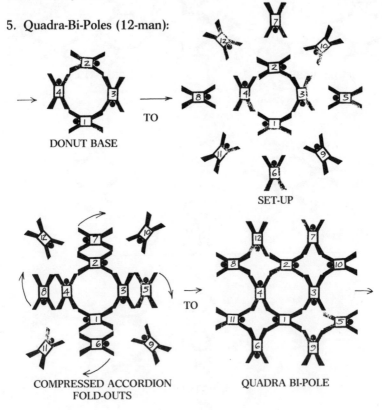

DONUT BASE

TO

SET-UP

COMPRESSED ACCORDION
FOLD-OUTS

QUADRA BI-POLE

6. The Jewel (16-man):

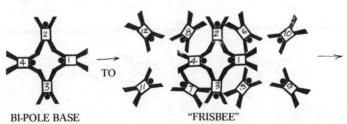

BI-POLE BASE

TO

"FRISBEE"

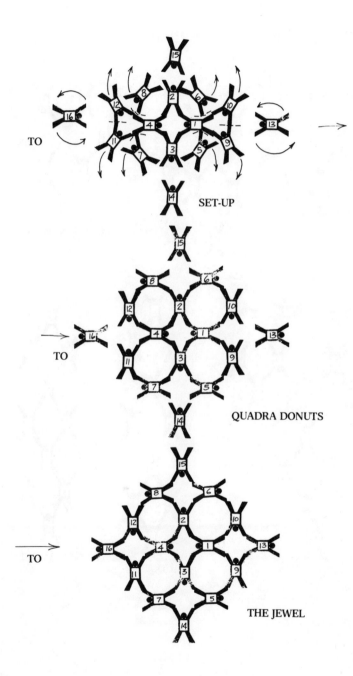

TO

SET-UP

TO

QUADRA DONUTS

TO

THE JEWEL

7. 10-Wedge To Triple Diamonds (10-man):

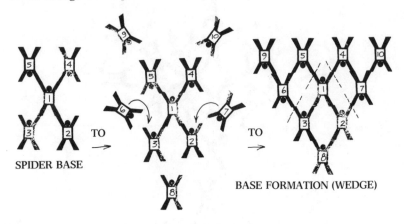

SPIDER BASE   TO   TO   BASE FORMATION (WEDGE)

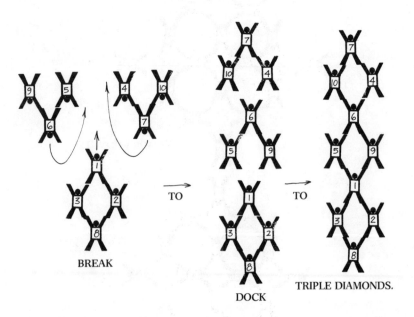

BREAK   TO   DOCK   TO   TRIPLE DIAMONDS.

8. In-Out (8-man):

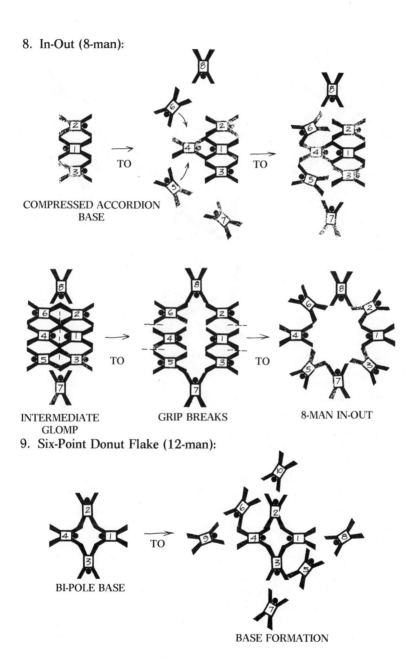

COMPRESSED ACCORDION
BASE

INTERMEDIATE
GLOMP

GRIP BREAKS

8-MAN IN-OUT

9. Six-Point Donut Flake (12-man):

BI-POLE BASE

BASE FORMATION

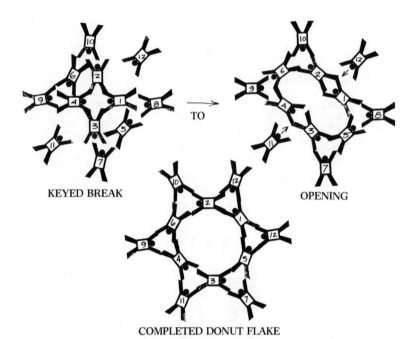

KEYED BREAK   TO   **OPENING**

COMPLETED DONUT FLAKE

These are not just possible arrangements of stick-men, they are representations of sequential routines that have already been completed. They are drawn here to show how basic sequential techniques can be used to accomplish sophisticated routines. Study these sequences to gain an understanding of how the dive builds from the base, and what changes and relationships are used to move from stage to stage. Walking through routines, as a group, on the ground is the best way to learn the sequence. This cannot be over-emphasized; it lends to understanding of routines that seem confusing in pictures and words.

Keyed Breaks and Transitions An important part of sequential relative work is the coordination of formation changes and the timing of breaks and transitions. There are three major ways to key sequences: 1. SHAKES, 2. HEAD NODS, and 3. ACTION KEY (when you see something happen.)

Each has disadvantages. Shakes take time to pass through a formation. They can be mistaken for someone repositioning a grip or a rough entry. Nods work only when people can face each other and work best with the fewest people at the shortest distance. Action Keys have a built-in perception-reaction time lag and cannot be used to key changes that must happen in different places at the same time.

All keys require *awareness.* Everyone must fully understand the sequence, be aware of when changes should happen, and know where to direct his attention.

Deciding how to key the sequence is a large part of the organizer's job. Ask yourself what is trying to be communicated? (i.e., I'm in, the formation is complete, change grips, foldout, break, etc.) Who has the information? Who needs to know it? By what means (shakes, nods, action) can it be sent? Again, walking through a sequence on the ground will make it easier to see the keys necessary.

Look at some of the complete explanations of the four-man series and follow the keys through them. Look at the complete explanations of the larger docking dives and see how the breaks are keyed. Keep the keys to any sequence as simple as possible.

Explanations For The Illustrated Sequential Dives.

1. Dare To Be Great (10-man)
1, 2, 3 build a three-man compressed accordion:

4 flys into position in front of 1. 1 shakes 2 and 3, who fold out 90°
4 then closes the bi-pole. 5 and 6 pin the poles (people facing out):

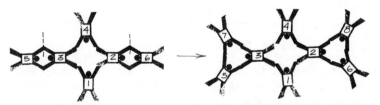

7 and 8 break on them to make three-man pods

9 and 10 enter on the legs of 1 and 4 to complete the base formation:

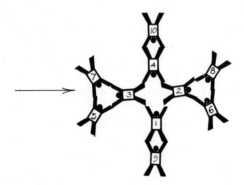

9 and 10 shake 1 and 4 as soon as they are in and see that the pods are built. 1 and 4 know the base formation is complete when they feel the shake. They look at each other and nod. If both are nodding, they shake 2 and 3 to let them know that the formation is breaking, then they release their grips. The formation breaks to two 3-man stars and two cats:

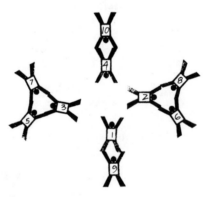

9 and 10 hold the cats momentarily as the formation breaks, then give a quick shake and release their grips. The point men (1 and 4) turn right, the tail men (9 and 10) turn left, and fly into the three-mans to make two five-man stars:

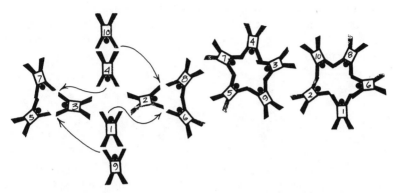

One of the five-mans has been pre-designated base. The other star breaks to a line facing the base, then breaks up and flies to the base to build a ten-star:

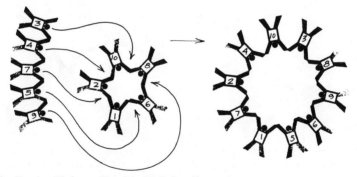

2. Donut Flake to Double Bi-Poles (8-man):

The donut base is built from a compressed accordion pin. 3 and 4 enter in front and back of the accordion to make a donut (opposed) diamond:

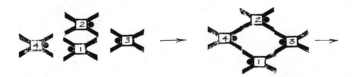

They turn the donut diamond into a donut by turning left as they place their right-hand man's hand on their right knee, then releasing the right hand grip and replacing their left hand grip with their right hand (donutize):

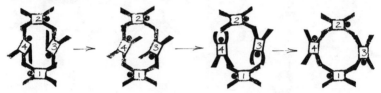

5 through 8 fly in and take a hand and a leg in each of the open donut slots. Donut—flake slots are assigned by designating who, in the donut, the flaker will be facing:

1 and 2 will control the key to the transition. When the flakers on the legs of 1 and 2 come in (5 and 8) they (5 and 8) give 1 and 2 a shake. As soon as they feel the shake and the flakes facing them are in, 1 and 2 look across the center of the donut at each other. When both are looking in, they nod, then 2 shakes 3 and 1 shakes 4. 3 and 4 nod to their flakes, who release their right grip. 1 and 2 nod to their flakes as soon as they have shaken 3 and 4. Their flakes release their right grips and fold left to make compressed accordions with 3 and 4. When 3 and 4 have caught the folders' legs, they give a shake and the folders continue their rotation to fold out 90°:

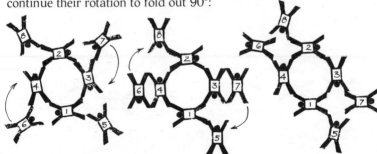

5 and 8 then swing and pick up the grips to complete the transition to the double bipole:

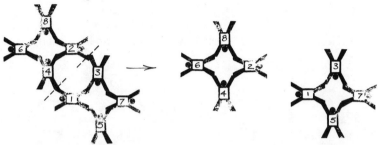

5 and 8 shake 1 and 2 when the transition is complete. 1 and 2 look inside at each other, nod, and release their grips. The formation breaks to two bipoles

3. Diamond Dock (9-man):

A spider base is built by 1 through 5. 6 and 7 do side approaches to fill the slots between 2 and 4, and 3 and 5. 4 and 5 catch the legs of the respective man as he comes into the slot. 8 and 9 close the ends to form the diamond:

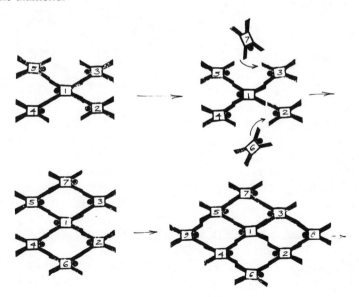

To back the four-man diamond out — 8 shakes 2 and 3, who relay it to 1, so he will know that the diamond is complete. 1 then nods to 4 and 5, who shake 6 and 7. 6 and 7 release their grips as soon as they feel the shake. 1 waits momentarily so 6 and 7 will have time to react, then releases his grips and the four-man diamond backs out of the Vee:

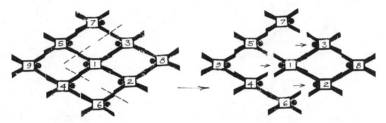

Air turbulence between the Vee and the four-man diamond pushes the diamond out — there is no need to shove off. Stop the diamond at about 20 feet out and re-dock it with the Vee to reform the nine-diamond. (When the four-diamond has first backed out, 4 and 5 can grab a grip to help stabilize the Vee and keep it from separating laterally):

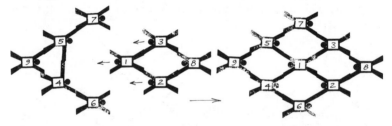

When the routine is working well, try doing a 360°turn with the four-diamond before re-docking, or build the 9-diamond with everyone facing the same way, then fly the 4-diamond out the front, do a 180° turn, and redock (note, when flying the small diamond, etc. the members should fly *with* each other, but do not counteract the movements of the others; flying it just as you would if you were by yourself.)

4. Triple Diamonds To a Double-Diamond Dock (10-man):

1 through 5 build a spider base. 6 fills the slot between 4 and 5. 7 and 8 take diamond wing slots on 6. 9 closes the back slot on 2 and 3.

10 closes the front between 7 and 8 to build the triple diamonds. 6 and 1 will control the break:

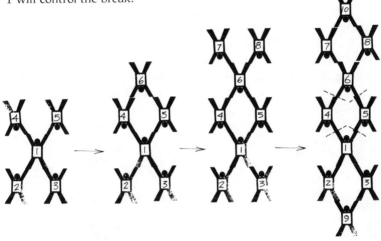

9 and 10 shake the formation-complete signal up to 1 and 6. 1 and 6 nod at each other and release their grips. The formation breaks to two four-man (facing) diamonds with 4 and 5 between them. 4 and 5 turn toward each other and hook up for a two-man base. The two diamonds dock on the base to complete the series:

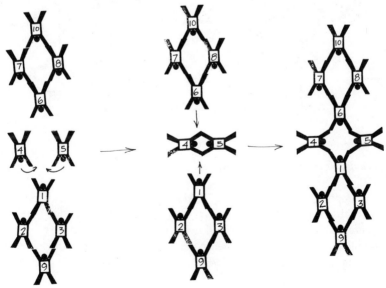

5. Quadra BiPoles

Donut base is built from a donut (opposed) diamond by 1 thru 4. 5 through 8 make compressed accordions with pre-assigned people in the donut. 9 thru 12 set up on pre-designated flake slots. As 1 through 4 see the flakes come into position, they shake each of the people holding compressed accordions who release their grips and fold out 90°. 9 through 12 enter as they fold into position to complete the formation:

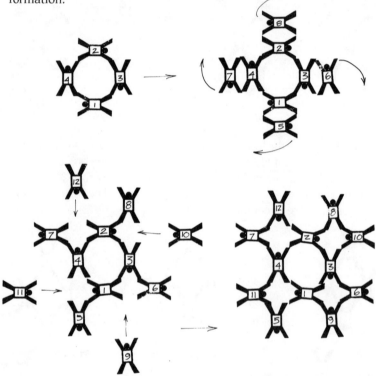

–*Matt Farmer, Spotter, May-June 1975*

Tempting our Imaginations: Making the Dives. For those divers with little experience in sequential relative work, and who are interested in pursuing it, the following has been designed as a familiarization of different methods which have been used to accomplish these and other skydives. A lot of what is printed here may easily be outdated by the time it is read, so a combination of these described methods, plus practice and more imagination will be necessary to establish a good base to work from.

The practice of putting the turkeys in the front of the load and the hot shots all going last will not work!

Being able to give and receive constructive criticism is an absolute necessity. As the ego is trimmed down, flying abilities improve respectively.

Keeping relaxed in freefall is a must. Not too loose, of course, just be relaxed.

The true secret of success if to fly to the place in the sky where your designated slot is and dock accordingly. Anyone can do this. It just takes the self-confidence, and not over-confidence, to believe you can do whatever you want to in freefall.

Grip switching and other intermediate steps which are often used to build the desired formations put undue stress and tension on the formation, causing it to warp and distort or even crumble.

Working with a group of four divers who all fall at the same relative speed produces the greatest learning process with the least hassles. A jump altitude of 10 grand or so is more than worth the added expense. Much more can be accomplished once everyone is working together. A 60-second delay is worth the experience learned in three 30-second delays, with the convenience of only one pack job.

As far as specific dives go, the following 4-Man formations are the building blocks for a majority of other formations including the dives for the World Cup sequences: the star, diamond, stairstep, donut, bipole, caterpillar and compressed accordion. In building these formations, each diver should fly to his designated position and stop. When all four divers have done this, the formation will be complete. If two divers are supposed to be flying at 90° to each other in the completed formation, they should dock at 90° to each other, such as in the star, stairstep, diamond, donut, and bipole.

If the first two divers into position are supposed to fly in line or parallel with each other, they should stop in that relative position and fly no-contact with each other, as the two remaining divers dock into their appropriate positions. This process of building formations proves to be the cleanest and quickest method, and can be used to build formations of any size or complexity. Of course this takes right-on approaches and fingertip docks or all chaos will break out.

Being able to fly formations with no-contact will help clean up body control considerably.

Some little tips on grips can help the success of these skydives, such as picking up a leg grip directly at the knee to give the gripped diver complete freedom of his leg movements. Also, outside knee grips should be used when gripping right hand to right knee or left hand to left knee. This grip is used when building donuts, bipoles, caterpillars and compressed accordions. Inside knee grips should be used when gripping right hand to left knee or left hand to right knee. This grip is used building facing stairsteps, wedges, diamonds, etc. An easy rule of thumb to remember this by is to always have "thumbs up" on all grips.

When building opposed stairsteps, wedges, and diamonds, etc. the arm grips should be inside elbow to inside elbow, as opposed to gripping at wrists or catching only one grip. Symmetrical grips by everyone at every grip point greatly improves the stability and flying characteristics of all formations.

It is often difficult to build bipoles by flying backwards directly to where your slot will be, but with practice it can be accomplished. An intermediate step which may be used with good results is to build a hook-up and then have the other divers take turns flying into their slots backwards in a pre-determined order. The secret here is to have good catchers in the hook-up, as it is much easier to turn around as you come into a slot, than it is for two catchers to simultaneously release the wrist grip and take a knee grip in one fluid move.

A good exercise in flying backwards may be practiced by building a bi-pole in the above-mentioned manner, and then to make a total break and switch positions to build a second bi-pole. Now, the original catchers fly backwards and the other two catch them. This can be continued until break-off. This is another very good exercise for cleaning up body control. Larger in-outs can be readily built by both these methods also.

Building and flying donuts is difficult. A common problem is that the donut will spin in the direction the divers are facing. One solution is to hold the outside arms out to the side at about 45° and slightly in front and above the shoulder to prevent the spin. A common cause for spinning donuts is poor grips and practice is the easiest way to solve this problem. The ideal way to build a donut, as previously mentioned, is to fly to your slot and dock on the designated knee with an outside grip. The last diver flying into position closes the donut.

When flying in and donutizing into an existing donut, the outside divers make caterpillar grips on a diver in the donut. The diver behind that person in the donut can then use a grip switch to enlarge the donut. When flaking a donut, remember to grip the leg before the arm if both cannot be reached at once, or it is apt to spin in the direction the divers are facing.

One of the most enjoyable forms of relative work is flying with a group of two or more divers gripped together and docking with other flying groups to form a single new formation ("flying pieces"). Only imagination will limit the size and number of these groups flying together. When two or more groups do relative work with each other, the same basic theories of individual flying hold true.

However, some special considerations must be taken into account. With two divers gripped together, there is twice the mass as compared to one diver falling alone. Along with this, the inertia is also doubled, so it takes twice the energy to start the two accelerating, and twice the braking power to stop this movement.

If both divers have complete freedom of movement, they can control their flying with the same methods and efforts they usually use flying individually. However, if either of the divers has restricted freedom of movement due to the grip or grips between them, then an exaggerated use of their remaining flying controls will be necessary. This does not pose much of a problem with two divers, but it will become much more evident the larger the flying groups become.

What about brakes? Once a large group is moving through the sky, it will have more momentum than an individual alone, and it will take more effort to slow it down. If, for example, a 4-man diamond needs to slow down, the lead person will not be able to use legs to help. The wing people will have marginal use of theirs, so it is up to the tail to do an exaggerated knee-drop, using the knees like flaps on an airplane or the tail feathers of a bird, causing the diamond to slow down. The wings on a 3-man wedge are able to use this same method to slow down, but they must brake simultaneously to avoid turning the wedge.

Correct and symmetrical grips are necessary to achieve maximum flying coordination. Also, symmetrical body sizes should be used as much as possible when two people are flying parallel to each other in a group. The less tension between the divers within a flying group, the easier it will be to fly together. Each diver should do his or her part to fly with the group, so there should not be anyone being dragged along for the ride. Don't over-fly your partner either.

A clean and symmetrical break is highly advantageous when splitting up a formation to form two smaller ones. First be sure that the original formation is complete before breaking it. Total eye contact with head nods and mouthing the "break" command works well.

A system of shakes to the divers with the controlling grips from the divers monitoring the completion of the formation is a good method when eye contact is not possible. This will take some concentrated ground practice to achieve good timing and symmetry with all the breaks. It is most important that the system used works accurately. Flying groups together is quite similar to flying individuals together. Each group flies to its designated slot and docks. As with individuals, it is important that the groups are able to fall at the same relative speed. Eye contact between each group is extremely important prior to docking, especially if the groups have been rotating and have lost eye contact for several seconds with one another. All the groups should work toward the lowest one if one is lower, and then aim toward a central point between themselves and dock simultaneously.

Otherwise, if two groups dock together and a third is still approaching, the two docked groups may tend to fall slower and float above the approaching group.

When docking groups in stages, certain additional procedures should be kept in mind. For example, in round 2 of the 8-man World Cup event, four 2-man stairsteps must separate from the original double 4-man diamonds and exchange partners to form two new 4-man diamonds. Two wing people from the original diamonds now become points on the new diamonds. They should move their heading 90 degrees toward their new partners and line up with each other on the same level. They should try to keep minimal separation between them in order to easily dock the two diamonds after they have been built separately with docking stairsteps.

If, after sorting your way through all this, you still feel that it is all fine and good for those advanced skydivers at the big DZ's, but that it really doesn't apply to your circle of friends jumping out of a Cessna on your small drop zone, stop sniveling until you put a little effort into it. A small drop zone and a Cessna add up to one of the best learning atmospheres possible if the skydivers apply themselves. It is a common fallacy to think that the elite group you read about is the only group who is good enough to do something. It has been proven over

and over that once a group finally tries something, they find out how easy it can be. Remember that it is easy for a group to be the best at something when they are the only ones doing what they are best at. It's all in the imagination! Think about it and then go for it!
–B.J. Worth, 1976

Tips on Starting a Sequential Team.

Reasonably expect *disappointing jumps for 15-25* jumps together. It will take that long to "click" but when it comes, it'll be so simple you'll wonder why you couldn't do it before.

You must *change your thinking about flying.* Sequential techniques are so much different from speed star techniques that you have to un-learn some things and completely relearn the new techniques.

Don't dwell on the details of the attempted jump until you can do the airwork. In other words, don't worry about the exit first. Perfection must precede speed.

Clean is good. Try to fly clean, not fast. Another difference between sequential and speed stars is that in 10-man you classify fast as good; the final determining factor on which you are judged is how fast it was. But in sequential, it's how clean the for .ation was, or it won't be judged as complete. Work on clean fir   , then fast.

Keep a team log.

Learn to fly tight but stable formations. Do not rush formations. From the very first maneuver, particularly the first maneuver because it's subterminal, you have to let the formation settle completely before you transition. If there's a ripple developing and someone lets go to sequence to the next formation, that ripple could fling everyone 30 feet apart. Practice holding each formation at least two seconds and feeling when it's completely stable.

Fly to help each other get into the formations. Don't rush the formations; build them clean; make sure your individual entry is clean and doesn't turn the formation, if you're one of the first ones in. Everyone has to fly themselves to help each other out. This sometimes means you fly the formation over, down or up to whoever isn't in. (Tricky, but learnable.) In speed stars, you're concentrating on wrists. In good sequential you have to think about your entry as it relates to the other people. If this means you have to fly slower than you are capable of, so you get there at the same time as everyone else does, then you fly slower. The base person of a formation should fly to equal distances between the other jumpers. The third person there should wait until the fourth person arrives before contact is made.

Good communication is vital. Give definite shakes. Learn to know when everyone feels the formation is stable and it's time to sequence.

Practice no-contact RW. A quick no-contact four-man star is necessary for throwing a donut. You're all there, no-contact, the key person nods and everyone turns and grabs. You also practice no-contact if you're the third person to a formation and #4 isn't there yet. You fly in position and wait til #4 arrives; then both people grab on.

Practice flying over top of other people without losing air or funnelling onto them.

–Pat & Jan Works

PART II — Quality Skydives versus Quantity of Skydivers — Big dives from small airplanes.

The Skydance Resonance
Start with the theme of local and global
  of doing the basics while keeping track
  of position and timing and matching rates
  and altitude and all the rest

And then explore the known dive pattern
  some variations and things
  to see how they really are
  with people who can do them

Make explicit
  the ideas, principles, techniques, outlook
  of the skydance approach
  to Boogie Mechanics

And after Easter we'll take off into the unknown.
–Skratch Garrison, 1978

Four-Man Sequential...or How to Have Fun from a Cessna.
The majority of drop zones don't have Twin Beeches or other 10-place aircraft. Every weekend more people dangle from Cessna struts than bunch inside small-door Beeches.

Still, large stars and fast 10-mans have received such wide acclaim that people on small drop zones sometimes feel they can't do good relative work because they can't get ten or more people up at the same time.

It's a quantitative view of relative work — bigger, faster, better. Certainly big stars and fast stars require good relative work, but there is also a qualitative approach to skydiving which holds that the sophistication, diversity and execution of a dive are more important than how big or how fast it is.

Sophistication and diversity are where sequential routines come in. People limited to four players by their Cessna can enjoy nearly unlimited challenge by using ever more difficult and diverse sequences. A four-man sequence uses some of the same formations as four-man competition, but instead of always back-looping from a star to a formation, a sequence moves smoothly from one formation to the next.

Sometimes just by changing grips. Sometimes by breaking and reforming. Sometimes by breaking to pairs and redocking. The idea is to fill the freefall with as much flying as possible.

A group can design its own sequences to challenge the ability and experience of its members. A group of inexperienced flyers may start by using the whole freefall to build one formation. They can then use that formation as a base from which to sequence and add onto as they gain experience.

A group with more experience will try a more difficult base formation, longer sequences, and more complex transitions. Whatever your experience level, sequential offers a chance to learn, a chance to expand the limits of our experience. Diversity in our interactions, sophistication of flying techniques; this is the way we learn and grow.

Here are some four-man bases and some of the possible transitions used to connect them. Stick-man drawings are an awkward way to represent skydives, so try to think of the drawings as symbols of real freefall experiences. Mostly, try some of these things in the air; that's where they belong and they make more sense up there.

FOUR-MAN BASES

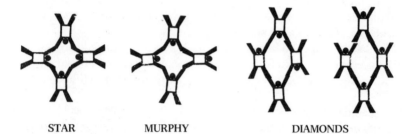

STAR   MURPHY   DIAMONDS

CAT   COMPRESSED ACCORDIONS

DONUT   BIPOLE   ZIPPER   BODY STAR

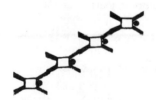

STAIRSTEPS   ACCORDION   SNOWFLAKE

The technique for building most of these bases is self-explanatory. Some, however, require relatively new techniques.

Bipoles and donuts stem from the compressed accordion pin. Compressed accordion pins can be tricky to learn. Practice them; try to catch each other at the knee at the same time. A bipole can be built from a three-man compressed accordion by opening the compressed accordion and having number four close the bipole.

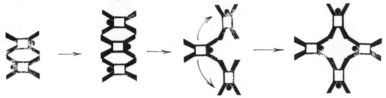

COMPRESSED ACCORDION PIN

A donut can be made by building a donut diamond from a compressed accordion pin and donutizing.

There are many ways to string these bases into sequences. Here are some of the possibilities:

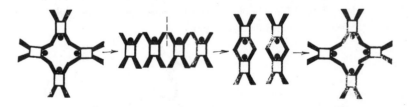

This star sequence is the oldest sequence around, and is still a good place to start if your group has never tried to do more than one formation per free fall.

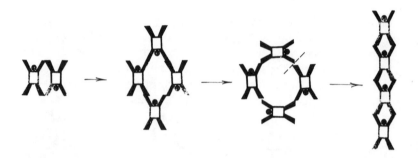

This is a simple donut sequence starting with a compressed accordion pin. It sequences by a series of grip changes. Once learned, the sequence can be extended like this.

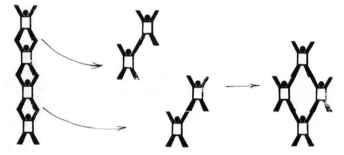

To move from a cat to stairsteps, the cat breaks to two cats, then grip-changes to stairsteps. The diamond is then built by docking the two stairsteps. Flying hooked up with others is really fun, and plays a large role in sequential relative work.

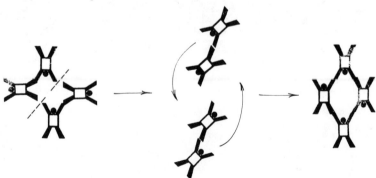

This sequence uses a bipole as the base formation. The bipole can be built from a three-man compressed accordion, or if you want to add a new flying technique, from a three-man Murphy with one man flying in backwards...

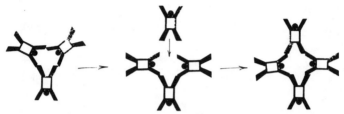

....or even from a two-man with two back-ins. Flying in backwards is not only possible but relatively easy and a whole lot of fun. The sequence could be lengthened to include a cat and another set of stairsteps to a diamond, as in the previous sequence.

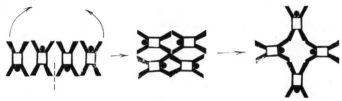

This sequence starts with a four-man compressed accordion, and uses fold-up, fold-out techniques to sequence. This set of moves, like many others, is reversible. You can go from a bipole to a double compressed accordion to a compressed accordion as easily as the other way around.

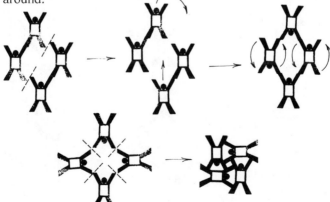

The base diamond can be broken to either left or right hand stairsteps. To move from a facing diamond to a four-man star, these grip changes can be used.

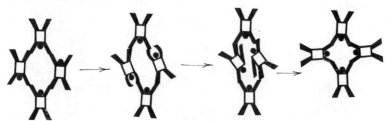

The star is then broken and reformed as a body star. Body stars are odd formations, tricky to build, with a high spin factor.

Once a few simple formations are learned and an understanding of some transitions is gained, the group can begin to design and execute more complex sequences. In designing sequences, remember that the important thing is to incorporate flying that is a challenge to your particular group. You can work up to more difficult sequences by planning practice sequences that repeat a specific move you're having trouble with, like building a stable donut or flying stairsteps or building bipoles or accordions.

Here are some examples of practice sequences:

1

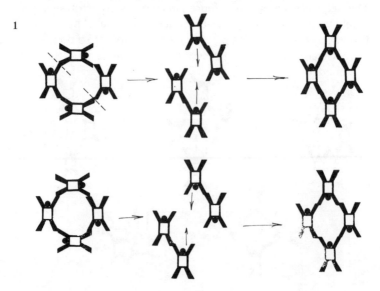

2

3

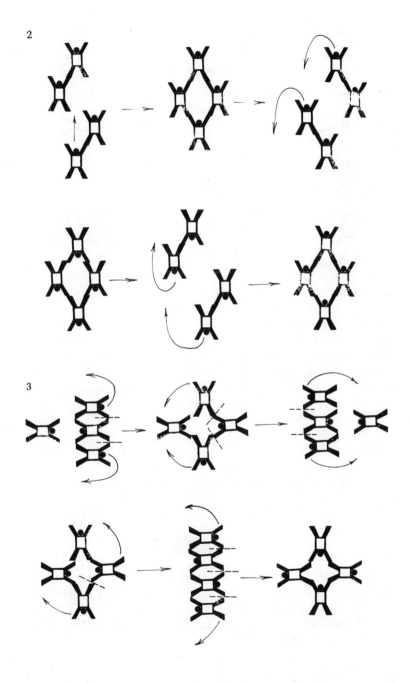

4

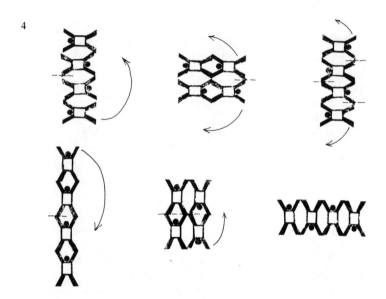

Remember, sequential routines require teamwork. Find some people willing to learn; people not afraid to blow a jump. Work together on a sequence to find the best timing, simple ways to key transitions, and the right grips. Plan a routine, then walk through it on the ground to work out the grips and keys. Talk your dives over as a group right after you land. Each player sees the routine from a different point of view, so work together to solve problems and to plan new techniques.

I hope this article will acquaint you with the mechanics of four-man sequences. It's up to your own imagination to make them become a real freefall experience. Four-man sequential is a format for good relative work, and good relative work is its own reward.

Editor's Note: Matt Farmer was a member of the 1975 United States Freefall Exhibition Team.

Matt Farmer, Parachutist, January 1976.

Quality Vs. Quantity & Serial Sequential. ... so there are only *three* spaces for a "filler load"... so the 182 is the only airplane on the drop zone and it will only carry *four*... so the Twin Beech is down and the 206 only carries *five* people... so you think *six* is a weird number to make formations with.

Why even bother jumping in those circumstances? First of all, because you love it. Secondly, you may well find yourself learning as much, if not more, on dives of this size than you do on the mega-loads that are the goal (or the routine) of so many jumpers. There are some among us who have moved much too quickly into dives of the two-figure magnitude or who, despite significant talent and experience, could benefit greatly from doing smaller and better things more often.

One of the hindrances to making small group dives efficient in terms of interest and experience gained is a lack on the part of the organizer of knowledge of the things that *can* be done. One of the advantages, however, of groups of this size is that there doesn't really have to be an organizer—you can just get together, decide on a dive plan that suits everybody, and discuss the moves during the dirt dive. With ten or more, that method usually takes hours and produces little.

The following sets of formations and maneuvers are for groups of from three to six. The names are attached simply for the purpose of communication. They have nothing to do with the way you do them, only with how you talk or write about them.

There are a *lot* of formations for *any* number of people and when you start combining them into sequences, you could do a lot of jumping without ever repeating a dive. One thing that may help is a change in perspective. Try to become less concerned with completions and more with doing better skydiving. Concentrate on:

—refined techniques.

—faster approaches with less (preferably *no)* momentum when a grip is taken.

—smoother flow in a sequence.

—less shaking and nodding signals, and more "sensing" when a formation is completed and knowing when it is time to transition.

All of these contribute to increased awareness and better flying and, if they aren't learned here, chances are they won't be learned at all.

Small formations are the pieces of which larger ones are made, and the techniques learned and experience gained on the "little" loads are the ones that all too often are shunned by new relative workers anxious to fly on the big formations out of the big airplanes with the "big boys."

There is a lot to be said for knowing where everybody on a load is, being able to see everything that is happening, having plenty of room at break-off time, not having to spend an hour and a half organizing and dirt diving, and being able to reconstruct a dive afterwards without chasing everybody down or listening to a dozen people talking at the same time.

As you look at these formations, and before you dash off to try the ones you haven't seen, think about them for a while—do some innovating *before* you get the load together.

You can, for instance, look at an entire set as an "eight minute skydive," done with several interruptions to air out your rig and repack it. Start out by arranging them in any order you want, then dirt dive a few of them as a sequence. Make the jump and see how far you get. That point can then be the beginning of the next dive.

Repeat the process until you finish the set, then reverse the order or mix them up and start again. One pass through will keep you busy for a bunch of weekends and by that time you will probably have thought of some more yourself. You could put each formation on one index card, shuffle the deck and draw several at random, doing them in that order.

Which brings up a point of view...I have always felt that any time you finish everything you have planned for a dive and have time (feet) left over, you are wasting time that could be used for learning more—enjoying it more—unless total completion was your primary goal. Plan more to do on a dive than you think the group has a reasonable chance of finishing; that "guarantees" that you will do all you can. You might be surprised.

Start looking for goals other than completing formations. If nothing else, you will stay in a better mood. Figure out the most efficient way to transition—grip switches or flying. Try doing them "contact, no grip" (just fly in position and occasionally tap the knee or elbow you would otherwise be gripping). Make vertical transitions when they are appropriate. *"Practice stopping completely in a slot,* then *taking a grip."*

Work on keeping the formations on a precise heading, or turning them to a pre-selected heading. Think about taking the first formation "out the door"—build it first, then fly it off the step or out the door. All these techniques are necessary or "nice-to-have" in doing large static or sequential flying, and small loads are where they are learned.

If you really want to get innovative, try some of the following:

—have one or more of the people in the formation fly inverted.

—roll a formation.
—track a formation, doing S-turns.
—mount riders on the people in a base formation.

Three-Person Formation Pool

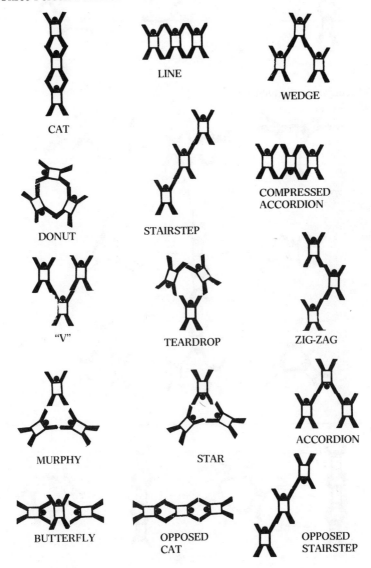

CAT

LINE

WEDGE

DONUT

STAIRSTEP

COMPRESSED
ACCORDION

"V"

TEARDROP

ZIG-ZAG

MURPHY

STAR

ACCORDION

BUTTERFLY

OPPOSED
CAT

OPPOSED
STAIRSTEP

"T" ZIPPER "S"

Three-Person Sequential

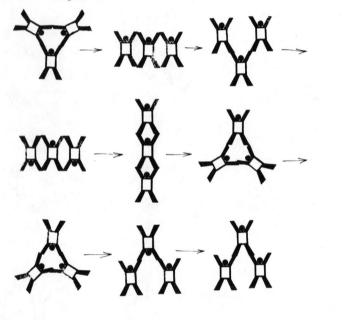

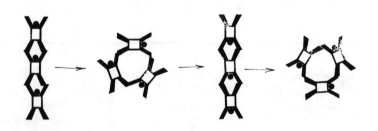

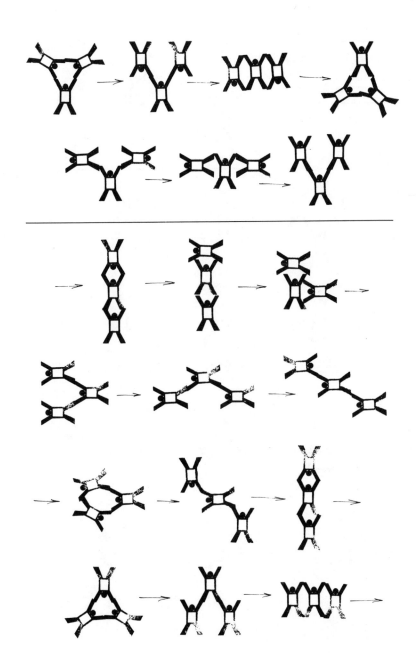

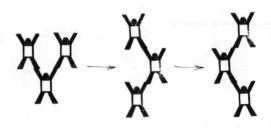

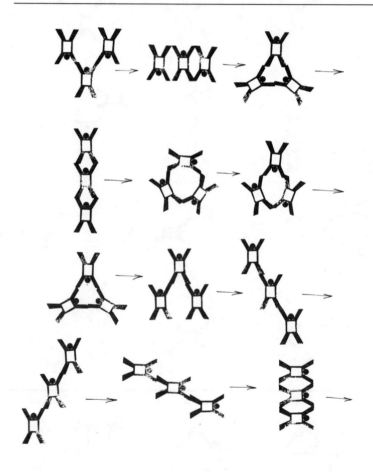

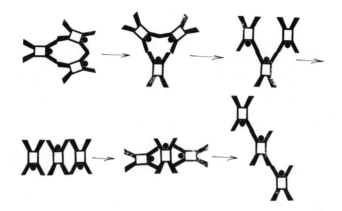

Four-Person Formation Pool

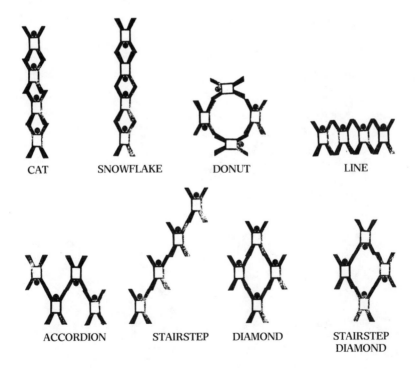

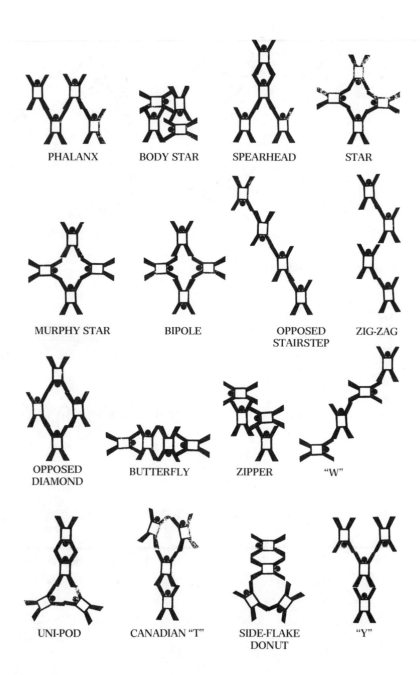

PHALANX   BODY STAR   SPEARHEAD   STAR

MURPHY STAR   BIPOLE   OPPOSED STAIRSTEP   ZIG-ZAG

OPPOSED DIAMOND   BUTTERFLY   ZIPPER   "W"

UNI-POD   CANADIAN "T"   SIDE-FLAKE DONUT   "Y"

Technique

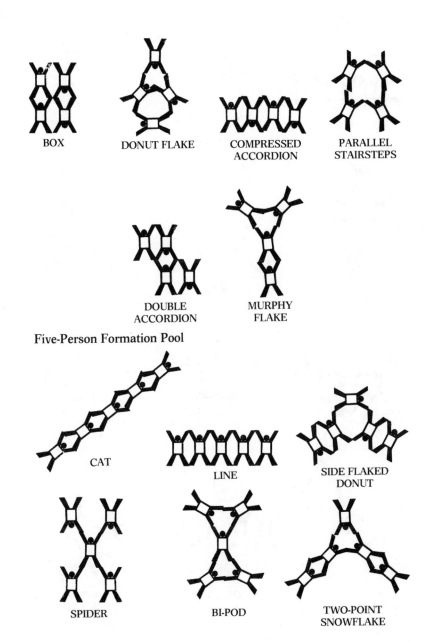

BOX

DONUT FLAKE

COMPRESSED
ACCORDION

PARALLEL
STAIRSTEPS

DOUBLE
ACCORDION

MURPHY
FLAKE

Five-Person Formation Pool

CAT

LINE

SIDE FLAKED
DONUT

SPIDER

BI-POD

TWO-POINT
SNOWFLAKE

53

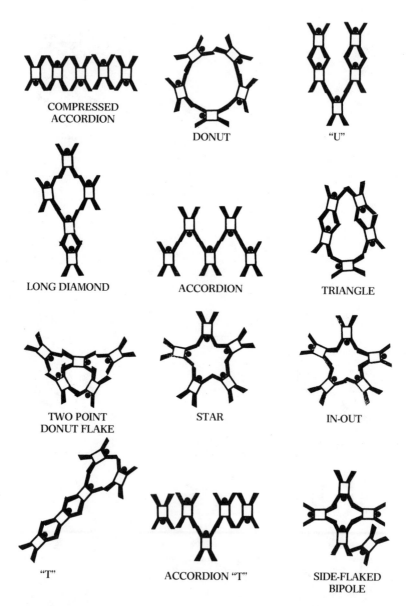

COMPRESSED
ACCORDION

DONUT

"U"

LONG DIAMOND

ACCORDION

TRIANGLE

TWO POINT
DONUT FLAKE

STAR

IN-OUT

"T"

ACCORDION "T"

SIDE-FLAKED
BIPOLE

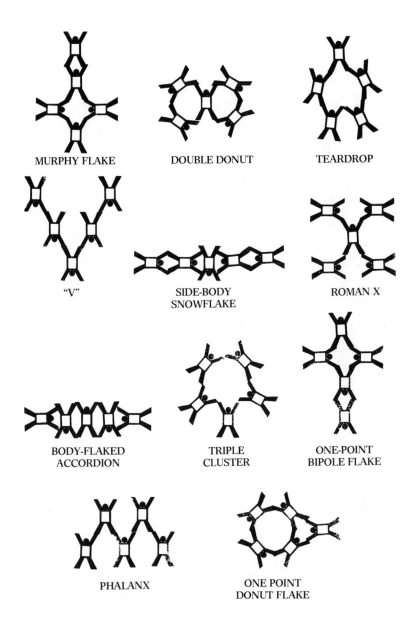

MURPHY FLAKE

DOUBLE DONUT

TEARDROP

"V"

SIDE-BODY
SNOWFLAKE

ROMAN X

BODY-FLAKED
ACCORDION

TRIPLE
CLUSTER

ONE-POINT
BIPOLE FLAKE

PHALANX

ONE POINT
DONUT FLAKE

Six-Person Formation Pool

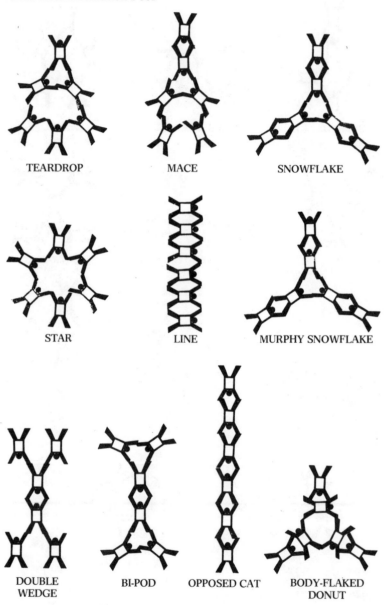

TEARDROP   MACE   SNOWFLAKE

STAR   LINE   MURPHY SNOWFLAKE

DOUBLE
WEDGE   BI-POD   OPPOSED CAT   BODY-FLAKED
DONUT

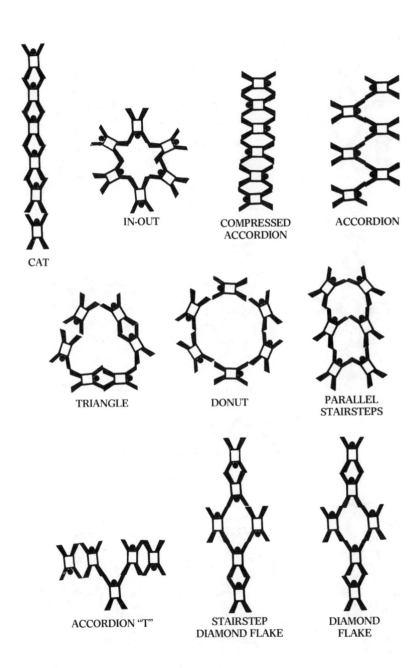

CAT

IN-OUT

COMPRESSED
ACCORDION

ACCORDION

TRIANGLE

DONUT

PARALLEL
STAIRSTEPS

ACCORDION "T"

STAIRSTEP
DIAMOND FLAKE

DIAMOND
FLAKE

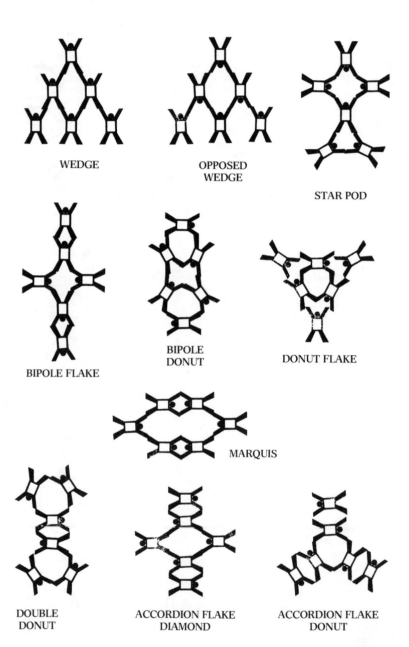

WEDGE

OPPOSED
WEDGE

STAR POD

BIPOLE FLAKE

BIPOLE
DONUT

DONUT FLAKE

MARQUIS

DOUBLE
DONUT

ACCORDION FLAKE
DIAMOND

ACCORDION FLAKE
DONUT

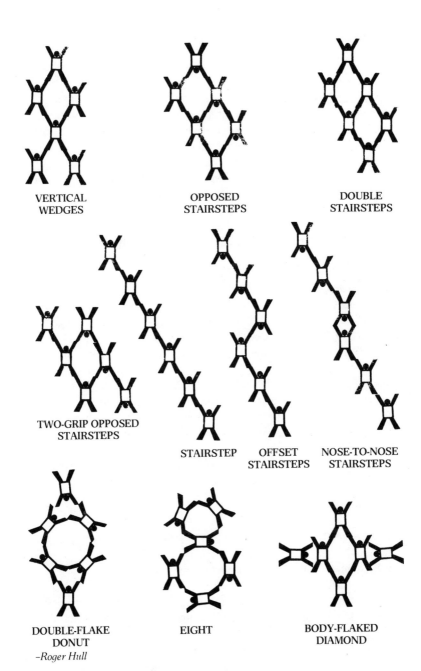

VERTICAL
WEDGES

OPPOSED
STAIRSTEPS

DOUBLE
STAIRSTEPS

TWO-GRIP OPPOSED
STAIRSTEPS

STAIRSTEP

OFFSET
STAIRSTEPS

NOSE-TO-NOSE
STAIRSTEPS

DOUBLE-FLAKE
DONUT
–Roger Hull

EIGHT

BODY-FLAKED
DIAMOND

A Voyage To Grabclutchland: Ground Practice. Ground practice in relative work can be an effective conditioner for both mind and body when done before every jump, whether a fun-jump or a team practice load.

It may be compared to rugby or football practice or any other team sport where coordinated interaction with one's teammates is required. You learn to work together and coordinate your movements on the ground so that every maneuver becomes reflexive, then the jump will fall together more easily in the air.

It requires a lot of jumps to develop group skill and team attitude and that is why you must supplement airwork with ground training. All good teams do ground practice. Even if you are planning just a "fun" jump with 4 or 5 people, a run-through on the ground before the jump will quickly reveal any traffic problems that may pop up in the air, and will help get everybody's head in the same place.

On the ground, *slowly* walk through the entire jump at least four times before every load. Have someone count the seconds out loud; listen to the cadence. Build the star (standing) just as you will in the air, starting from the plane. Imagine that you are in freefall. Don't build a star in four seconds if you usually take 8-10 seconds in freefall.

If you're doing 4-man RW, key off the sequences just as you do in the air. Walk into the next formation in proper sequence and timing. Then imagine break-off time and practice pull sequence.

It is a lot easier to learn the various formations of 4-man RW on the ground rather than wasting a lot of time in the air. Spend a lot of ground practice learning the mechanical steps. More importantly, spend some time to learn the *cadence* of the jump so that you all feel together every maneuver. Do it the same way each time.

Pat Works, RWu, June 1974

PART III—Your Relative Work Technique—Hints for Neophytes

To Be Faster, Don't Think Speed...Think Good RW

"You will begin to touch heaven, Jonathan, in the moment that you touch perfect speed. And that isn't flying a thousand miles an hour, or a million. Because any number is a limit, and perfection doesn't have limits.

Perfect speed, my son, is being there."

From Chiang's advice to Jonathan Livingston Seagull (Richard Bach)

Peak Function

Peak-Function—That is what a skydive is—
A place where you can peak-function—
A time when you can be...all there—
With simultaneous awareness—
Of all the different aspects—
The intellectual calculation of alternatives—
The laws of physics...And experience—
And feeling the flow of the air with your whole body—
And the sense of...quality...artistry—
That makes you choose one path—
From all the many that are possible—
To put it all together—
As a thing of flowing beauty—
Peak-Function...Skydiving—
–Skratch Garrison, August 1, 1975

Hints For Neophytes, Or, Why You Is A Spastic Clod at RW. There are at least four reasons why you are a toad in the air:
1) You're so tense from trying too hard and being generally freaked out that you don't have energy or coordination left to do a clean swoop.
2) You aren't aware of the differences between momentum and non-momentum RW.
3) You are basically dumb and your reactions are on par with a sloth.
4) Your *friends* are basically dumb and can't use the language well enough to give you a meaningful critique.
Of the above, we'll deal with only the first two.
On Being A Stiff. The state of being overly tense and uptight requires the expenditure of both psychic and physical energy. Since you have only a limited amount of these energies available to you, *any* excess expenditure must be subtracted from energy you oughta be using for RW. As a result of being tense, you can't think or react properly and so, you screw up.
Since screwing up makes you even more tense, you may actually seem to get worse in your RW. So you're tense on your next swoop...etc.
Tenseness also has a mechanical ill-effect. Any rigid object is hard to

control in a wind blast of 120 mph. Try this simple experiment: Make two jumps. On the first carry a 4-ft. length of lumber with you. On the second carry a like-sized piece of cardboard. Now, which was easier to control in freefall? The point is, if you keep your body rigid and tense you'll have the same kind of control problems you had with the lumber.

Obviously you have neither the energy nor the control skill to stay rigid and tense during RW. So relax! While RW-ing you should be no tenser than you are in the bathtub (except when you need to *move* as in a track or when braking, etc.) This relaxedness should be mental, too.

Later on, when you become a super-dynamite, ace-expert, sky-god RW King, you will discover that certain types of rigidity can help. Some rigidity, i.e. pushing the air rather than always letting it push you can, in many circumstances, make you faster, more precise, and improve your general RW ability. But for the beginner the most important thing to do is relax.

"Easy for you to say," you say, "but how?" True, telling someone to relax does not insure that the novice can do it. Often it has just the opposite effect. Telling a jumper, "Look, if you don't relax in the air this time I'd better not see ya when we get to the ground, cuz I'll bust your head," probably won't help him relax unless he's a special case. A jumper can, however, learn to devise methods of relaxing that work for him. One of the most common devices is to take a few deep breaths a few seconds before exiting — it really works. Some jumpers like to move around and shake a bit to get the heart going and the blood circulating; others have devices that are very personal but work for them.

Take a relaxed, aggressive "attitude" toward RW and you'll be faster. More importantly, relaxing in the star makes the star fly better and thus makes it easier for the guys you burned to get in. ("Perfect speed...is being there."—J.L.S.)

SPECIAL NOTE to feather/asses who tend to get in OK but float like a potato chip once they touch wrists. If your entry is not too high to start with and your ass floats up no matter what you do, then you are probably tense in the waist, back and legs. Even when you bring your knees in you float 'cause you bend your back, too. Arch your back and relax your waist, letting your legs to limp and blow up out of the way on your ass. Keep your hands *higher* than your head.

FLOATING TYPE

NON-FLOATER   FLOATING TYPE NON-FLOATER
(SIDE VIEW) (TOP VIEW)

Types of RW. There are four types of RW: terminal, sub-terminal, momentum and non-momentum. You gotta be good at 'em all. You know all about terminal and subterminal (or think you do).

Non-momentum RW is the kind of RW you learned to do first. You get within about 30 feet of the dude you want to relate with and are at his level. You stop dead-still and then hand-track over; you have no velocity or speed left over from your descent track.

This type of RW (non-momentum) is difficult to do well. Experts at it seem to have a motor and can dance on the columns of air beneath them. You need to be good at non-momentum RW to try to enter a really weird and squirrelly star or you won't get in.

Momentum RW is the kind of RW you learned to do (or will learn to do) when you build competition stars. In momentum RW you never stop or slow down; you maintain track-generated velocity and redirect it to enter. Your approach angle is very high. You must be very aggressive, and your chances of a wipe-out are higher. You generally use the "mush" entry in momentum RW. The "mush" is a high-angle, high-velocity approach, differing from an at-level approach.

So you gotta be good at non-momentum RW for the last couple of feet if the star is building fast, or is squirrelly. Also, heaven forbid, you might be so fast you go below and the only thing that will get you in is non-momentum RW. On the other hand, if you're gonna *be* as fast as you already think you are, then you gotta be hot at momentum RW, too. But, unless you can do a subterminal 4-man, you are not good at any RW anyhow, and need help and practice.

Exit Tip. If you Z out on exit, try to totally relax and let yourself start to go limp. You'll find yourself stable a lot sooner. Realizing that your *initial* exit is done on air pushed by the propellers rather than the ground should clean up your act quickly.

NOTE TO INEXPERIENCED STAR-MASTERS. Put at *least* three *good* people up front for a serious attempt. If you're making a serious RW attempt, these slots are absolutely key. Putting a toad base, pin or third will mean you have a poor-falling, slow-building mess. OK, now smile, relax and swoop lots!

REMEMBER: Everyone is a one-man star. To build something bigger, you gotta do RW.
Pat Works, RWu, January 1973.

Body Dynamics. This condensed fairytale is for novices who do not yet fully understand body aerodynamics.

BASICALLY, YOUR ARMS CONTROL YOUR ALTITUDE AND YOUR LEGS CONTROL YOUR SPEED.

It's hard learning to control your legs properly because you cannot see them. Get the feel of the positions they're in. Practice bending, straightening, and pointing your toes on the ground. YOU HAVE TO BE ABLE TO THINK OF WHAT YOUR BODY'S DOING BEFORE YOU CAN IMPROVE YOUR RW.

Tracking. Your arms control your descent to the formation below. On a 90 degree approach, you should bend at the waist in a reverse arch and place your arms behind your back. Arms should be straight and your hands should be above your shoulder blades. Check diagram below.

SIDE VIEW

On a 45 degree approach, your arms should be in a medium delta.

SIDE VIEW   TOP VIEW

And on a level approach, your arms should be in an "Iron Cross" position to gain maximum lift. Your drive towards the formation is obtained by straightening the legs and pointing the toes.

SIDE VIEW   TOP VIEW

Adjust your arms according to the position (angle) you find yourself on. It'll be different every jump.

Approach. Always look where you want to go. Your body will follow your head. Your approach should be relaxing into a frog position and coasting toward the formation with speed generated from your dive.

If you are going to overshoot and go over the top of it, (arrow) pull your knees up to sink you out.

If you are sinking out (arrow), extend your legs and assume the "Iron Cross" position. Keep coasting towards the formation.

If you are sliding to the left or right, and not straight at the formation, you have to tilt your body to correct. A slide to the right is corrected by tilting to the left.

This is accomplished by pushing your left arm down, lower than your right arm. Your body will slide in the direction of the lower shoulder.

Final Approach. Final approach is made by relaxing and keeping your elbows bent and down in front of your chest. If you extend your arms to reach for wrists, your armpits will inflate and blow you out of the slot.

If you're having trouble, explain the jump to an experienced jumper and ask his advice.

If you want to get in quickly, you'll have to learn to control your swoop with speed from your dive. Hand tracking should only be used as a secondary technique when you miss on your first swoop.

Roger Nelson, Freak Brother Flyer #3

In the Star. If you're a lightweight and have trouble flying in the star, take heed!

It's been customary to tuck up the knees to keep proper altitude in the star. This only creates tension and makes it nearly impossible to retain your grip. You must refrain from inflating the armpits of your jumpsuit. To prevent this, keep your forearms parallel and below your body by bending your elbows. Arch your back, keeping the head high and bend your knees so that your lower legs are in the burble from your thighs. Point your toes straight up (to keep an awareness of the position of your legs).

The faster you need to fall, the more you pull your head and body into the inner circle of the star.

RIGHT WRONG

Practice this on the ground. It's a lot cheaper than practicing it in the air. I weigh 180 lbs. fully geared, jump bells, and haven't found a star that I float in. If you don't believe me, try it. It's a lot easier.
Carl Nelson, Freak Brother Flyer #2

More Approach Talk. So you're having trouble getting in. You seem to be coming in nice but all of a sudden, you're jamming past in a heavy left slide. On your next jump, all you can remember is seeing the star flyers tuck their heads in their shoulders and make an 8-man look like a 4-man as the colors quickly rushed by.

As a new swooper, you now must realize the people holding it don't like being bowling pins, and that going 100-feet below is just wasting your precious $. Believe me, it's a lot better to use your working time coming in rather than in a reverse arch. Go slow and don't expect to get in every jump. But with practice, you'll soon get closer and closer. And soon, with about 300 swoops, you'll be at the gate of "Skygod."

There are two basic approaches, momentum and non-momentum. The momentum being not stopping until entry. This is an approach only recommended for Skygods.

Now to break down on the approach. I personally feel there's three variations on an approach angle, one being the "L" approach when the diver drops his head out the door and dives to pick up working speed called the down and over.

The next is one I mostly recommend, the "straight-line" approach. This is when the diver gains visibility of the star after prop blast and never takes his eyes off it. Going into a turtle type position steering with head and shoulder enables this approach to be a lot quicker than the down and over. The swooper comes out of his dive and aims for a slot by the feet having much salvage increase of shift and slide.

The last is the one I use and recommend for speed stars or when you get a 30-second exit. It's the "over and down" approach. This is done on exit; the diver flares in the prop blast and goes into a rolled-back shoulders position with his arms pushed about 6" past his trunk, eyes straight, tracking over and at the star with this being a more true, straight approach at the star. Once you've reached over the star, you can sit up and use your speed to drop into the slot. This approach is the quickest, using gravity to its fullest extent; it is also the easiest way to bomb the star. The breaking impact is pushing down on the star instead of in on it towards the middle. Even though this is the easiest to blow, it has a lot of salvage if you don't panic and slide or shift with the star. You'll still burn in there faster than you can imagine.

I recommend never taking your eyes off your target (unless it's a turn for a pre-star) 'cause the instant you do, you're not making a straight line.

A tip for everyone including Skygods: keep a better consciousness of your legs for a maximum track, feet and legs together with toes pointed, this is the best and fastest gliding position. Many people only *think* they know what their legs are doing, and many good people are limited because of this. I've found from studying Karate that exercising gives you a better awareness of your exact body position.

The quickest way between two points is a straight line. The straight line approach is a good one for getting there quickly to set up a slot or to await your approach in a maneuver. It leaves you high for easy setting.

When you find yourself awaiting people designated to form the base, consider pre-stars. They're a lot of fun and give you more flying per jump.

Roger Nelson, Freak Brother Flyer #7

Flying A Hot Piece. You can 360 and redock your diamond, wedge or stairstep really *fast* if you do it the easy way.

The *only* grip suitable for formations is made by interlocking your "elbow pits" in your teammates "knee pits." This makes your formation rock-solid, and it will fly as a unit. This grip also prevents the formation from floating, and allows each individual to move their limbs freely, vital for successful formation flying.

If you grab someone below the knee (higher up on the leg as you look at it in the air), you will put tension on your formation and prevent it from flying as a unit. The higher you grab, the more leverage you'll have to screw up the person in front of you.

If you're flying properly, you shouldn't be able to see the complete formation, only the crotch of the person in front of you. Upon mastering level flight, with correct grips, you can make the transition to redocking and tracking your formation.

Let's use a triple diamond formation as an example. The formation is made up from three separate diamonds, each consisting of a point, two wings and a tail. The point people are docked together in a 3-person star. Shaking is necessary when the tail docks to inform the points that their individual diamond is complete. The points use their vision to perceive completion of the other diamonds.

The base three-man is flown with the elbows bent at 90 degree angles, making swoop cords loose. If you fly the base three-man "stiff-armed," you will cause the formation to float, and when making the break to redock, you will backslide and gain unnecessary separation.

The break is made simply by letting go. No shaking is necessary as everyone usually gets the idea when they see one diamond burning them into the turn. The turn for 360 and redock, and the 90 and track are made in the same direction. Ground practice is necessary so everyone knows right from left. (Especially after a joint safety meeting.)

The 360 is accomplished by the points doing a body turn (twisting the trunk and making the arms asymmetrical.) The point is the only person to do so. Everyone else does a *knee turn* by pulling one knee up toward the chest (right turn is made by pulling the right knee, etc.). The wing people put their arms out 90 degrees to their side to prevent the formation from banking (which creates a slide and unnecessary separation). If the formation doesn't make a level turn, you probably won't redock. The turn should be completed before driving forward until you get a little experience, and hence, a consistent turn. If you're more than 15 to 20 feet apart after completing the 360, you either backslid on the break or did a banking turn.

Driving forward to redock is accomplished by the tail of the diamond putting legs together and pointing toes, while floating a little above the rest of the diamond. The tail should be able to see everyone's backpack, and be calculating the "rush" during the redock approach along with the point and wing people. (This takes some experience, as a 4-person diamond can drive forward faster than one person alone.)

The tail is responsible for braking the diamond's forward drive. This is accomplished by changing from slightly above the diamond to slightly below it. The tail is kind of like the front disc brake of a motorcycle in comparison to braking efficiency. Keep this in mind, as the tail can back the entire formation out of range by sitting up and going a touch below prematurely. The wings can use their hands, forearms and bodies, decelerating in unison with the tail prior to contact at the point.

As soon as contact is made, the tail extends legs and floats the diamond to the level of the newly completed formation. At this point, if you're any kind of Skygod, you can 360 and do it again. If not, you can make a 90 degree turn and track the diamond across the sky.

The most effective track is accomplished by driving horizontally, and avoiding a vertical descent to gain speed. The point *slowly* goes into a medium delta (maximum sweep of 45 degrees) as everyone places their legs together and points their toes. The tail pulls the right and left wing people close together so that both of the wings' inside legs are close together. This makes the diamond narrow and more aerodynamic. The tail also extends arms, eliminating the elbow pit grip, and maintains position with a secondary hand grip (on the thighs, not the calfs). The tail should now look like George Reeves from the Superman TV series.

From this position, the tail goes head down, nose facing the ground while at the same time shrugging the shoulders and very slightly reversing the arch of the upper torso by sucking the stomach in. Now the tail is driving horizontally at maximum speed.

If everyone else uses their *entire body* instead of just the extremities in their track, horizontal speed will be around 60 mph. The other diamonds tracking in different directions will be accelerating likewise, creating a bombburst effect with a 120 mph relative speed! This one's great to blow the Geeks away on your next demo, provided of course, that you all have square canopies.

Freak Brother Flyer, Fall 1976

Additional Tips on Flying Formations and Maneuvers. Learn to fly using your legs as well as your arms, especially for holding position with a one-handed grip.

When gripping legs, grip the side of the knee or above the knee on the back of the leg, to allow the person you're gripping freedom of lower leg movement for flying. Getting the ankle or foot stretches the leg, increasing float and instability, distorts the maneuver, and restricts the person's flyability.

When forming a cluster, those hooking up between legs have a long reach if the base formation is a 3 or 4 man star. It will help to grip the outside of your man's leg, to decrease the reach distance between you and the man on the other leg.

When building a diamond, an inside knee/leg grip is more appropriate for the wing people. If doing a 4-man diamond or wedge flying and docking, this will keep the unit tighter and falling faster, and provide greater stability in the formation for better maneuverability.

When flying formations, all members must fly smooth and together. For example, in the diamond, fly smoothly the same as you would fly on your own. Don't counteract for the others in the formation. The point man typically controls most of the *turn,* with assistance from the wingmen. The point can drop the front or sit up and brake (though most of the braking is done by the tail man). The tail controls the forward speed of the diamond, by extending his legs and picking up the back end of the formation to move forward; and sitting up and flaring the diamond to brake. Anticipate the necessary corrections— don't do anything radical—be smooth and deliberate.

Don't try to salvage a bad approach by hanging on and swinging or climbing up legs. Let go and fly back into the formation. Trying such a salvage often results in a turning base or a righteous funnel. This is especially important in flying a straight-in slot, where the tendency is to correct excess momentum (speed) by grabbing on and swinging wide, then swinging back into position. THIS DISRUPTS THE MANEUVER!!

Try to fly large maneuvers in waves or stages, i.e. in a donut-flake, the flakers should set up and wait until the base unit is *complete* and *stable* — don't enter your slot if your side is complete and the other side isn't.

Although our medium is air—don't forget the ground. If you are in a base formation or a docking maneuver, cross-reference the ground to keep from turning or sliding, and don't turn unless necessary.

If you think it's easy to forget about altitude in star-work, it's much, much easier to do so in flying formations, sequential and docking maneuvers. Designate *at least* one person to be responsible for the breakup of the maneuver. Design your break-off altitude according to the type and size of maneuver. There's a lot different spacing and tracking required of a 16-man diamond than of a 16-star.

Design a system of communications for each jump. If you're facing out on an In-Out, for example, just watch the horizon using peripheral vision to pick up the legs beside you, and let the In-men tell you to correct — to tuck up and bring it down by a shake of your legs. If you turn around to see them, you'll probably sit up and backslide into the center.

Take your time. Be smooth. Most people would rather have an incomplete jump because of slowness, than be on the bottom of a righteous funnel at 6 thousand feet, or sit 50 feet away and watch a spinning, sliding base.

Rande Deluca, Spotter, May-June 1975

Wedge Speed. *According to Ed Mosher, the Marshall, Mich. police clocked an Exitus team 16-man Wedge on radar. The radar timed the formation at 78 MPH. All the jumpers were wearing Brand X jumpsuits.*

Relative Wind, Western Conference newsletter, March 1977

Malfunctions. I personally believe in this particular theory in an emergency procedure whether jumping pig or otherwise.

Due to funnels, separation, high breaks and reforms, many relative workers pull between 2500 and 1500 ft. That leaves approximately 8 to 12 seconds of emergency working time.

It is extremely important that the jumper know how he wants to handle each situation. Questioning emergency procedures or hesitations can easily lead to high-speed impact with the dirt. (Which doesn't hurt but makes you look mighty dumb in front of your friends.) Even though you must play all malfunctions by ear, you can still plan an escape and study your ideas until you have true confidence. Recommended minimum pulling altitude is 2000 ft. The reason you pull at that altitude is so you have time to employ your emergency procedures. It's reaction time — meaning if you dump, get jerked upright and look up at garbage, immediately proceed with your streamer procedures. Dumping at 2,000 feet leaves *no* time for shaking risers or playing with lines.

Many hot dogs will argue that they have shook at streamers many times and probably have. But just one malfunction doesn't put you in the hole. You can only make so many mistakes before it catches up with you. For instance, you look up late at a streamer and have a Capewell hang-up, then going unstable and missing your ripcord will get you in trouble. Fast malfunctions are *nothing to mess with!*

A good procedure is to watch your "shit" leave your back to know you don't have a total. Then, check your canopy during or immediately after opening shock.

Riding a line-over or similar malfunction gives you a bit more time but sitting under it wishing don't do nothing but cost you. So get rid of it or shake and hope.

A malfunction is nothing to panic about although it's hard to tell your adrenalin that at times. You pull at altitudes anticipating problems so if you got a problem, go about the proper methods to fix it!

A malfunction costs time, money and sometimes life. Remember when cutting away: *"Don't delay, do it today, cut it away and live to fly another day."*

Roger Nelson, Freak Brother Flyer #6

How to Track Like a Peregrine Falcon.

Introduction: Among many other parachuting credits, Tom was a member of Jerry Bird's All-Stars team which won the first US RW Nationals in '72. An old California jumper, he was a rigger for the U.S. Air Force Academy parachute team before his untimely death in 1974. The fastest tracker in the West, he won the Elsinore Scrambles tracking contest for two straight years. Most of us track. Tom knew how to max-track... The faster you get there, the more time you have for RW. Herein he reveals his secrets...

Last September, during the SCR Scrambles at Elsinore, jumpers and whuffos alike were shown what three Beech loads tracking with smoke looked like. The crowd response on the ground sounded as if it were a 20-plus star. There were 10 ribbons of smoke strung across the valley...three times. A year before there were only 10 people and nobody had smoke. As is true in all cases, when you can use a little smoke, everything looks better.

I've never read any dates concerning the first time that someone realized he didn't just have to fall stable. A reliable source from the Northwest once told me that a student of aerodynamics bet Loy Brydon that it was quite impossible to change one's angle of trajectory from anything but straight down. As the story goes, Sgt. Brydon went up and ordered the wind to blow him across the sky.

I believe that large-star RW was largely responsible for refining the more effective methods of using one's body as an airfoil. We use a track not only to get down and over, but also to ensure separation after the star. Everyone who has done it knows what it is like to go on someone else's bad spot and not realize how bad it is until after the star breaks. I've found that most people will put out more effort and track harder and farther when it's a matter of avoiding known hazards. If you want something bad enough, you'll begin to ask yourself what forces are involved when you are covering the most ground. The subject is speed.

Sources of experience sometime take on unusual disguises. Most people who share the sky in freefall would listen to a man with 4,000 plus jumps. A Russian by the name of Igor sounds like a jump story. I met him at the '72 World Meet, and after watching him do some hand balancing, I spoke to him of balance and muscle control in freefall, which led to the subject of tracking.

We babble-rapped awhile before I got him to tell me how he did it. He contended that his best track position could be practiced on the ground, by finding your center of gravity, approximately one inch below your breast bone, and balancing all your weight on a three-inch tent pole. By holding your body in this rigid position, you can duplicate the strain it takes to hold the perfect angle.

It didn't take but a few full-tilt, boogie tracks to feel the muscles Igor was talking about. To date, my best tracking efforts have been followed by at least three days of sore legs, back and shoulders. I can't think of anything else that you could do that would allow you to flex all the muscles in your body for 60 seconds and not touch anything but the sky.

I have found that the prospect of solitary concentration seldom presents itself in freefall as intensely as it does while tracking. Once I have the position which affords me maximum lift, I hold my body motionless and rigid. To find, keep and hold this position requires the awareness of one's own head. As a mass, your cloth, leather, fiberglass or uncovered head controls the subtle changes of body attitude which affect one's particular lift efficiency. Arm and leg positions can vary as much as the gear people wear.

The most common method goes something like this:
Lay on your stomach on the floor, put heels six inches apart and

point your toes until your calf muscles hurt. Put arms three inches from the hips.

In freefall, big gloves work nicely. After all is said and done in the pursuit of your best track, you'll find that it is in your head. Put it in the right place and it'll take you there.

If you have become complacent about tracking or you feel you are already doing everything as well as you can, then I suggest a half dozen purposely mis-spotted tracks for motivation. Because there are no secrets outside the physical size and gear except experience. You must track to get better at it.

Tom Phillips, SCR-236, RWu, June 1974

Down & Dirty — A Discussion of One Side of Skydiving: The Underside. Look at the little man down there. He looks like a dead spider. There he is, looking up at you, watching you through the 50 feet of sky between him and his slot...

The slot that would complete your 32-person mega-cluster-blot for a new world's record and your SCR.

You wonder: "Why doesn't he come back up here? What is he doing down there?"

Going below is the most common mistake in relative work. 75 jumps, 1500 jumps; 200 pounds, 130 pounds; male and female; belly-wart and piggy-back — they *all* go below. If they haven't, they will.

Why? That's a tough question. There are immediate, short-term answers: experience, currency and concentration are important. But in the long run it's not clear why this one problem stays with us so doggedly. We've taught ourselves to fly backwards and upside down — but we haven't learned how to keep from going below. Our relative work techniques have definitely advanced, but we've brought our oldest mistake with us.

But it doesn't matter so much *why* skydivers struggle with the problems of going below so long as we can teach ourselves to stop the habit.

(It should be noted here that a relative worker who was out of sight above the formation "didn't get in." The skydiver who didn't get in, but was seen flailing beneath his slot, is said to have "gone below.")

(That's pronounced: "Yeccchhh!")

Last Sunday, a friend of mine had trouble on almost every skydive.

We agreed to sit down later and talk about it; I thought I could help. Lucky for me in the meantime I was able to get below a mega-blot and see the problem first-hand.

It's a bitch.

The hardest approach to a formation—any formation—is from below. (This doesn't include floaters, who have an entirely different skydive.) When you're caught below, you become dead in the air as you start your recovery: you must sacrifice all your horizontal control to go back up. If you're moving sideways on the way up, you're not going up as fast as possible.

A basic law: horizontal movement uses vertical advantage. If you want to go sideways, you're going to have to give up altitude to do it. And, if you're below, the last thing you want to give up is altitude.

If you're below, you're in a reverse arch (or should be) with your head pressed down over that ball of air (nowhere else will do, not even an apologetic glance at your pals above you and the only way you can see anything is between your legs).

It's very difficult to seek your slot from such a position. And very embarrassing.

But, recall the image of the dead spider below your mega-blot and consider the first rule for not going below:

1) Do all your awkward positions above the formation. This means you must take those drastic actions to stop your descent to your slot the instant you see you're getting down close to it.

See, there's a glide path between where you are and where you're going: it's your glideslope. The best glideslope is that one which allows you maximum control range. If you're below your best glideslope, you have to fly a flat shallow path to the formation: a path that requires a big, awkward body position, a position that doesn't allow much control.

If you get stuck flying shallow like that, the only control you have left is the ability to go down faster. And if something messes with your approach (as usually happens) all you've got left is the opportunity to go below.

Don't ever try to flatten your glideslope. You can't. Don't ever accept a flat angle to your slot: you're just asking for trouble.

The instant you see that you're flying a flat path to your slot, FLARE. STOP. REVERSE ARCH UP TO YOUR GLIDE SLOPE. START AGAIN FROM THERE. Don't intercept your glideslope on the way to the slot; enter your glideslope, *then* take it to your slot. It's much easier that way. Honest.

If there is a first rule about not going below, there must be a second one.

2) Go to your assigned slot the instant it's ready for you. This is just good skydiving practice. It means you should be ready to fill your slot as soon as it's there. (Air traffic controllers space traffic so the runway is clear as soon as the airplane behind is ready for it.) If your slot is there and you aren't, not only do you stall the skydivers behind you, but you're giving the formation more time to do something flakey — like slow down and "float" on you (and embarrass you).

The third rule is easy:

3) If you're 10 feet up, be ready to take your slot. Ten feet is not enough altitude for most people to sacrifice flying sideways around a formation looking for the right approach. Remember: horizontal movement uses vertical advantage. If you're just ten feet up without a slot in sight, well, it's likely you just can't get there from here.

But, if you're ten feet up and discover you have to go somewhere, the secret is to get *big first* and get the altitude you'll need (the glideslope you want) for a nice swoop to our slot.

Altitude is advantage.

Then, if you're one of those of us who've had the frustration of seeing neat skydives from their belly-side, there's rule #4. It's specially useful to people who've gone below more than a little.

The rule is a head trip. An attitude adjustment for all our skydives. Follow it closely, carefully, and every skydive can be a newer and fresher experience; you'll do more and learn more.

4) Don't repeat what you already know. If you've been below — really down & dirty and grippin' it — you know how to do that. So don't do it anymore. You've seen the glideslope that will take you to that frustrating air beneath your slot. You must never again get on that glideslope.

Sure.

The problem is one of recognition — being able to pick out what you did that put you off your best glideslope: deciding what was mistake and what was skydiving. It's difficult. There's no one with us watching our every move; and our friends notice us only after we've blown the approach; too late to help.

That's why more has been written on how to do reverse arches than has been said about ways to avoid needing them.

Fogged goggles will not make you go below. Neither will the sun in your eyes, your new Strato-star or the guy behind you in the exit. And, although jumpsuits are important, they aren't to blame nearly as often as many people would like to believe.

Your position in the air is subject to your control. Your body goes where *you* fly it. If you end up below, *you* did something with your body sometime during your skydive that put you there.

Pay attention, Think about what you did. Try to remember the flight path that took you below, then stay off that particular glideslope forevermore.

A fine skydiver once said to me after he went below a large formation: "I flared high enough, but it was just falling too slowly for me." *Wrong!* It may have been falling slowly, but he obviously didn't flare (awkward position) high enough or else he wouldn't have gone below. Period.

Unwanted results point to improper techniques and are called "mistakes."

To recognize mistakes, backtrack from the unwanted results. What did you do before you went by the wedge? And what did you do just before that? You had a clean shot out the door and then, somewhere between your exit and your reverse arch, you did something that put you down & dirty. What was that something?

When you think you know what put you beneath last week's mega-blot (your exit? your dive? your last ten feet? your flare? whatever?) don't do that anymore. Or do it differently. Pay attention! Change something, do something, even if it's wrong. At least you'll be trying something new.

You can't sit back with the same old mistakes that put you below. Go up, and seek your slot from above!

Matching Exit to Aircraft. She'd been having a real tough weekend. The score was Slot: 1, Below: 4. Not very satisfying skydiving.

It was hard to figure. She tried more jumpsuit, less weight, an earlier slot. Nothing seemed to help. She continued to go below.

So we went up to have a look. It turned out she went out the door in one of the most aggressive head-down dives I'd seen in a while. But, she never took a glance at where she was going.

That was what she was taught four years ago out of Twin Beeches:

exit, dive head down for four seconds, look up and flare. She did the whole routine superbly, flawlessly.

But that exit is for Beeches, not for the DC-3 we were skydiving from. The 3's higher airspeed and the longer exits for the large formations we were building — coupled with some light-weight skydivers — simply made her exit technique the first and worst mistake. She was going below the proper glideslope immediately out the door!

If she got out and GOT BIG IMMEDIATELY, she would have flown up to a much more comfortable flight plan. No jumpsuit in the world, no featherweight gear can salvage a slot unless you give it a decent chance: the right glide path in the first place!

Path To Glory. Just because you're higher than the formation doesn't mean you've stayed above it.

Usually we're surprised to find ourselves below. One minute I'm in fat city coming to the slot and in an instant I'm trying my best reverse arch.

Why can't we see it coming earlier?

It's important to realize what is below and what is above. There is a best guideslope that radiates outward and upward from every slot; that is your best path to your position. It's different for every skydiver and every formation.

Around that glideslope is a "Cone of Best Control" — defined as that area where you can easily get back to your glideslope and your approach to the slot.

If you get below the cone of control, you're grippin' it: You've given your vertical advantage away and can't move horizontally to the slot. You have to stop and go back up into the cone of control. If you don't, you'll go below.

You can't stretch your glideslope. No, not ever.

Kevin Shea, Parachutist, December 1976.

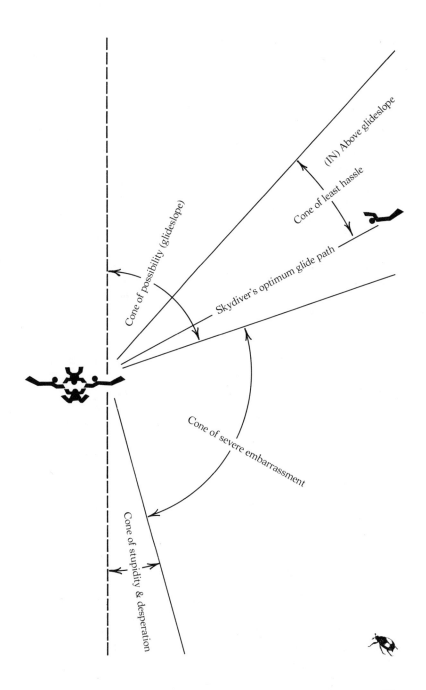

(IN) Above glideslope

Cone of least hassle

Cone of possibility (glideslope)

Skydiver's optimum glide path

Cone of severe embarrassment

Cone of stupidity & desperation

Subterminally Relatively Working. Exiting slow-moving aircraft, at say, 60 knots, and flying in thin, subterminal air just after exit, with only the prop blast for support, is tricky. If your group can build a 4-man in six seconds, hanging from a Cessna, then you're good at subterminal RW.

The original Greene County 4-man team could do it in less than 4.5 seconds from a C-180. Out of a Twin Beech, Captain Hook & the Sky Pirates builds 'em in under 10 seconds with full separation on exit.

True subterminal RW is one-shot relative work...there's no going back. You gotta do it all on a thin Relative Wind. That means the wind you're working on originates from the aircraft speed (the prop blast). It takes about 10 seconds to shift so that the wind you're working on is "blowing" from below you as you hit terminal velocity instead of coming from ahead of you as it is on exit.

Here are some things to remember about doing subterminal RW, whether you're jumping a base, pin, floater or flyer position:

1. There is no "base" in subterminal RW. At subterminal every RW'er is either a floater or a diver. A good base is actually a good floater who floats up to where the pin-man will be when they meet in the quiet air.

2. Be aware that your working air starts from the prop blast (your direction of travel).

3. After exit, just lay against the prop blast for an instant; feel it. If you want to move down toward the maneuver, flare briefly against the Relative Wind of the prop blast. This helps kill off the aircraft's speed so that you can start going the other way. You only start to move away from the aircraft's flight path and toward the star when you've dissipated the velocity imparted to you by the aircraft.

4. Then dive downward with a relaxed attitude, making sure you cover any horizontal distance required. Settle into the vertical via an RW Stable configuration (see "The Art of Freefall Relative Work" for a diagram of this position). Settle into your slot and enter.

5. To avoid landing on a backpack or somebody else's body on an expanding or sliding star, modify the vertical settling of your RW Stable into a short horizontal swoop. In other words, use the kinetic energy of your relatively faster drop rate to glide horizontally and enter.

6. If you're good at it, you can drop into a slot from directly above. To do this, you "elevator" down between the columns of vacuum left

by your skymates on either side. Locate their body burble with your hands. Feel its pressure on each hand from the bodies on each side of your slot. Dance down the column of air between them using your arms, feet and body to settle in. (By the way, this is a VERY ADVANCED TECHNIQUE and you're stupid to try to use it unless it will work 100% for you. It's a skill you will lose quickly if you lay off jumping, even for only a couple of months.)

7. Instead of trying to "get to" somebody, you should concentrate on where you're supposed to be: A point in space that lies in future time.

8. In order to float, exit in a relaxed manner so you can body surf up the wind blast from the prop to reach the maneuver. Use this technique whether you're a "floating" base man or a "floating" flyer.

Pat Works, RWu, October 1975

Special Rocky J. Squirrel Hot RW Hint. There are three basic track-approach techniques used on competition 10-mans... 1) down, then across and enter; 2) straight 45° angle from the airplane and in; and 3) horizontally, then dive down vertically.

The first is the slowest, and while safer for novices, is actually hard to control. I can't figure out if #2 or #3 is the faster. #3 sure is fun tho... you have your eye on the star the whole time. (Any traditionalists who might want to argue... I didn't develop these... I just copied some people who consistently get in sooner than other people.)

You have any ideas? If you're good at RW theory, share it with other RW· nuts.

Pat Works, RWu, Fall 1972

* * * *

King Kong Died For Our Sins

Flying in a New Dimension: Burbles
"He stole my air."
"Somebody went low and took it out."
"I Z'd in the burble and couldn't get back up."
...all expressions of disgust uttered by "victims" of the turbulence which follows most anything that moves through a fluid, like a jumper through the air.

One thing we as jumpers have in common with others who share the air is an awareness and appreciation for three-dimensional relationships and movement in space. Unfortunately, many of us have spent too much time looking at RW through narrow-slit snow goggles. Witness the poor soul who always tends to approach a formation from a level setup and therefore often "tends" to go low. Those who are consistently "in" have an appreciation and understanding of glide slopes and altitude in reserve and decelerating formations. However, little has been done until recently with *designing* the third dimension into formations and the transitions between formations.

Not to say that a lot of people haven't flown "over the top" to dock on the far side of a formation when that suddenly became the appropriate way to go, but how often was it planned? Flying under a formation is a more or less universal taboo and has been the source of many an up and coming relative worker's being ostracized from several subsequent loads.

To try to change the trend of thought on the subject, let's talk about some of the things that *have* been done with an eye toward what *can* be done.

Four people set up a no-contact skirmish line with about a meter of lateral separation. The jumper on one end dropped down about two or three feet and sideslid underneath the other three people with the intention of floating up into place on the opposite end. As it turned out, his burble successively dropped each of the other three down the same two or three feet and the flyer was in place as soon as he got across without climbing back up. Nobody "Z'd in the burble" and three people completed the cycle in turn.

Lesson #1: *When you are expecting the burble from someone flying underneath with lateral momentum, its effect is negligible and short-lived, and can be compensated for.*

Four people set up a Polish accordion (zig-zag with hand to hand grips). The jumper on one end let go, floated up about a meter, flew *directly* over the person next to him and down into the opposite end slot. The objective was to stabilize directly over the slot and sink straight down to dock, instead of making a conventional approach. It worked. All four people made the transition and the only complication arose when one flyer concentrated too much on the slot he was headed for and not enough on generating sufficient initial vertical separation. His knees brushed the jumper he was crossing over and the flyer had to recover and fly up to re-enter. The formation was unaffected.

Lesson #2: *When flying over people one at a time with moderate momentum, the burble will drop you down about two or three feet, so that much vertical separation needs to be generated before starting across. If you wind up level with the formation on the far side, then you have* used *the burble instead of fearing it.*

Five people built a "V," with the point facing the other four. One of the end people let go, flew down the line over three people and docked on the point's leg. Then the other end person did the same thing, docking on the point's other leg. The other two people did the same transition and completed a "V" with everybody facing the same direction.

Next, four people built a straight diamond. The tail let go of the leg of the left wing who then dropped his grip on the point, floated up, straight across and down onto the right wing's leg. Then the point was released and he flew up, over and down to be the new tail. The cycle was repeated three times with people who were not that experienced and had *never heard* of vertical transitions.

Lesson #3: *This stuff is not hard to do.*

Five people built a spider. The two people on legs nodded at each other and dropped grips. One flew diagonally under the formation and the other one went over the top, simultaneously, then up and down, respectively, to dock on the "top right" person's legs. The "top left" person then dropped his grip and flew over the top to the new center person's right leg, forming a new spider. Three cycles were completed on one dive with burbles everywhere and no funnel.

Lesson #4: *This stuff is fun to do.*

The beauty of all these dives is that they are open-ended. There is no such thing as a completion. Motion is the essence of multi-dimensional maneuvering, and a stopping point is counter to that idea. Once a cycle results in the original formation, repeat it without hesitation. Let break-off be the only interruption. Keeping up with what has to be done next is good for developing situation awareness. The dives just described were done by a variety of jumpers, some in this country and some in Scandinavia where they were just learning how to do basic sequential.

Vertical transitions not only work, they are in many cases the fastest, easiest and most logical way to get to a new slot during a change in formations. Whether a flyer goes over or under a formation need only depend on which is best for *his* maneuvering potential, as long as when he flys underneath, the people in the formation either see him or are expecting him to be there.

Burble Basics. In investigating the burble over an individual jumper (try it) you will find that it is a well-defined *narrowing* column of air that can be felt, anticipated and maneuvered around. *Think* about it while flying over someone and you will *feel* it on your face, then your chest and finally down your legs.

The effect on the air is much the same as what you see when you put your hand flat on the surface of a swimming pool then submerge it rapidly. The *narrow* column of bubbles that follows your hand is caused by the same sort of trailing vortex that is over your back in freefall.

This burble does make things inside it fall faster relative to things outside it, so the trick is to maintain a moderate lateral momentum when moving directly over or under someone. Of course, the faster you move the less the effect on the guy on top, but tracking speeds are totally unnecessary. Just don't stagnate. Over large "dense" formations with small spaces between people there may be one large column of turbulence instead of several small ones, so flying over the top may be potentially disastrous. Use some discretion about easing over the next 21-wedge you happen to encounter.

But with small or moderately-sized formations where a vertical transition might be useful, plan it and use it. You will develop a keener sense of perspective and awareness of the vertical dimension that might previously have escaped your attention.

People are now working on large formation sequential with pieces or groups of flyers making vertical transitions. It is just one more direction we can go, one more avenue for creativity, one more aspect of the ultimate awareness.

Roger Hull, Parachutist, January 1977

Your Condition's Condition
Second of a series on *How NOT to Do 4-Man RW* **or, "Doing It With Your Rig On."** Have you ever witnessed someone leave the plane, do three unintentional left turns and a back loop just before he goes into a barrrel roll — arms & legs flopping all over the sky — before he gets his act together?

Have you ever hurled your body at a star in such a fire-breathing, body-beating track that you had trouble getting your arms away from your sides to flare? If so, you've got a case of the "unqualified muscle" — a disease that can strike anyone. It's muscle that's not ready, or qualified, to do what you want it to. And I'm including it in this discussion about equipment because equipment, as I see it, is everything you leave the plane with. A good mental attitude and good physical muscle tone are as much a part of your equipment as your rig. While a good jumper can acclimate himself to any combination of rig, jumpsuit and boots, very few can overcome a broken mainspring between their ears or a defective body.

Optimum body conditioning is necessary to excell in RW because you have to be able to hold your body in configurations necessary to alter given trajectories while in freefall for the purpose of relating to other people. Your muscle structure relates to the weight and mass of your body of course, but whatever it is, it should be in good shape.

Three things are vital to good RW: 1) physical conditioning; 2) mental alertness; 3) a good parachute so you can do it again.

The skydiver must be able to push the air around him. That's why the aforementioned wind dummy who was Z-ing out all over the sky won't make a good relative worker until he cures his unqualified muscle.

If you have a four-man team, you should consider adopting a vigorous exercise program (yoga, calisthenics, jogging) together; it will make working and thinking together easier, too. Or, each individual should do it on his own.

Unqualified muscle also afflicts the brain "muscle." Mental preparation is more difficult but sometimes just realizing the source of a head problem is a start toward clearing it up. All relative work starts in the head and if the head is hassled (fights with the old lady, or the boss, $$$ problems) it'll show in your RW. When you bail out to do sequential RW you need 100 percent concentration on your job.

The head can't be separated from the physical person. Physical fitness to many means taking care of everything but the brain. But when the body is run down or out of order, the head usually is too. When the body is beautiful and the head is a blank — that doesn't work either. The body and the brain are inseparable and must be worked on together.

Some people seem to do RW by turning off their head and jumping out the door. That's how stars are busted, grips are lost, formations do not fly well, etc., etc. RW requires constant awareness and attention to what is going on.

Man didn't survive the dinosaur age because he was stronger than the dinosaurs and could force them to do his will. He survived because he was smarter and used his intelligence better than did those prehistoric beasts. So, when you leave the plane, don't be a dinosaur.

Equipment for the most part is a personal matter. Almost any gear can be successfully used for relative work, but it is most important that you be able to fly the equipment you have rather than letting the equipment fly you. It's of relatively little importance whether you are the coolest-looking dude in the air or have the smallest, largest, weirdest equipment on the team. Your equipment should relate to the job you have to do in the air.

Marc Cohen, RWu, October 1973

Be Safe. We've lost some of our fellow RWers in parachuting accidents... unfortunately tragic deaths because they could have been prevented so easily — with a little *carefulness.*

Are we forgetting some of the basic safety rules in RW jumping? When a star breaks, turn 180°... and track (don't *everybody* track for the spot either)... wave off... never dump right in the pack.

When the relative work stops, don't stop thinking.

RWu, June 1973

Using The First Seven Seconds. Revelation: sub-terminal isn't sub-terminal any more. We exit at terminal.* It is the direction of the relative wind, not slower speed, that makes it look like we do things differently out the door.

If you step out at 12,000 feet, accelerate to the advertised 120 mph in eleven seconds and get it out after 70 seconds in the air, somebody else will have to log what was just your last skydive. But you say, "We do fall that long and manage to open higher than high-speed dirt."

Obviously we are falling slower than 120 mph. How much slower? Around 90 to 100 mph appears to be right for the times we are getting. Applying Newton's laws — the physics of falling bodies — shows that one square foot of surface area (like wings) added to your shadow will knock off about seven miles per hour for the same body position. Start with 180 pounds of total weight, reduce it by ten pounds and you will decelerate three more mph. Add those two speeds together and you have ten mph—more than enough to put you below (or take out) any formation. Ten mph is how fast you run if you can do a six-minute mile. The point?

The trend toward larger jumpsuits and weight-conscious skydivers has made a substantial difference in the "average" terminal rate-of-descent. So much so that we now fall at or near the exit speed of the aircraft we jump out of.** The best relative work that has ever been done is being done today and it is being done at the speed we used to call sub-terminal (because it was). We used to think it was a region of poor control where flying had to be done entirely differently, with exaggerated body movements. Some people still think that way.

For the post-exit transition to be smooth and under total control, you have to start the relative work inside the airplane and continue it out the door. You have to present yourself to the relative wind without trying to force yourself into a visual preconception of where your body should be. It shouldn't make any difference to you what the airplane is doing when you get out or where it is after you have left.

If you look at a good single-file exit just as the last person leaves the door, you will notice that each jumper is successively more inclined with respect to the horizon.

How inclined? Being the hot divers they are, they probably don't even notice. They don't care about the horizon. It isn't important or even relevant. It's the wind.

Each of these flyers, either seeing or "knowing" where the formation is, adjusts his attitude and does whatever maneuvering is necessary to get there.

So fly into the relative wind. Ignore the airplane and the horizon. If you want to dive, float, track or whatever, *feel the wind first,* then do it. The lead who exits and wants to cut down on the time required to form a base-pin can track toward the pin. He looks like he is tracking up, but we know now that he is actually head down into the wind he feels.

Changing from an apparent head-up position to an apparent head-down position just out the door is a *flat* turn with respect to the wind and it is done the same way as it would be later on in the dive when you *are* flat. It just *looks* like a cartwheel.

People who fly differently simply because they have just exited are probably the same ones who come off a freeway on-ramp at 40 mph when the traffic is at 55.

A student who does a rearward door exit from a Cessna in a good arch, then suddenly starts tumbling, probably thinks he is unstable when he sees the sky behind him, underneath himself and then de-arches, when actually he is in only a moderate head-down dive into the wind.

His eyes deceive him because he has not yet learned to feel the wind and to trust his body position. People who always keep at least one foot on the ground normally use vision as their primary reference for attitude orientation. Beginning jumpers (and relative workers) typically continue to depend on it.

More number-crunching reveals that we slow down very slightly after exit for only about nine-tenths of a second, then our total velocity increases slowly to whatever terminal is for the combination of air, weight, jumpsuit, gear and body position. The difference in speed would be virtually imperceptible if you had your eyes closed.

Some folks who take big things right out the door even say you have your best contol at exit because that is when you are at your *fastest* airspeed. I'll buy that. It means the airplane is flying faster at exit than the terminal velocity for whatever goes out the door.

Forward throw is only significant for about seven seconds. By that time drag has reduced your horizontal speed essentially to zero and gravity has accelerated your vertical speed from zero to terminal, "replacing" the horizontal component. You don't fly on vertical wind alone so you don't have to wait until it builds up. The resultant of the two speeds (horizontal and vertical) is called the relative wind and it is there at the moment of exit.

That is a lot of talking about a small portion of a dive. "All this for the first seven seconds?" you ask. "Yes!" When you leave the airplane, forget about "mushy air" and exaggerated contol movements and sub-terminal sub-awareness. Look around, sure. But to fly...you need to feel.

Damn few of us have enough time in freefall to call it a day. Skydives are expensive and seven seconds is ten percent of a high one. When we are at the point of doing relative work inside the airplane and continuing it out the door, the dead time on the top is eliminated. Freefall with your friends is a rare privilege. Use it *all.* Enjoy it. More peak function time...more total awareness.

Editors' Note: Roger is referring to the desirable high exit speed. Of course, exit speeds of less than 90 mph involve sub-terminal RW, which requires different techniques.

Roger Hull, Parachutist, November 1977, and Can-Para, September 1977.

**More than 80 mph for a DC-3, C-47 or Twin Otter. Exit speed from a Cessna 170 or 180 series, or a helicopter is around 60 mph. No matter what airplane you jump from, a high exit speed is desirable.

PART IV Exits — better exits for better skydives.

You Got Me Floatin'

"Well, you got me floatin',
Around and around.
Always up, you never let me down.
Across and through,
You make me float right on up to you."

These are words from the immortal Jimmy Hendrix who perhaps knew more than many credit him for.

The most important variable in floating is *TIMING*. You must exit at the exact same time as the base and should be on the side of the formation opposite the direction of flight. This eliminates congestion with the divers.

If you're not on the proper side after exit, you should immediately sit up and get your chest into the prop blast. This will push you into the proper position very effectively. Needing to use your swoop-cords instead of your chest indicates poor timing on exit. If you sit up after you clear the prop blast, you'll sink out which is the opposite of what you're trying to do.

That first 3 seconds after exit is what you must learn to use. If you don't use the benefits of the prop blast, you'll have to wait for your airspeed to build up before you can manuever quickly and you'll take a long time to dock.

Here's the easy way to float:

1. Climb out quickly so you don't overshoot the spot.
2. Hug the plane close and it won't be difficult to hang on.
3. Watch (or listen) to the countdown and exit at the *exact* same time as the base never taking your eyes off him. You should be 10 to 20 feet away at maximum. If not, you need better timing.
4. Exit in the frog position and assume the same position as the base. Correct as necessary and make up the *horizontal* distance in the prop blast.
5. Do not try to float up before you clear the prop blast as you'll inflate

your swoop cords and back-track out of position.
6. When the base "planes out" (chest parallel with the ground), extend your feet, legs together and toes pointed. As soon as *you* plane out, put your arms in the Iron Cross position (straight out, 90 degrees to your sides). Float up using forward drive from your legs only.
7. If you are above the base, you can dive (delta) down to it. Remember, you should be on the back side before and after your dive.

Once you perfect this subterminal flying, you can experiment with competition exits (base back-sliding as little as possible), and you'll have excellent technique for fast pre-stars before the maneuver.

Carl Nelson, Freak Brother Flyer #6

How to be a Floating Base. Just exit and move into a relaxed delta (rather than flaring into the relative wind of the prop blast, as a flyer might do). Said another way, after exit let your arms blow behind you and relax your chest as you arch slightly. Like the feathers on an arrow, your arms and legs will "weathervane" you toward the airplane. As a result, *you* don't turn to face the pin, rather you let the *wind* turn you to dock with the pin.

Pat Works, RWu, October 1975

Exits. Exit is an interface, a boundary, the place where things touch, and everything happens. Exit is the interface between the cocoon of the aircraft and flight on freefall's relative wind.

Exit is the most violent and sudden of aerodynamic, physical and mental shocks you'll encounter during your skydive. When we dive out or let go, we leave one situation for another, and the transition isn't easy.

If you think your skydive begins after your exit, you're missing the point.

The point: your skydive begins when you tighten you leg straps. And, next to canopy opening, exit is the most crucial part of your skydive.

Because it's so violent, sudden and variable, exit is the one place where you're most likely to lose control during your skydive. (If you don't agree, turn around and look behind you on your next run-out-the-door exit.)

Because it's the one place where you have the most opportunity for control, it's crucial to pay attention to it. Exit is the first, best, and perhaps the *only* place you can sneak past the rules of freefall aerodynamics.

Exit is the short instant where you can use the aircraft to your advantage. Right after you leave — less than a second — the airplane no longer has a direct affect on you. But during exit you can summon power from your relationship to the airplane: *leverage*.

Leverage: the quality of push, pull, friction, inertia and momentum. Aircraft aluminum provides much better leverage than air.

Help is all around us just when we need it most. The more we pay attention to exit and its relationships (to each other, to the plane, to the wind), the less surprised we'll be as we leave the airplane. And the more stable.

What follows is a guide to making your own exits better. It works for three people, twenty people, Lodestars and Cessnas. You can apply and adapt it to whatever skydiving you'll be doing this weekend. If you do, you'll find that exits are fun.

Approaching exits. Speed exits are not only for speed stars. Why?

Think of exit as psychological preparation for the rest of your skydive.

Fast exits make everyone's freefall time easier and more productive. Because of the very nature of a hot exit, it sets the tone and pace of the rest of the skydive.

If you have to wait to get out the door, you'll probably have to wait for your turn to execute your slot.

Exploding out the door forces your concentration, tunes your awareness to your next move. The speed of the exit is carried over to the rest of the skydive: a fast pin/base *only* follows an explosive exit.

Ultimately, the pin/base and the rest of the skydive become part of the exit.

Four things make good, fast exits:

1 — Low Volume
2 — Common Motion/Momentum
3 — Presentation to Air/Relative Wind
4 — Comfort & Safety

1) Low Volume. It's important to get the last man in line (or on the step) as close as possible to the first man out the door.

Inches in the airplane factor into yards in the propblast. The factor varies according to the design of the door through which the exit must pass. Every door/floor/fuselage/airspeed combination is unique in how it spreads skydivers across the sky. Small-door Beeches have a high factor; Cessnas and Skyvans have a low factor.

Pay attention to aircraft. Every plane has a different potential. Beechcraft exits waste the space a DC-3 or Lodestar offers. A 182 exit doesn't work as well if you're jumping a 180 or a 206. Fit the exit to the airplane.

To get low volume: A. Determine your door picture. How wide and how high is the open space in front of you? There are two approaches to this.

An angled exit permits a longer, smoother flow but narrows the door picture. A straight, perpendicular line uses the maximum door width but limits the number of people in the line.

Similarly, a tall, standing line-up uses the full height of the door, but forces the people in front to perform long turns as they enter the prop-blast.

Either approach can work well. Choose one according to the skydive that's planned.

B. Have everyone present themselves to the door, *then* present themselves to the man in front of them. Allow no space.

Don't crouch and shove your butt out (moving the man behind you further back). Keep your trunk vertical, squat and slide under and against the man in front of you, press your legs and belly against his pack.

Space is distance and distance is time. Time is what makes a slow exit. Allow no space.

C. Compress your line physically. Hold on to something in front of you and push/pull yourself to it. As the entire line does this (all the way back to the 22nd diver) it'll shrink 15% — and the last man will be closer to the first man. And get to his slot sooner.

D. Hang people outside of the airplane. Practice low volume with each person wearing what they wear jumping (and cinched down tightly). Five minutes doing this before your skydive will be worth it. Honest.

2) Common Motion/Momentum. There's no point in leaving the plane right next to someone if that someone is going away from you.

Plan the exit (particularly the front pack) so it is flung away from the plane like a handful of marbles. Everybody leaps into the airstream individually together.

It's something we learn, unconsciously, from Cessna struts, then somehow forget when we try on different airplanes.

If the man in front of you dives down while you jump up, you're already going away from one another. If you both hop out (or off) in the same direction, your momentum is the same — and it takes just small flying forces to bring yourselves together.

Compare it to orbital spacecraft docks. When they're already in the same orbit (momentum), satellites use teeny thrusters to dock. But massive boosters are required to get separate spacecraft into the same momentum.

If you exit with common motion/momentum, you leave the airplane on final approach to your slot.

To get there, you need:

Good count. A simultaneous, controlled count. Tradition has it that 3, 2, 1, GO works best. Assign certain people their counts and motions according to their position in the exit. (Sometimes if the front initiates their motion *between* 1 and GO, the exit flows faster with less resistance. Late divers need not count, just react to the pack in front of them. Floaters need to be told when "GO" happens.)

Good picture. Plan ahead how to share the door picture. Find out where the man in front of you plans to pass through the door, then plan to take some other part of the door (if it's big enough). If you plan how to alternate and share portions of the fuselage and door, you'll reduce bumps and friction, and exit faster.

Good push. Join your exit force with the common exit force. The direction and flow should be in a line as straight as possible out the door. Curves and angles squeeze people out of line and should be reduced or eliminated where possible. Don't push anyone anywhere but through the door. Always move for the door.

Good grips. Grips help exits. Flying something off the step or out the door is exciting and challenging and gets your skydiving/flying started faster. Grips are your sensors that tell you the direction of the momentum of the exit in front of you. The better you get at it, the less tugging/friction/resistance the exit gives you and, eventually, you're *not* hanging on — you're just *there.* With your hands on the exit to prove it!

3) Presentation to the Relative Wind. The exit must give every member control (leverage, either aluminum or relative wind) to, through and outside the door.

Sometimes it's not easy. There's a stiff, sudden, horizontal wind outside the airplane. Don't be surprised by it.

Think about how your exit will introduce your body to the slipstream. Where is your body while you're still inside or on the fuselage? Where is your head? Where are your eyes looking? And where is your slot?

Get on the optimum relative wind for your slot immediately. Imagine your slot and the very best body position you'll need for a clean swoop to it. Then, *jump* from your airplane exit position *to* that swoop body position in the airstream.

It's important to use the airplane's slipstream and take advantage of the most wind (control) just when you need it. You'll be through the slipstream before you have time to react to it, so plan how you're going to meet it (your presentation) *before* you leave the plane.

Fast, good exits get everyone flying on the same air sooner. By reducing the differences in exit members' relative winds, fast exits reduce variables and confusion. The faster the exit, the sooner things happen.

4) Comfort and Safety. Skydiving is more fun when we don't get hurt and it's easier and safer for us when we don't abuse our gear. Exit has to achieve the first three factors and still maintain comfort and safety.

Low volume isn't meant to injure people or damage gear; good push isn't good push if it opens containers or canopy releases. There are ways of getting out of an airplane without sacrificing our bodies.

How? If you pay attention to the first factors: low volume, good motion and your presentation to the relative wind, and invest a short time working them out, they provide comfort and safety in themselves.

Look for the sloppy, loose areas in the lineup that *will* (I promise they will!) bump around and expand and rub and make your line-up stop and start and hurt someone. Eliminate those spaces, then you have good low volume.

Look for each member's presentation to the air. If he has it, he has control. If he doesn't have it, he's out of control — and that's when we get hurt. Good presentation is comfortable and safe.

Look for everyone's motion to take them out the door. Get a good door picture, get everybody moving for the door. Together. Good motion means no one is aimed for the door jam, means there are no bumps and grinds to interrupt your skydive.

Look for the hooks and snags that will (even if they never have before) snag, tear or rip something or someone. Look over the airplane and yourselves. Look to see that you'll make it out of the plane in one piece.

Fix it, tape it, hammer it down or take it off, make it right *before* you get in the plane. There's no point in letting some silly oversight interrupt someone's skydive.

And that's the point: your skydive begins when you tighten your leg straps, and it ends when you *close* your container. Don't allow any interruptions.

Approach your skydive as a whole thing, so you can enjoy the whole thing.

Kevin Shea, Parachutist, April 1977

Captain Hook Sez:

Captain Hook (Al Krueger) of "Captain Hook & the Sky Pirates" has this exit hint; "Never touch the door sill or frame with your hands on exit. It will slow you down."

RWu, June 1974

2

RW Gear

Creative New Gear. The Human Factor. Build a better
mousetrap...design something into a piece of parachuting equipment
that is a new, different, faster or lighter way to "do the job," and you
enhance its marketability. Unfortunately, sales appeal does not
always bear a direct relationship to improvement, especially when
improvement is cast in terms of safety, efficiency and susceptibility to
human error — the human factor.

Throw-out and hand-deployed pilot chutes, plastic hardware,
new-concept canopy releases, ram-air canopies — all highly innovative
ideas from industrious and conscientious equipment manufacturers
and jumpers — have caused major shifts in thinking and capability in
the jumping community with respect to the gear we use. The process of
evolution that took place between the B-4 and the Top Secret or
Wonder Hog has resulted in something akin to Toffler's "Future
Shock." Specifically, a lot of jumpers at widely diverse levels of
experience and talent are using equipment without an adequate
knowledge of
  — how the equipment actually works,
  — what the inherent dangers are,
  — how to deal with malfunctions peculiar to the particular piece of
    gear,
  — most importantly, how susceptible the gear and its sub-systems
    are to errors in assembly or use.
In many cases the ignorance is so profound that they don't even know
enough to ask questions or imagine problems.

I do not in any way want to imply here that the equipment
manufacturers and innovators have designed or are designing gear

that is deficient in accomplishing the function for which it was intended. (Some of it *may* be deficient, but that is another topic.) However, some equipment is designed with apparent inattention to, disregard of, or ignorance of the way it is actually employed.

Let's look for a minute at the process through which most equipment innovations pass before getting "out on the street."

— Someone, a manufacturer or just some jumper, has an idea, a "better way," usually due to some dissatisfaction with what he has.

— He toys with the idea, designs and makes a prototype or alters his present equipment.

— He asks himself, "Will it work?", "Can it break?", "What happens if it doesn't work or does break?", and "Is it really better (lighter, faster, easier to use) or is it just different?"

— If the answers to his self-posed questions are optimistic, he proceeds to make one, then jumps it.

— He "tests" it using "reasonable" safety precautions. The tests may vary from "I'm alive so it must work," to full-blown FAA-dictated strength tests or drop tests with supporting test design reports and data submitted for approval and TSO.

— In the tests of the equipment, he is highly prone either to test it himself or solicit the help of highly experienced friends or employees to make the test jumps "because they know how to evaluate it."

— If the results appear favorable, he markets the gear and watches to see if unforeseen problems develop and if the community response is also favorable.

— Maybe, many months later, the USPA Safety and Training people or some interested jumper/writer will do an equipment article for *Parachutist* explaining their test results and describing how to use the gear properly.

This process, which differs in detail in every case, has some positive, constructive results. With some exceptions, we have equipment which is

— safer
— better looking
— "cleaner" aerodynamically
— more comfortable
— lighter in weight

— more durable

— less prone to malfunction

— occasionally, less expensive.

But there is a negative side. Things do go wrong with new equipment for various reasons. People do get hurt and killed, or more frequently, just scare themselves. Worst of all, people with little to no knowledge of equipment manufacturing and testing or of the nature and intent of a new design or especially of human factors, do attempt to copy new equipment design features in order to save themselves time or money.

I saw *seven* hand-deploy or throw-out pilot chutes "in tow" that necessitated reserve deployments at the last Turkey Meet. They occurred with a variety of rigs, some just crude imitations of good gear. Most of them were due to "people errors."

At least two people are dead because they confused a Capewell cover with a blast handle after a cut-away (same shape and feel, four inches apart).

People have deployed reserves because they could not find the plastic golf ball or the "little red tab" on the end of an external pilot chute.

People do thread chest straps through ripcord handles. It's easy!

I have seen and used equipment with critical functional features that were easy to *see* but hard to locate and use by *feel* alone.

When an equipment manufacturer sees a malfunction on gear he made and investigates the cause, then chuckles and writes it off with a statement like, "You just assembled it incorrectly. There is nothing I can do about that," he is missing the point. He is admitting that he is making laboratory equipment — a system that works well in the absence of all the "extraneous variables" like wind and cold and funnels and fast pack jobs to make the next load. If the gear can be mis-used, mis-rigged or mis-handled, *it will be.* It is the nature of the human, even if he is sharp enough to be a good skydiver.

We have to consider the physiological sense or combination of senses that are depended upon to operate a piece of equipment and the actual situation in which it will be used. As in many other situations where habit patterns of complex movements are involved, we become more dependent on feel than on visual control of those movements, especially when there are other high demands on our visual system, like ground rush.

Equipment testing cannot be considered adequate when it is restricted to the manufacturer himself or other experienced people who completely understand the system. There must be some determination of the susceptibility to human error when used by much less experienced and less aware jumpers who may not understand the system at all.

There is no more excuse for placing the total blame on a jumper who makes an error in the use of his equipment than there was to place the total blame on pilots of WWII vintage aircraft who landed with the wheels up when the landing gear and flap levers were exactly alike and side-by-side. Both worked the way they were supposed to, but the susceptibility for error was high.

The human factor in system design must be considered from the beginning and all the way through in the development of new equipment, from connector links to complete assemblies.

Some of this consideration becomes rather involved. For instance, pulling a ripcord requires conscious *effort* (as opposed to breathing, which is sub-conscious) but it may not require your *attention,* given enough experience. How often have you initially reached for a ripcord where it used to be before you changed systems? It is the reason we tell students to look at the ripcord before pulling. It forces attention to the task at hand and reduced the chances of pulling the reserve ripcord, Stevens' lanyard, or main lift web in error. With increased experience, attention is usually not required to perform a routine task, but if an error is made, then attention is required to correct it. Equipment must be built for consistent, non-attentive, proper use with a low probability of error, *by design.*

So there is a problem... what do we do about it? There is gear on the market that comes with no written operating instructions or owners manual, with the usual exception of packing instructions, and these are often only for the reserve. There are no restrictions imposed by anyone on the sale or purchase of equipment and few restrictions (in this country) on the use of advanced or high-performance equipment or sub-systems. I don't think we need or want restrictions, primarily because they are virtually unenforceable except in tightly controlled situations. But there is a way.

A jumper who makes enough mistakes on RW loads doesn't get asked on very many more until he improves his performance — *self-regulation by the community.*

People don't loan money to a known deadbeat — *strength of reputation.*

The turkey who buries a disc and leaves it there catches a ration of grief from the next guy in who "had it wired" — *peer pressure.*

Ripcord stops finally fell by the wayside — *organizational pressure, not regulation.*

The novice jumper who wants the latest gear is more likely to hold off buying it if he is told he *can't* get it by some "authority" — *appeal to basic motivation, group acceptance.*

The high puller, the railroader, the dude with the foul pits — they all *lose face* eventually.

People who design and manufacture new equipment have to make a profit and they deserve it. Potential loss of profit is an effective motivator. If a new gear is shown, publicly, to be highly susceptible to human error of serious consequence, it will be improved or it will be ostracized by the community at large.

Manufacturers can improve the situation by asking themselves throughout the development process, "How likely is it that an overly ambitious, half-lit jumper with little experience and a lot of pressure will use this equipment incorrectly, and how much trouble will he be in if he does?" and "How can I design it to minimize that risk?"

The user of the equipment can keep himself healthier by asking "What sort of mistakes *might* I make with this gear?" "How can I check myself *before* time is critical?" "What will happen if I *do* mis-use it?" "Am I comfortable enough with my equipment that concern about it won't distract from the other things I want to do in the air?"

Time dedicated to thinking through potential equipment problems is time well spent. If you can conceive of some unusual situations and think through the corrective actions thoroughly, mentally rehearsing them step-by-step, chances are when the situations do occur, you will follow the procedures "instinctively" with little demand on your attention. Retrieval of the steps from memory will not require your attention; only their execution will and you will have bought yourself more time. It's a good investment.

Communication is the process by which reputations and group opinions are formed. If you make a mistake with your gear, if it "breaks" or you see a potential problem with it, admit it; make it public; help somebody else avoid it, remembering that it may not be simply a dumb mistake or a freak occurrence. You might have been partially victimized. At least with someone else to blame it is easier to talk about it.

So let's continue to innovate, redesign and improve the equipment we use. Those who do so are making substantial contributions to the sport and its overall progress. But that progress is multi-faceted and it must not be made at the expense of safety.

Roger Hull, Sport Parachutist, April 1977

Great music is like RW...
"O death, all conquering one,
Now you are conquered!
With wings I have won for myself,
Striving in fervent love
I shall soar
To the light no eye
Has seen!"

Gustav Mahler's tumultuous "Resurrection" Symphony #2 in G

The Evolution of the RW Jumpsuit...Or, You are What You Fly

Today's relative work is reflected in the jumpsuits we wear. Precision RW has evolved through the development of the jumpsuit as a functional piece of flying equipment.

Today a belled, puff-sleeve jumpsuit with swoop cords and 12-inch underarm extensions is a MUST-HAVE piece of RW equipment.

In the early 60's jumpsuits were nearly universally Sears & Roebuck white painters' coveralls. These coveralls were first cleaned up by cutting off the hammer loop and belt. Then, to improve their looks, the unsightly baggy material around the body and legs was tapered for a chic, tailored look. The purpose of these jumpsuits was to stop the wind of freefall from messing up your shirt, to keep your jeans clean, and to look cool, man.

In the mid 60's the tight-fitting Pioneer jumpsuits were popular. They looked nice and had nifty double zippers that allowed you to put on your jumpsuit AFTER you had already put your boots on! Revolutionary!

In the late 60's, the picture changed in Southern California when Ward-Venegas entered the scene with the weird philosophy that "A jumpsuit can never be too big for you...and the bigger the better." These were definitely a relative worker's jumpsuit. However, few people were really into the esoterics of hot RW.

About 1970, at the very beginning of his jumping career, Joe Garcia, a master tailor and material-molder since childhood, started making his own jumpsuits to help correct his stability problems. As a pilot, Joe knew he needed more control surfaces. So he started in an obvious place and put flares, or bells, on the arms and legs.

At the first USPA 10-man National Championships in 1972, less than half of the competitors wore bells, as I recall. Bird's team won, all wearing bells.

In 1976, just about all relative workers were wearing bells. In 1974, the United States Freefall Exhibition Team popularized the concept of the fully functional "flying" RW jumpsuit — with extensions, swoop cords, and lots of bagginess. This idea was apparently developed by Seattle area jumpers.

It is now generally accepted that the jumpsuit is the single most important piece of equipment for relative work.

RW created a demand for a good jumpsuit. Good jumpsuits enable good relative workers to fly closer to their respective limits of perfection.

HERE'S THE STORY OF THE JUMPSUIT THAT REVOLU-TIONIZED JUMPSUIT THINKING:

Once upon a time, not so long ago, there was a kid who was really poor. I mean, he didn't even have decent clothes to wear to school. But his folks did have a sewing machine. So this kid made his own shirt to wear to school.

He made Christmas presents for his relatives, too. And for his girlfriends, he made nice coats of fur and leather. Pretty soon, people were paying him to make the stuff.

At age 15, Joe Garcia made a basic business decision. He looked at what he was making, compared it to the salary of graduates, and quit school to start his own business. His specialty was making anything of fabric.

He started out making leather accessories for motorcyclists. Later he became a pilot and bought an airplane. One of his shops was located near an airfield that also housed jumpers. A place called Elsinore, California. Lots of gliders and parachutists.

Joe got interested in jumping. He says, "I had a stability problem in my early jumps. As a private pilot, I knew I needed more control surface, so I made my own jumpsuit and put bells on the sleeves and

legs. I had about 40 jumps. People laughed at my first jumpsuits. Then Jim Heydorn and Pete Gruber had me build jumpsuits for them. I did. And they worked."
Pat Works, RWu, June 1976

Ultra-Lightweight RW Gear...An Objectively Subjective Evaluation...AN UPDATE

Sir Isaac Newton should get all the blame for the lightweight RW gear revolution. It was he who discovered gravity and MOMENTUM. (I think it was Wildman who discovered light RW gear. Hank Asciutto, John Sherman and others have made it a reality.)

Momentum is easier to understand if you know that it is somewhat like speed. Speed is measured in miles per hour. At terminal velocity, your speed is about 120 mph. Momentum is a *quantity* that is equal to the product of your weight multiplied by your speed. Momentum changes whenever your weight or speed changes. The less you weigh the less momentum you have and so the easier it is to reach maximum speed in an approach, and the easier it is to stop quickly, too.

For example, say you jump lightweight gear:

your weight	165 lbs.	
gear weight	27 lbs.	
TOTAL	192 lbs.	times your speed (120 mph) equals your momentum **23,040**

Or if you jump regular weight gear:

your weight	165 lbs.	
gear weight	42 lbs.	
TOTAL	207 lbs.	times your speed (120 mph) equals your momentum **24,840**

There's a quantity of 1800 — a 7 percent difference. Aw, screw the numbers, it all boils down to the fact that one pound of weight is worth a 51 percent bonus in momentum. And, the lighter you are, the more your gear weight affects your momentum. So to conclude, IT'S GOOD TO HAVE LIGHTWEIGHT GEAR.

Here are *RWu's* impressions of some current lightweight systems and canopies:

ParaCommander — Introduced in 1964. With its high performance characteristics, was then what the square is today. However, the good ol' PC is too bulky and too heavy for present-day RW.

RW-PC — A light-weight Para-Commander. Packs up slightly bulkier and is a tad heavier than the Sierra. The RW-PC is the canopy of choice for heavier jumpers who insist on a round. Handles very smoothly; is forgiving on landing. Good accuracy canopy.

Sierra — Lighter than and packs up smaller than an RW-PC. Costs less. Flies smooth although not as stable as the RW-PC. A pleasure to jump. Recommended for RW jumpers who prefer a round canopy.

Piglet II — The original lightweight RW canopy and system. Still the best hard-core system for the serious competitor who wants a simple, ultra-reliable round. Lands briskly. Very easy to pack. *RWu* recommended for serious competitors who do not weigh a lot and prefer a round canopy.

Piglet 23' — "Big Man's Piglet," a larger canopy for the heavier jumper and for those who want softer landings than the smaller Piglet II delivers. Easy to pack, reliable; not an accuracy canopy but a fine general use RW canopy. Recommended.

Paradactyl — The lightest RW canopy available. Presently one of the least expensive because of its unpredictable opening and flight characteristics. Treat with respect! Older models are chancy on opening. All delta-shape wings can fold up in flight. Not recommended.

Strato-Flyer — The Strato-Star's little brother. Flies faster and lands a bit harder than the Star. Very light; packs up very small. Cannot be free-packed. Considered to be the square canopy of choice for the hard-core RW competitor. Is relatively touchy at flare point compared to larger squares.

Strato-Star — The square that revolutionized RW by putting canopy control back into the jump. Easy to free-pack fast. Packs up smallish; all-white versions are only a pound or so heavier that the Flyer. Good accuracy canopy. Very reliable openings. Said to be slightly easier to fly than the Flyer. A good all-around canopy.

Strato-Cloud — the "Cadillac" of squares. The best accuracy canopy. Although heavier than either the Flyer or Star, total canopy (all-white) weight is only 4 or 5 pounds more than a Flyer. Very reliable openings. The easiest square to fly. The best no-wind canopy. The sofest landing canopy. Easy to free-pack fast. Good for canopy RW. The best all-around canopy.

	Canopy Weight	Opening Shock	Flight Characteristics	Low Turns	Landing Shock	No-Wind Landings	Packing Difficulty	Opening Reliability	Price	RWu SCORE*
Para-Commander	3	9	7	5	6	4	5	6	3	48
Lightweight PC	6	6	6	4	7	4	5	6	4	48
Strato-Star	6	6	9	1	9	6	8	9	3	57
Piglet II	10	5	5	2	4	3	8	9	8	54
Piglet 23'	8	6	6	2	5	4	7	9	6	53
Sierra	7	6	6	3	5	4	6	5	7	49
Strato-Cloud	5	10	10	1	10	9	7	9	2	63
Viking	6	10	10	1	10	9	7	9	3	65
Strato-Flyer	10	8	8	1	7	3	7	6	3	53
Paradactyl	10	4	1	1	4	3	7	3	10	43

* Key to Score: 1 = Unacceptable   5 = Fair/Good   10 = Excellent

Recommended ultra-light weight reserves
Security/Sierra Light (Security also makes the same reserve for
National and others)
Strong Lopo
Piglet
Preserve
   Cheap Alternatives — If you haven't much money, then here are
some low-cost options:
   1. Jump a reserve as a main canopy. 4-line release. Lightweights
      only!
   2. Jump a 28-foot that has been "gutted" (see details later). 4-line
      release.
Updated from RWu, October 1975

   RW Gear Of The Future. Tomorrow is now in RW. Toads used to
jump sloppy fitting gear and skintight jumpsuits and do "ok"...me for
one. But now gear does make a difference. Here are some tried and true
ideas for RW gear:
   Jumpsuit...Custom-made for you; fits well; bells & big as the
situation requires.
   Harness...Snug-fitting harness system that doesn't weigh over 35
lbs. *total* (including backpack & canopies).
   Main canopy...A type that lets you down easy and is
maneuverable; packs up small.
   Reserve...Reliable and light.
   Main and Reserve Container...Tandem or "piggyback" type, shape
determined by canopy, *light*.
   Boots/Shoes ...Adidas or similar athletic shoes, Puma pole vaulting
boots, Indian moccasins (wrap-type) or other lightweight,
feel-your-feet coverings.
   Gloves...Thin (aviator's, water skier's or handballer's) or none.
   Helmet...One that doesn't get in the way — wear a soft one, a
semi-rigid one or a hockey helmet. You gotta be able to SEE!
   Goggles ...Some that allow good vision. Jockey goggles and boogie
goggles are good.
RWu June '73

   Lighter Gear + Faster Stars = Longer Freefall Time. Relative work
10-man teams and judges around the country are finding that freefall

times are considerably higher than the old 10,500 equals 45 seconds formula usually applied.

The Beechnuts team from Michigan reports, for example, that they average 47-49 seconds of freefall time from 8,000 ft. exit to 2,500 ft. opening altitude. And the judges at the recent Rumbleseat Meet in California recorded freefall times averaging 52 seconds from 9,500 ft. down to 2,500 ft.

These increases are probably attributable to larger jumpsuits; smaller, more lightweight gear; and faster stars. It appears that the faster you build your star, the more freefall time you get.

RWu, December 1974

Song of the Godfrogs

Oh come with me and we'll go up there
Where the wind blows cold and there ain't much air,
Where the clouds are ice and your blood runs thin...
But don't worry, toad, we're comin' down again.
Like a frog, a screamin' Godfrog!

When the airplane gets so high she won't go no more
With a laugh and a holler it's out the door;
Down amongst them clouds to play
Like that ol' eagle who does nothin' else all day.

Then back on the ground, when the Whuffo's ask "how come?"
And you really don't know,
And you are feelin' sorta dumb...
Well, you may wonder, but I know why —
You're a screamin' Godfrog and you love the sky.

C. G. Godfrog

Helmet Regulations: To Bell or Not to Bell. Some people like to wear helmets for jumping—some do not. Currently there's a lot of fuss and bother because the helmet wearers are afraid their soft-headed friends will hurt themselves. They want to legislate personal safety. *RWu* believes that crash helmets should be worn for safety reasons by everyone who *chooses* to, and those of us who choose not to wear helmets shouldn't have to.

Mike Schultz, manager of Pelicanland, top ranked competitor in style and accuracy, has some thoughts on helmets. We're excerpting from his letter to USPA's Board of Directors of October 25, 1973.

"The history of USPA has been reactionary, which is good! It was born and has been guided in reaction to arbitrary and injurious bureaucratic activities. Its evolution and course have been influenced by the vanguard activities of the jumpers/members who have pioneered in equipment and techniques for bettering and furthering the interest of sport adventures.

In my opinion, one of the greater advances recently has been the advent of the smaller, non-rigid head coverings. They have considerable advantage over the rigid, crash-oriented helmets which have dominated in the past, but which restrict head motion and vision in freefall, as well as creating neck problems for some, due to jerk on opening.

I would like to create the issue of the hurt head at Pepperell on the light of narrow thinking, as follows:

There is no assurance that the same gentleman who went to the hospital in Pepperell would have fared any better with a Bell helmet on. I feel that the design structure of the Bell is focused on impacts strong enough to crack the protective covering. Otherwise, the protection is only that provided by the internal padding.

The conditions that day at Pepperell (I was there!) were gusty and the gentleman who hurt himself made a low turn after running to pass some low wires. No body equipment recommended by the BSR's guarantees immunity to injury under *any* conditions, much less questionable judgement or unusual circumstances.

So much for a technical argument! My opposition transcends this lonely issue and encompasses a broader concern for the specious thinking that highlights it. If we are to maintain a viable profile in the reactionary community, we can't rush to the legislative desk over every isolated incident that arises and attempt to create obstacles to the enjoyment of our sport for our own members.

The impact of this issue reached me as I was thinking about equipment for 10-man RW and style. I felt offended that the occurrence to a man with 200 jumps should be extrapolated to include me with 2,700 and many others with more than that. I like the non-rigid helmet. There is no question it is safer for me and helps to improve my performance, and moreover, I *want* to jump it.

Gentlemen, please consider all aspects of the issue and influence your S&T committee to adjust their thinking to include all members of

the parachuting community. Don't allow arbitrary outside bureaucratic actions to affect the entire Board of Directors. Perhaps rigid helmets are beneficial to non-licensed jumpers or other inexperienced levels! I certainly wouldn't allow the student jumpers at our DZ to wear non-rigid helmets, but I don't see the immediate relationship to my style jump or to my 125th RW jump with the same people on a 10-man team, or with persons of equal ability.
Michael E. Schultz, RWu, December 1973

Tips on Gear

A Swoop Cord Tip… With an elasticized swoop cord, or most any other type of swoop cord, you can adjust your wing area by how tight you wear the cuff. For example, if you want to put some slack in the wing area so you'll fall faster, fasten the cuff velcro more loosley.

Shortline Your Reserve… Security 26-ft. reserves may be safely shortlined three feet without affecting descent rate or opening reliability. Result; a lighter, smaller reserve. (Check with your master rigger.)

1.1 Canopies Can Land Softer… Simply sew shut the apex of a regular 1.1 main canopy. Seems to slow the descent more than 10%.

Swooping Shoes… Adidas tennis shoes are neat for serious RW. Makes you feel like you got hands on your feet. The best are those made out of nylon, and are consequently washable in — guess what — a way to eliminate the devastating foot stink — Woolite and cold water. This is especially important since most of us don't wear socks. In fact, sometimes we don't shower, no siree, just step outside and stomp a skunk first thing in the mornin'."
RWu

Gutting your Cheapo — You can reduce bulk in your cheapo by "gutting" the 550 cord that runs through your canopy. Running inside the braided tube that makes up 550 are seven 35 lb. test lines (testing out to 245). This means that the outer braid is 305 lbs. test.

Using a seam ripper, open up the canopy just enough to get the 550 out. Make the incision 1 inch below the zig zag stitching near the skirt. Pull the line out (4 inches or so) for easier access. Using a hard lead pencil, separate the weave of the braid. (This braid is similar to Chinese finger cuffs.) Increase the size of the pencil hole by using a football inflater or *dull* penny nail. Pull out, *count,* and cut the 7 inner lines. Tie a surgeon's knot so the cut lines won't slip back in.

Repeat the above (except tying the knot) 1 inch above the highest zig zag stitch near the apex. Put tension on the canopy. The knot near the skirt will put the lines back in the canopy while it's under tension. Make sure the lines go back into the canopy so you can pull the "guts" *straight out,* or the "finger cuffs" principle will work against you. Have someone pull the guts out *slowly* while you stroke the canopy as needed.

Total bulk reduced is about the size of a football. The remaining braided tube will be sufficient to carry the load required. It'll take you about 2-3 hours to do.

Also, you can shortline your cheapo two feet. Then, open (or loosen) your chest strap after opening and it will fly the same. This will save you one line stow. If you shortline more than 2 feet, you'll ruin the flight characteristics of your canopy.

The 28-ft. is too large to get any real benefit from inverting the apex. You'll come down slower, but you won't get much drive.

Carl Nelson, Freak Brothers Flyer #3

Washing your Jumpsuit

Power to the Putrid! Yeah, there's nothing like those hot summer days, packed three across in a humid Lodestar. Smells about as good as a pair of old sneakers after a summer's jumping. The truth is, everyone wants to fly good, not smell good, and it seems that everyone's afraid to wash their jumpsuit.

If you own a polyester suit (Dynasoar, Brand X, etc.) you can wash it in cold water. First, stick all the velcro together so it doesn't get full of lint and thread. Soak overnight in cold water with ½ cup Biz or Axion. Wash the next day in the same water, rinse in cold and hang it up to dry. It won't fade or shrink a bit. Starch helps your "float-power."

If you own a cotton suit (Classon, Strong, etc.) it must be dry-cleaned. Even if you try cold water, it will shrink for sure unless you like knickers. If you try hot water or a dryer, the only thing your suit will fit is a Barbie doll. Use laundry starch to revive the material's original stiffness and body.

If you're in the market for a new suit, white shows up the best against the sky, then yellow and orange. The other colors are more difficult for judges and spectators to see, with black being the worst.

Now is the time to get ready for the spring thaw and may everyone smell good this summer.

Freak Brothers Flyer #6

Air Brakes. There are a number of jumpsuits designed with the RW person in mind. The fact is that they don't usually work really efficiently.

Photos prove that any excess material crafted into the suit will only blow back in freefall. Swoopcords will eliminate this problem and will permit the suit to function in the manner it was designed. You can make a set starting with a pair of elastic motorcycle tie downs and removing the metal hooks. Then feed 1,000 lb. tubular nylon through both ends (this step is very aggravating). The nylon on one end should be sewn together as big around as your hand. The other nylon should be sewn (or tied) so it's about 18" long and can be tied to your belt. Adjust the tension so that the cords are loose in the frog position and become taut when the elbows are extended into the flare position.

Wear them under your jumpsuit and notice how nice they work. Once you get used to them, you really get a heavy rush on your approach.

C. Nelson, Freak Brothers Flyer #3

Ride on the Wind
Out into the blinding sky
Floating, soaring figures fly
As a silent airplane falls up.
Vertical dive on your back
Like a hunting eagle,
As earth-pushed air roars.

Arch back, and the roar dive becomes swoop
While the formation and you freight train on railroad tracks of air.

You flare to coast as the joy wells and flows into the sinewy dance
Of flyers on magical columns of air.
To dock with single-pointed mind that ecstasies into an electric smile
As you shake and break to enter.
And the power flows through the formation 'til it explodes
Into fragments which blossom all the colors of spring
And the World starts, again.

Pat Works

The Gear Scaries.
Sometimes my gear scares me
It's a long way up
To be hanging from strings and rags
So I think really hard
And figure it all out again
And everything goes fine
For a while
And then I go do something
Scary again
Like watch someone open
Do I really believe that?
I better
Because it's my turn now
I just keep going through the process
Because I started when I was too
Young to know any better
And now I can't stop.
Skratch Garrison .

3

Canopy RW

Dear Roger, and Skratch and you,

Hello!

Well yes. But of course. Um humm? I used to do it but quit when Joe fell off the left edge of a vertical 20-person double wedge canopy dock. Yessir, it was right after they 360°-ed and re-docked. The point man had just locked his legs in when Joe fell into Tom's inflated jumpsuit. The force of the vacuum opened his chest strap and he forgot to turn right. Everyone stalled into the collision and somebody panicked and started a riser dive that took out both left wings. Boy, you shoulda seen ol' Top Swooper try and flare with parts of the tail group suspended from his ankle!

Yes, before that we all jumped cotton canopies with no reserves. Using one or no altimeters on each jump helped keep the cliques down. Fortunately, all the gear belongs to the state now and nothing exciting has happened since Iron Tooth eliminated everyone on his 4-man team but himself... he woulda got the Honorable Medal for Late Timing, with cluster, but he had to split when they drove up to his parents place in a tank. He ran down the railroad tracks and didn't stop 'til he got to Texas. Heroopa!

Love and maximum RW,

Pat Works

Canopy RW — Relative Work in Slow Motion.

"If only I could do it again, knowing what I know now!" Imagine how much easier it would be to go back through high school or a first jump course if no one knew you had already done it once. Now we have a chance to do just that. Learning canopy relative work is like learning freefall RW all over again, only in slow motion this time.

All of us who are involved in freefall RW went through some sort of time-consuming and expensive process that may or may not have involved any actual training, and from which we learned how to maneuver ourselves relative to each other in the air. Every new technique learned was a step away from apprehension and ignorance and toward understanding and enjoyment, expanding our awareness and whetting the appetite for more and better flying.

We have all finished a skydive, landed and said, "If there had only been a few more seconds, we could have completed that formation!" It is common now for canopy relative workers to do a clear and pull at 9500 feet, land and say, "If we had only had a few more *minutes,* we could have gotten it together!"

It is just like freefall RW. All the elements are there: dives, swoops, no-contact flying, non-momentum docks, vertical transitions, sequential formations . . . and intensity.

Intensity — a way to maintain the peak function awareness of a skydive *after* the freefall. Now we can get several more minutes of adrenalin time for not a penny more.

It has not been that many years since people were apprehensive about relative work, and often for good reason. When it was not very well understood (or done) there were fears of collisions, funnels, exit injuries and canopy entanglements. Most of the fears based on ignorance have been replaced by respect born of knowledge. The knowledge has come from communication, reasoned experimentation, experience, eagerness to learn and willingness to share. We certainly have not "arrived" in freefall RW, but we aren't scared of it anymore.

Now the process is just beginning for canopy RW. Step one is to get over the ignorance and fear of it while at the same time not moving so quickly into it that disasters occur and the fears again become well-founded.

So where do you start? Optimally, find someone who has done a lot of it and pick his brains. Ask for his knowledge — tap his experience—share his time. Without that opportunity, there is a way, but it ought to be done cautiously. All you need is a friend, two square canopies and mutual curiosity. It will be a safer evolution if you both have enough dives on your canopies to be really comfortable with them.

Start by learning to maneuver your canopies close together (close enough to talk to each other) with no relative motion except for whatever difference there is in the rates of descent. At some point in the process of getting together, one canopy will become the target and the other the aggressor. Although that may simply be a matter of which one is higher, it will be more efficient if your positions are known ahead of time—like in freefall RW.

Although the CRW is easily "added to" the bottom end of a freefall RW dive, it is probably best *learned* when done as the only thing on a dive, clear of the interference by other non-participating canopies and with the chance to open at a much higher altitude, giving you more time to work slowly or to do several hook-ups, or alternate roles, prior to landing (sequential anyone?).

Unless you have made a successful hook-up and are in stable flight, it is unwise to be doing CRW below an altitude at which you could not breakaway successfully if problems develop. Like *at least* 1000 feet.

Do as much planning and discussion on the ground as you would for an involved sequential RW dive. As an exit for two people, you might consider a three-second interval between exits for lateral separation.

Find each other and make whatever turns are appropriate to get into the same general airspace. If the two canopies are level a turning front-riser descent is the most efficient way to get down. The target should stabilize with the aggressor off to one side, low, on the same heading and inside his radius of turn, then fly in a *very slow* turn toward the aggressor. It is called a "lead pursuit curve" and is a technique that pilots found out years ago is the most efficient way to rendezvous two airplanes, friendly or otherwise.

It has to do with the geometry of equal radius circles with offset centers, and allows the two canopies to rendezvous at equal speeds and rates of descent—something you can't do on a constant heading unless you are side-by-side to start with.

Once you have made several CRW dives together the need for verbal communication will diminish and you will begin to sense what needs to be done to effect the building of the formation. The need for small corrections will be obvious and the canopies will flow together with both of you moving to the same rhythm...like in freefall.

Getting there is the most important thing to learn. Just fly no-contact side-by-side. Make some very slow formation turns. Practice staying in position. You'll find that moving your toggles up or down briskly will cause your canopy to move vertically long before it changes speed (moves forward or backward with respect to the other canopy). A "pump" stall will move you down very nicely a few feet.

Once you are used to having a sky full of nylon right next to you and feel comfortable flying into position and staying there, it's time to start working on docking the canopies. A hook-up is most easily manageable when the person on top is standing up with his feet tucked *into* the center cell (either channel) of the lower canopy so he can steer normally. If you are merely standing on top of the canopy, the formation has no structural integrity and if you drift back there is a danger of getting a foot tangled in the pilot chute bridle with potentially disastrous results.

A canopy in steady-state flight is in a condition of equilibrium so its velocity or relative position can be changed in *any* direction with a small force. However, large enough forces can exceed the ability of the canopy to accelerate and will cause it to distort or change its shape. Changing shape is the mechanism by which a square canopy changes its flight characteristics and is something to avoid if you want the two canopies to continue flying in unison. If you are the person on top, you should feel only very slight pressure on your feet. They may actually slide slowly up and down along the inside of the channel with no pressure at all on the upper or lower surfaces.

There is only one area on a canopy that can be gripped by the man on top with any hope of transitioning to a hook-up. That area is the *top leading edge of the upper surface.*

WARNING: Taking a grip on the tail, stabilizers, suspension lines or pilot chute bridle can result in anything from the inability to move elsewhere to sudden, spinning, whirling mess and impending disaster.

"Anyone who has had a bull by the tail knows five or six things more than someone who hasn't."–Mark Twain.

If in the process of docking, one or more cells of the bottom canopy collapse, you can simply shift over to it, lift the upper surface of the cell and re-inflate it. If it is only one cell, just ignore it, unless your friend is uneasy. It won't affect the handling of his canopy at all.

WARNING: *Never* approach or exceed the stall point with docked canopies. Both canopies will probably stall simultaneously with easily imaginable results.

You can maneuver the canopies to a point landing just as you do with one if you keep in mind that you have to allow about fifteen extra feet below you for your friend, which he won't be if you drag him across a fence or into a van. We land stacked canopies in the peas regularly and have gotten a dead center when the guy on the bottom was not even steering. With a moderate wind, two jumpers could probably get the same disc from a hooked-up approach and landing.

Because of the difficulty in judging the flare point for the guy on the bottom, look down and watch his hands or have him yell out "Flare!" When he yells or starts the flare, kick out and get off. If you stay hooked-up and continue to fly to *your* flare point, you will drive him helplessly into the ground. If you flare early to let him land smoothly, you will wind up fifteen feet in the air all out of airspeed and ideas. Done properly, you can make gentle dual stand-ups even on no-wind days because of the additional speed that can be bled off in the flare. It works well to stay at full drive until the flare is initiated, but it isn't necessary.

When two or more canopies are docked, the formation has a somewhat faster (maybe 10% more) forward speed and rate of descent. The reason is that the relative wind due to the normal forward speed acts on a vertical moment arm that is twice as long. In steady-state flight, you are always tilted forward slightly (like your canopy is towing you) although you probably don't even notice it. With a hook-up, you are tilted forward even more because the wind drag on the lower person is acting on a point twice as far away from your canopy (like a longer lever). Because of the extra tilt, your canopy is in essence trimmed more nose down and therefore flies a little faster.

Which brings us to another important point. There are two types of square drivers: those who have had their canopies collapse in flight...and those who will. It usually happens downwind of a large obstruction or at the edge of a thermal. The "book" says to stay away from full drive or near-stall toggle settings in strong gusty winds. If the canopy is subject to dynamic collapse at full drive in a gust, it will be more susceptible if it is flying even faster.

WARNING: Don't do CRW in strong gusty winds. You can

overstress the lower canopy when the oscillations get out of phase and you are subject to having two people and two *collapsed* canopies trying to occupy the same airspace.

A stack of several flies like a stack of two. You just have to allow more distance beneath you when you set up the landing approach. It is like flaring a 747 when you are used to a Cessna. People are disengaged off the bottom one at a time and land straight ahead.

So where are we going with this stuff? What is the goal? I sincerely hope we *can't* answer those questions. If we set a limit, we'll reach it, and that isn't worth much. It is what we do along the way that will make it worthwhile. You have accomplished little if in reaching the top of a mountain you miss the intensity of a climb taken step by step...the expanded awareness that comes from total mental and emotional involvement...and the adrenalin rush that comes from doing something requiring ability of which you were not certain.

CRW has vastly unimagined, much less unrealized, potential for all these things. And we have only just begun. Think about freefall RW. This is the same thing...in slow motion. The rendezvous in "2001..." was done to a Strauss waltz and it made all the difference.

Roger Hull, Parachutist, May 1977

Canopy RW — West Coast Style. It's now generally well established that canopy RW started on the East coast, either at Deland or Z-Hills sometime back in 1975. During the next two years after its beginnings, however, it was performed by only a handful of zealots who practiced either vertical hookups, generally by closing beside the other canopy and sliding across to the center cell, or side docks in which the two canopies would fly side by side, held by the top pilot.

The next step in the progress of canopy RW, naturally, was the making of the world's first three-stack. Informed sources report that in the spring of 1977, a three-stack was formed over Stormville, NY by Dave Strickland, Mark Baird and Gary Pond. It is difficult to verify whether it was prior to a couple of West Coast three-stacks which were formed over Pope Valley, Calif. by Roger Hull, Marty Martin and Ken Beaudin. On June 15, 1977 the Know-Sense team put together their first three-stack. The stack was completed by Steve Haley, Paul Rober and Norton Thomas.

The importance of the three-stack performed by the Know-Sense people was not whether or not it was "the first," but the fact that it incorporated an entirely new concept in canopy RW — closing from below and behind.

Within the next four months, this concept was responsible for enabling the Know-Sense team to build their first four-stack, five-stack, several six-stacks and a seven-stack. As the stacks progressed, it became obvious that putting the first eight-stack together would simply be a matter of time. The basics for building it were now established through months of trial and error by Haley and Norton.

Haley was the official "stack pilot," always on top of the stack and directing the movement of the stack to pick up pursuers as month after month the size of the stacks grew larger. Norton, often at odds with concepts Haley would propose, offered the balance needed to progress to larger stacks. Invariably, Norton would hold out, directing others into position to close on the stack, then close last. Always being last, Norton had the "honor" and distinction of being the team bowling ball, often times being drilled into the ground as the stack was flown to the ground and landed without being in trim.

The importance of "trimming up" the stack became apparent as the size of the stacks progressed. One of the major obstacles to building larger stacks was the problem of oscillation. As a jumper approached the stack, attempting to line his center cell up on the bottom man's feet, the stack would start swaying. Concentrating on the feet, the approaching jumper would give a little left toggle or right toggle to compensate, only to find the stack swaying back in the opposite direction by the time his canopy responded.

Oftentimes the bottom man on the stack, seeing that the jumper on approach was slightly off target, would attempt to compensate by a toggle adjustment. This, too, would just serve to aggravate the problem.

The important point learned was for the jumper on approach to maintain his line of flight, slow down and wait for the stack to oscillate back to center. This called for split second timing, being in "the slot" just at the right second. If the oscillation was too violent, an approach could not be safely made without the distinct possiblity that the canopy on approach would collapse upon impact with the bottom jumper.

In order to prevent or stop an oscillation, unequal tension within the stack has to be eliminated. To do this, the stack pilot calls down to the jumper below to "come up" or "go down" as appropriate. "Coming up" is accomplished by going deeper into brakes, thus giving the canopy more lift and relieving the tension on the upper man's feet.

On the other hand the lower jumper's canopy may be "floating" too much, causing the top man to loose his foot grip. This is rectified by letting up on the toggles enough to create the additional drag needed to hold the proper amount of tension between the two canopies. The top man gives the "OK" when the tension is proper.

The sequence is then repeated sequentially on down the stack, with the No. 2 man giving instructions to No. 3 to trim up, No. 3 to No. 4, etc. The proper "trim position" is held by each jumper by locking his hands onto his harness or risers in whatever position his toggles are at the time he is advised this trim is proper.

Soft toggles make holding proper trim for extended periods of time a lot easier. Also, the use of riser trim tabs can even eliminate the need to hold toggles at all, once in the formation and locked into proper position.

Holding the stack in a definite slight turn is especially important so that those pursuing the stack can intersect its flight path in a minimum amount of distance. Another point to bear in mind is to not fly a stack in half brakes, especially if the top canopy is a Strato-Star. Clouds trying to close down the stack have problems because it is almost impossible to slow the Cloud's closing speed enough to avoid flying through and wrapping around the person on the bottom of the stack. Optimal flight mode for the stack pilot generally seems to be somewhere close to quarter-brakes.

In large stacks it is essential to utilize a large surface area canopy (Cloud, Foil, whatever) on the top (base) to insure stability.

–*Tom Courbat, CCR-9 Starcrest, Oct-Dec 1977.*

Basic Canopy RW Techniques

Building Sequence. From top to bottom is smoothest, cleanest, quickest way (adding to bottom of stack).

Experienced pilots should be able to build speed-stack with simultaneous dockings top and bottom (will require some experience in closing both ways—top is risky).

Docking. Closing from below — top canopy in ¼-½ brake mode — top canopy pilot may hold *both* toggles in one hand to free other hand for docking — soft toggles are great for this. Riser trim tabs may also be used but are not essential. Less than ¼ brakes causes too much chase (horizontal time); more than ½ brakes causes excessive lift of top canopy.

Aggressor (bottom canopy) approaches in full-flight mode from behind and about 10-15 ft. below—*must* flare to dock—not too early or inadequate lift—not too late or top pilot will go thru (collapse) bottom canopy. *Never* approach from above and behind turbulent air flow at 45 degrees vertical angle to tail.

—(turbulent air flow.)

45°

Additionally, pilot chutes sometimes hang out in that general vicinity.

If approaching from above, side slip *very slowly* after establishing non-contact side mode. In an approach from above, it is extremely difficult to get the top canopy to drop the distance necessary to dock without gaining too much forward speed and getting ahead of lower canopy. Any time you are ahead of another canopy, *turn off;* do not under any circumstances attempt to "back-up" into the lower canopy. (Note: alert pilot on bottom canopy should be able to "flare up" to top canopy to effect proper dock if circumstances permit, i.e., not likely if lower canopy is the top of a 5-stack.)

Grips. Basic no-no's on grips—absolutely no grips on stabilizers, tail, pilot chute (or bridle) or lines—*ONLY* on top leading edge of upper surface. Once docked, use hands if necessary to grab center cells and plant feet securely. Wrap cell walls *firmly and securely* around entire foot. This is essential; loss of grip at 20 ft. if bottom canopy is collapsed could be fatal. If one grip is lost, *resecure* remaining foot hold, then work on regrip for lost foot. A completely collapsed canopy can be landed safely if the top canopy is flying properly.

End Cell Problems. Pilot on top can reinflate a totally or partially collapsed canopy by reaching down and pulling up on top of cells closest to him—then on each cell going out toward edge of canopy on both sides. DON'T PANIC!

Approach. If you are on final, go for it as long as there is no traffic jam. If you find yourself stuck in the slot for over 60 seconds on a large attempt, turn off and allow another canopy to close. You can make several efforts later and not jeopardize putting the stack together because everyone else had to wait for you. The bottom man on a stack can rotate his *body* (not canopy) 180 degrees and watch the next man's approach if visibility is a problem. He can "catch" the approaching canopy this way and then turn back on heading.

Docking/Grips. Once docked but prior to securing the grip, bottom man has responsibility to tell top man whether or not he is centered on bottom canopy. If not, bottom man uses simple, brief commands—"move right"—top man may sit on canopy and slide over a cell, or may be standing inside cell and with firm hand grips on tops of cell, pull feet out and reposition in proper cells. Keep communication to absolute minimum—only essential commands to avoid confusion.

Top Man. Top man completely controls the entire formation although he cannot of his own accord stop an oscillating stack. Top man must take responsibility for locating (with assistance of bottom man acting as lookout) canopies on approach and setting up easily accessible approach course for those coming in (up). Important not to be running away from your pursuers the whole jump...very frustrating for those who are chasing! Fly heads up when on top.

Good general idea: initiate *slow* steady turn to left or right so that pursuers can intercept path as quickly as possible and get hooked up. Fly at about ¼-½ brakes to maximize factors for those approaching. *Don't* keep altering your flight mode—people shouldn't have to second-guess you.

Tom Courbat, 9-30-77

Caution: Canopy RW Can Be Hazardous to Your Health

Here are some of the "rules" that have developed after many canopy RW jumps. Each one seemed to write itself in response to real or foreseen emergencies. It's an incomplete guide, because canopy RW is still mostly uncharted territory.

1. Clear all other canopy traffic before, during and after canopy RW. If you're flying a hookup, remember that the bottom man is controlled by the top man. The top man is responsible for the lower canopy, too.

2. Don't attempt canopy RW unless that parachutist knows you're there and works with you.

3. Be cautious in rough or bumpy air. Ram-air canopies react to gusts independently and can throw their suspended weights (you!) violently into one another.

4. Canopies doing RW should be flown at half-brakes. This allows you to go faster or slower to pursue your target or escape collision.

5. Don't attempt to hookup until there is no significant motion

between person and parachute. Non-momentum docks are essential.

6. Never grasp another canopy with a steering toggle in your hand, but keep steering control with your other hand. It works this way: if you're hooking up to a canopy on your right, release that toggle and keep the left toggle. Then, in case of trouble, your right hand is uncluttered to fend off a collision—and you can still turn left, away from that collision with left toggle.

7. Pay attention to your feet. Be aware of other canopy's lines that may try to snare you. Consider that the military teaches a spread eagle position to prevent your body from passing between another canopy's lines.

8. Don't do canopy RW any lower than you'd like to cut away from. 1,000 feet is a nice break-off altitude: the place to stop trying to hookup. Once hooked up, two canopies are pretty stable and can go lower—but it's risky to initiate RW below a grand.

9. Remember, the guidelines we've developed for freefall RW are all applicable to canopy RW. The importance of grips, non-momentum docks, wake turbulence and rules of right-of-way apply equally to canopy RW. Think of them before you go up.

10. Canopy RW isn't difficult. It's the same as accuracy, but the disk is moving! This list of "don'ts" isn't intended to show how dangerous it is. They're here just to help us enjoy canopy RW without getting hurt.

Kevin Shea, Parachutist, March 1977

Canopy Contact Relative Work: Revolution or Evolution? The 1976 U.S. National Parachuting Championships revealed new equipment, incredible skill and, perhaps, even a look to the future of the sport. Accuracy was all tied up after ten rounds with monotonous dead centers; it went more than 20 rounds to break the eventual two man tie. Style was a blur of sixes, the fastest ever. 10-way speed stars are so fast that one must ask whether subterminal flying is really "relative work." 4-way sequential has developed into "group style." Now there is talk of movable targets for accuracy, of dropping style altogether, 4-way and 8-way accuracy stacks; there are many proposals.

After a number of impromptu demonstrations, the conversation turned to the possibility of a new team event to take place after opening: CCRW, or "Canopy Contact Relative Work." A basic explanation is simple: After opening, jumpers line up for contact formation flying by holding onto the outboard leading edge of the next canopy. Though very little in this area has been done, the record already is four. The possibilities are limitless and the addition of CCRW to parachuting events certainly warrants more thought.

New Competition Event. CCRW is an obvious addition to freefall team events as it allows teams to compete during the canopy descent part of the jump as well. Otherwise, this segment of parachuting is, more or less, wasted. It is projected that 4-way and 8-way teams will begin with speed "V"s, the basic hookup maneuver, for time. Watches would start on the appearance of the first pilot chute and stop as the last jumper makes contact. In a few years when times are fast and other countries begin to catch on, it will be time to change the event. Next we'll progress to sequential maneuvers, eliminating the speed hookup "problems." Starting from a basic "V" formation, all jumpers will make a 360 degree turn to dock in a second formation for time.

The reactions to CCRW were as varied as they were widespread. The Chute Shop immediately began offering tee shirts imprinted with: "Grab a square in the air if you've got the hair." POOPS (Parachutists Of/Over Phorty Society) is reportedly considering a special hard core event for their annual meet for the aged, a 1.1 cheapo version of CCRW. The USPA Competition Committee began drafting rules for the new event. Publication is expected for the 1980 season. Si Fraser promised to upstage the national organization once again by adding the event to the annual Z-Hills November team competition. U.S. Team Leader George Krieger sent a card from Team training in Bimini stating that Team Fund donations would have to pick up if the Team was expected to train for another event, too. John Sherman has been practicing a way to open hooked up. This involves reaching into the next jumper's pack before dumping. Tricky! Jim Stoyas has already filed a protest.

Another event promises even greater spectator appeal. If it can be merchandised as tennis was, the sport of parachuting may be on the threshold of great publicity and resulting expansion. It utilizes two teams with ram-air canopies and one jumper under a Piglet for a game of aerial soccer. The object is to fly past the Piglet canopy, kicking it to the opposing team's side of the drop zone. The "honor" of flying the Piglet usually goes to the lowest ranking license holder.

Basic 3-way "V" being docked on to
form a 5-way "W." Adding one more would
from a 6-way accordion, and so on.

New World Records. Parachuting record categories will have to be
expanded again. Basically, all will consist of the greatest number of
participants in a contact formation but there will be several altitude
classifications: they'll be attempted from 1,000 meters, 2,000 meters,
4,000 meters, etc. Naturally, it is easier to make a four man formation
from 4,000 meters than a 12-way formation from 1,000 meters.
Photographic documentation (primarily X-ray) will be required. It is
rumored that the staff in Orange, Massachusetts is busy packing
lunches. The plan is to make a record attempt from a slow-climbing
Norseman.

New Equipment. With the development of speed 10-way jumping
over the last few years, the emphasis has been on the weight and
volume of parachuting equipment; each manufacturer has been going
smaller and lighter. CCRW, however, will require a completely new
line of equipment as the competitive mission is completely different.
Harnesses and containers won't be so important. It will be necessary
to develop canopies of various sizes to equalize the descent rates of
various size jumpers. Advance models will sport spoilers to allow a
jumper to increase his descent rate smoothly and at-will in order to
position himself at the proper docking altitude. New turning systems
will have to be designed to free the hands for docking with adjacent
canopies.

Top view of 16-way wagon wheel.

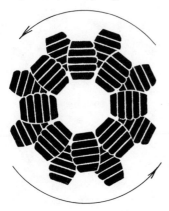

Laura MacKenzie, USPA Assistant Director, casually washed down another bon bon with a slug of Coors and declared: "I'm glad to hear there is a team event where an *increase* in weight is important." Then she dialed Jeanni McCombs who is rumored to be gathering an all-girl CCRW team. Letters poured in from Mary Thornton, Editor of the *Spotter,* Sherry Schrimsher, Editor of the SW *Conference Newsletter,* Betty Giarrusso, Editor of the *Flyletter* and others; all vowed their support.

The word from New Jersey is that Steve Snyder took a break from his drawing board to call both his banker and his broker with the good news. Dick Morgan scheduled classes. In Chicago, Lowell Bachman rushed to the printer with a new catalog.

One newsletter teased that some teams may be adding Velcro to their gloves and to the edges of their canopies. (One Florida team made the mistake of sewing hook Velcro to one glove and pile Velcro to the other. Not only did they have a problem with improper mating with the canopy, some have landed in an uncontrolled, palm to palm, praying position.) The FAA is considering some sort of standardization, perhaps under the TSO procedure.

And while on the FAA, it is feared by some that all this attention to the increased maneuverability of parachutes might prompt the FAA to require licensing and "N" numbers as they do with other aircraft. The writer contacted USPA Vice-President Stretch Harris, a San Diego attorney for an opinion. Harris suggested an office appointment and commented that "free legal advice is often worth exactly what you pay for it."

Some Southern California jumpers have come up with a less expensive descent equalizing system: each carries the required amount of compensating water ballast. If a jumper finds himself too low after opening, he simply jettisons some ballast by turning a valve. Fortunately, this is done over sparsely populated areas. On a recent jump, a visiting Canadian figured he'd knock off "two birds," being thirsty too, he drank the water!

Up in Massachusetts, Ted Strong reports that business is booming since he began installing Sure-Grips on Strato Stars. And, Hank Asciutto of Henry's Weight Reduction Salon in Perris, California, is designing a canopy with fewer lines — to reduce entanglements. Jim West ordered a dozen, in green (e). PI adopted a "wait and see" policy.

Of course, it's imperative that all canopies open on precisely the same level. This requires good equipment and close timing. In Florida, Bill Booth is developing the "Tangle Hog" with hand deployed, Velcroed pilot chutes. According to Booth, the team flies together to form a star, then they pull out their pilot chutes and stick them all together prior to release. He promises test reports as soon as he can find a team to jump the system.

Meanwhile, over at Para-Duplicators, they were waiting to see what the competition might produce. The design staff of Wing, Whang and Wong are said to be able to come up with great equipment faster than a speeding Xerox machine. In Dallas, McElfish announced a new imported prehensile boot while the RW Shop in New Hampshire is offering a new canopy made entirely of patchwork TSO tags. Apparently they got quite a deal on a closeout from Cesar Aguilar who was deported again. "It's all a mistake" wires the Hondurican from his native country.

8-way diamond. Particularly beautiful when the top three dock with the lower five. Good airspeed must be maintained to avoid wake turbulence.

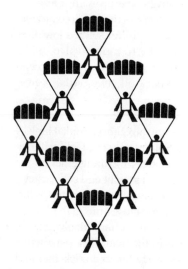

Safety Considerations. One obvious question does arise: Safety-wise, is this a step forward or a step back? Of course, some new Basic Safety Regulations will be necessary and some have already been proposed to the USPA Safety and Training Committee.

*100.31: Canopy Contact Relative Work.

(a) Shall not be engaged in by those holding less than a C license.

(b) Breakoff Altitudes
1. With four participants or less: 200 feet AGL
2. With five participants or more: 300 feet AGL

(c) Night formations will require regulation navigation lights and a red rotating beacon.

As with any new activity, there will be some growing pains. Parachuting officials will have to be wary in order to maintain an acceptable level of safety. It is imperative that they be able to react swiftly rather than have to go through a lengthy litigation process. Hereafter, minor infractions will be handled immediately by the Area Safety Officer, usually with a grounding. In major cases, the Executive Director is authorized to exchange the offender's "D" license for one with seven digits. Repeated infractions call for an unlisted number.

J. Scott Hamilton, Chairman of the Safety and Training Committee, appeared happy with the new activity, saying "This should eliminate the low pull problem now that everyone is opening high for the new event." He went on to note that if some CCRW maneuvers were to be included in future license requirements, Denver area jumpers might petition for an exemption as descent rates are much higher in the "Mile High City." Then he scheduled a meeting of the Committee to discuss another foreseeable problem: canopy to canopy transfers. A letter from the Gulch claims this was mastered over a year ago. It was, however, signed by only one of the participants.

In Deland, Gary Dupuis was heard to say: "Shucks, I don't care who gets into my DC-3 or where they get out as long as they buy a ticket." Major Chris Needels suggested some changes to the Army's Parachuting Regulations AR 95-19. Larry Sides began offering a special CCRW team insurance policy; it features million-dollar coverage and a two-jumper deductable.

Recognition, Organization, and Low Numbers. Don Beach, USPA Executive Director, said "While I like the idea of CCRW personally, the moving of the Headquarters to Washington has been a greater task than anticipated and the office staff just does not have the time to devote to any new projects." He kicked it back to the Competition Committee. Some investigation, however, revealed that most of his time has been spent in a running battle with USPA President Curt Curtis. It seems that both want their own portrait on the 1977 membership cards.

Australian Claude Gillard writes that the new formations will be particularly difficult to perform upside-down, but that the Aussies will give it a go. South Africa has already forwarded a bid for the First World Cup of CCRW.

Mike Truffer, new Editor of *Parachutist* magazine, was too busy to comment. He had just received 14 articles from Bill Ottley. Somehow Bill always suffers from "hyper-typewriter" in Board election years. Ron Young elected to wait for the movie. (And Dan Poynter immediately began writing a book on the subject. — Ed.)

Starcrust Magazine announced that Willie Knewall was prepared to run the CCRW World Headquaters from his villa in Acapulco. He will issue numbers and maintain the registration file. Looking to the future, he proclaimed that anyone entering a wagon wheel formation eighth or later would qualify for a "CCS" award, a "canopy contact solo." It is reported that he has been trying to fly Strato-stars through hoops. Chet Poland began peddling belt buckles. Asked for an observation, Skratch Garrison commented "I think this is where I came in."

The "Bud Man," USPA Treasurer Jack Bergman, said: "I don't care what the events are as long as the Nationals get one buck off the top." And of course, Jacques Istel claims that he brought the event from France in 1953 and that "CCRW" is one of his trademarks.

Betty's husband, Dick Giarrusso, says: "CCRW is where it's at," while Betty is demanding special, separate certification for the judges working the new event. A recent edition of *RW Underground* said, in part: "...so in conclusion, we demand that the USPA Board add CCRW to the Nationals in 1977. This important segment of parachuting cannot be ignored any longer..." A completely illegible petition (except for the profanities) arrived at USPA Headquarters from Elsinore while Gene Paul Tacker kept dumping style loads at Raeford. Then the latest edition of *T.N.T.* arrived...

From Pope Valley, USPA President Curtis penned an editorial for *Parachutist* which went something like this: "My Fellow Parachutists, ask not what the USPA can do for you, ask what you can do for the USPA. The question of CCRW is not a we-vs-they controversy. After all, we all jump out of the same airplanes..." And it went on and on and on.

Dan Poynter, Parachutist, November 1976

With Eagles

"To be again where the angels play
In the endless halls of space,
To race again the whistling wind
With the sun hot in my face.

To top the golden tinted clouds
To see the distant rain,
To ride the rainbow's spectra band
To just be alive again.

To fly thru halls of towering clouds
Where the ancient Gods once Played,
To lose myself in the milk-white haze
To lose weeks or years or days.

To roll down from the shining sun
Toward the stagnant earth below,
On a high side pass from two miles up
And the bright round amber glow.

To ride again the calm still air
When the universe stands still,
To fight the jolting, bucking stack
That tests your every skill..."
Charlie Straightarrow

4

Competition

Sometimes competition skydiving seems to be a separate type of parachuting. Competition involves high energy, high calibre skydives and good team relations. Here are stories relating to competition. Since annual events have a history, older articles are included so that the continuing change inherent in freefall competitions is evident.

Nexus — Nexus —
And the time winds wail —
Analyze —
  What teams do to get good —
  With their daily doses of balanced diet —
  Donutize, back-in & hop-over —
  The basic ingredients —
  And the timing practice for crosses & weaves —
And analyze —
  Those special times past —
  When the fantasy flowed and the dives were hot —
  The USFET magic was a frame of mind —
  There because we believed in it —
Analyze —
  The quadra-bipole flash —
  And the mood components of organized dives —
Analyze, too —
  The 道 — the path — the ASC —
  The jump run feeling of tuning in —
  And that explosive expansion of awareness —
  When you're still going fast —
  And the world slows down —
  To canopy speed —

Analyze —
   Competition —
   The energy trap —
   The price of that edge —
   Is a focus too narrow —
   No fantasy —
   How good a donut —
   Do you really want to make —
Analyze —
   Journeys and goals and equating the two —
   And the multiplex balance —
   Of practice and challenge —
   Focus — variety —
   Choosing and drifting —
   On an edge —
   Not out —
   But in —
Analyze —
   The air flow and yours —
   Swooping and swarming and all that milling —
   Valences — slaloms — infinities — pulsars —
   Lurk loads — maneuver flakes —
   Lounge exits — air flow days —
   Demo dives —
   And coordination boogies —
Analyze —
   Until —
It's time —
   You'll have to pardon me now —
   But I'm getting off here —
   It was fun writing here —
   Analyzing with you —
   But that's dirt dive offramp —
   And I've a fantasy to do —
   –Skratch Garrison

Team Chaos at a Sequential Meet. And *now,* folks, here comes Confusion and Terminal Chaos at the North American Sequential Sweepstakes.

Introductory Preliminaries. Chaos reigned! Our 8-man team out at Elsinore (part of the old "Element of Chance") had only six people...and we couldn't do round #3 of the International 8-man. The big meet up at Fort Lewis, Wash., lost helicopter support, and it was rumored you were supposed to wear helmets for all dirt dives. We had only three weeks of practice left before the meet. That meant that our 4-man team wasn't going to get any practice at all, except in the van. Nevertheless, the big question was "How do you do 8-man team freefall with only six people??"

Ahhh! Dave Wilds (Mr. Clean) joins up with our crew after his 8-man team splits up. As his contribution to our chaos, Dave brought good morals, energy, and a tremendous amount of speed-star experience...something like 800 jumps with Captain Hook. Gary Boardman counterbalanced this when he joined, skateboarding through ground practice and announcing that he loved sequential and boys.

Goodie, now we had 8 people...*if* Bob Schafer (of the USFET) could make it over from the Gulch. Since we hadn't jumped together as a team, ground practice would be a neat way to start out. Schafer arrives, but Doctor Death (Vic Ayres of the "Exitus" team), having wrecked his car, is still at home when the first load is called. Finally he arrives, and we're able to start ground practice by 10:00 a.m.

Ground Practice. Otis Vanderkolk acts as Captain Chaos to keep ground practice down to a four-way shouting match. Dave Wilds asks if we can't replace the moldy team battle cry: "Blue Sky, Black Death!" with his own version: "Lions and Tigers and Bears, Oh my!" The stunned reception is taken for agreement, and team practice starts.

In order to save time, part of the team adopts the Arizona (USFET/Gulch) team's 8-man techniques. In order to preserve chaos, the rest of the team doesn't.

Team Practice Jumps. Compulsory #3 is giving us problems, but through diligent lack of organization, we have about an 80 percent completion rate on the 21 practice dives we put in before the meet.

In order to keep things interesting, we change the exit order for each of the compulsory jumps. We hang three people outside the DC-3. They act as floaters or base, depending on whose turn it is. To add glamor to whoever is going base on a particular jump, they are termed the "Heroes" of the dive. Where practical, or fun, we carry a three-man hook-up out the door.

To instill team spirit, the exit command is "Get out thar, Stupid!" One guy, a dope-smokin' Tennessee ridge-runner, being about seven feet tall, introduces the team to the "animal" exit by planting his feet against the wall opposite the door and lunging out the door with almost everyone in his arms. Since it was fun, and felt good, we kept it up. This tall guy claims his name is Greg Giles, but we call him "Long Death" 'cause it's easy to remember.

People keep forgetting the sequences in the air, so we all promise to "get serious" about ground practice at the meet. (In a show of togetherness, three team members have malfunctions and/or blow up their mains on one single day.)

At last, the final day of practice ends and we plan to leave for the Big Sequential $10,000 Meet at Fort Lewis! Our final team meeting was wonderful. Several of us want to know "Where is Fort Lewis?" (It's 1,250 miles away.) John Hager, from Oklahoma, has a better question "How are we going to get there?"

Getting There is *Not* Half The Fun. Wednesday night late, we're zooming toward the North and the competition, looking forward to a 24-hour drive, a good meet, and some hot mega-dives afterwards. The trusty old van is outfitted with a stereo, headphones, CB radio, cruise control, and part of the team. We stop just twice for major repairs. To keep sane, I do yoga in the parking lot, standing on my head, while Gary rides his skateboard around standing on his hands. Gary's CB radio handle, "The Queen of Palos Verdes," makes for some interesting CB talk and adds new dimension to modulation in general.

At Fort Lewis at last, we pitch camp, make four practice dives, and say a great *big* "hello" to a whole mess of old friends from all over everywhere. Goddamn, it's great to see everyone again!

Pre-meet gossip has it that it will be a close meet, with the top teams likely being Seattle's "Clear Eye," with "years" of practice; Texas' "Kaleidoscope," with 130 practice jumps; the Arizona/Gulch/USFET team (who called itself "Fish" because they were always getting hooked into traveling across the United States at the promise of "all the free helicopter jumps you can make"); and our Elsinore team which somebody understandably has registered as "Terminal Chaos."

In addition, Curt Curtis' team, "All the President's Men," (Pope Valley) were looking good, and people from the "Seagull Squad," Utah, sounded good, too. In all, there were 12 teams entered out of about 20 who had paid the registration but didn't show, due in part to the last minute confusion about helicopters and meet location.

There was a whole slew of 4-man teams registered, but many withdrew, discouraged by the cost of the event and the fact that the four-man teams were given low priority by the meet director. Some 4-man teams had to wait five days to make a jump.

The Big Meet, At Last. I just love competition. It's one of the best kinds of RW jumping for me. Since it's all "organized" already, all you gotta do is show up, pay your entry fee, wait for your load to be called, and party. Everyone is doing their best flying, and there are judges and videotape TV to keep track of what happens in the air and who is able to fly best as a team.

Dave Singer did a good job organizing the meet. He had some of the best RW judges (including Diane Kelly, Betty Giarrusso, Lorrie Young and Bob MacDermott) lined up, plus the TV videotape from Elsinore.

The Army did an outstanding support job, in spite of the Department of Defense ruling cancelling the helicopters. The Fort Lewis Army Parachute Clubs were beautiful! They gave up their entire Labor Day weekend to help run the meet, hold a barbecue, and support the relative workers! Yea!

As a Bicentennial tribute to the turkey, several teams clutched and blew the first dive. Arizona funnelled and blew their chances. The base formation for the first dive was an 8-man star. We decided that competition was a great place to add a fourth man to our somewhat successful 3-man-out-the-door. It didn't work and the 8-man reform was backward and garbled from what it was supposed to be for flying the wedges 360° to redock. Everybody just shrugged, played it by ear, and it worked...we got full points!

By the time we reached the last round, we had "max-ed out" all our dives, getting full points within working time. On round six we had a slow jump when one man went low on a sequence. We completed the dive but figured we were between 49 and 51 seconds on working time.

But several of the judges had missed our jump, so we weren't sure where we stood. At a team meeting we decided not to protest the jump in the interests of promoting the sport and good vibes, etc. etc....(We were tied with "Clear Eye" for first.) However, when Texas was moved up with us for a three-way tie after getting credit for a questionable judging, we protested, too. The judges and jury upheld our protest.

Enter Clouds and a Day of Rain. Dave Singer began to feel the pressure and seemed to flip out for awhile, declaring that since it was *his* meet, he would run it the way *he* wanted to. The judges said they couldn't let that happen, since what *he* wanted to do was overrule the judge's decisions.

Jumping stopped for about a day of daylight until the judges and Singer reached an agreement. Dave would direct the meet, but the judges would keep the official score and the jury would decide protests and post the final standings as they judged them.

So on Tuesday afternoon, when everyone is supposed to be back at work, we rejump and blow it, going 4 seconds overtime with another man low. This puts "Clear Eye" and Texas into a *sudden death* (weird choice of words, huh?) jump-off for first place. "Terminal Chaos" and "Seagull Squad" also went into sudden death for third place.

Seattle's Clear Eye took first. Texas completed the maneuver, but went overtime and took second. "Seagull Squad" completed their maneuvers, too, but went overtime. We chaosed our jump, and blew the dive. Chaos reigns!

It was a fun meet in the air. I'm looking forward to the next 8-man competition. One thing we learned for sure was that our very intense ground practice helped us a lot in the air.

FINAL STANDINGS

1. Clear Eye Express, Seattle   } Tie, jump-off
2. Kaleidoscope, Texas
3. Seagull Squad, Utah   } Tie, jump-off
4. Terminal Chaos, Elsinore
5. Country Hod & the Fish, Arizona
6. Rush
7. Skydive, Canada
8. Swine Flu
9. Western Hemisphere, Utah
10. All the President's Men, Pope Valley
11. Alien Eight
12. All of the Above, Seattle

Pat Works, Spotter Magazine, Nov.-Dec. 1976

The Team
Oh, yes, a guy bounced.
He fell onto the mountainside.
Comfortably far away. Nice that I didn't know him.
Only slowed the meet down a tad.

Otherwise the best part of the meet were the crazy turquoise lakes
and brown mountain/hills
that magically turn rich green on opening
and blossom into birds and flowers when you land.

You land wondering *what in the hell just happened up there?*
Gathering bright soft nylon into the routine bundle
you muse on what you flew
and wonder
about the reality of the actual dive
while speculating on what will become the official debriefing story.

Seeing you all land, the monster swings its head and watches
the separate figures walking back in after the competition jump.
It sees the team members as Ego: integral parts of its primeval self.

The monster stirs and its mindless head sets the stage
for the reunion of the Skygods. A Television stageset self-constructs
and single members become one as they gather,
merge and metamorphosis into
THE TEAM.

Peer pressure. Dodging, feinting, swinging the adrenalin-charged
whip of criticism in unthinking frenzy,
the team meeting blots out the sun with its Karma;
creating its fleeting thought-clouds upon the eternal sky.

The monster flexes, luxuriating in the exertion of the skydive
as each team member reenters the monster that has many names.

"I AM CALLED THE TEAM!!!," cries the monster to all.
"My birth was in the sacred gathering of my members who are my Self.
"My character is ordained by ego.
"My only reality occurs before and after the flow that is called 'the
    jump'."

"I die on exit as each member climaxes
into sequenced perfection
of joy, love and flight.

"I wake after the landings, when the gathering and conversation come.
"HEAR THEN, MY MEMBERS, HEAR AND LEARN BY WHAT
    PERIODS I COUNT MY TIME."

"My seeds lie in hope. I exist only because
no man is the whole of himself...
his friends are the rest of him.

"While all my members are present in me, I am present in none of
them. This is my divine mystery.

"I have no mind and I roam where I please,
heedless of reality.

"I honor only that which I choose to recognize,
and act accordingly.

"Pride synergizes with ego and the euphoria of any success,
so that I AM POWERFUL.

"I decide the how, the when and the where of my existence
in a benign dictatorship.

"Tradition bound, I always live for the future, forgetting always the
everpresent Now.

"My members work around me,
giving me size, coloration and smell.

"I become what they are. Whatever they think they see
is only a reflection of themselves
from the mirror I hold up to their hopeful gaze.

"I satisfy,
but cannot be satisfied.

"I move without direction. By answering to everyone,
I answer to no one.

"I am Chaos."

"Fly Me."
–Pat Works

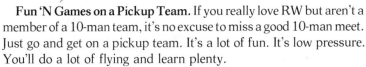

Fun 'N Games on a Pickup Team. If you really love RW but aren't a member of a 10-man team, it's no excuse to miss a good 10-man meet. Just go and get on a pickup team. It's a lot of fun. It's low pressure. You'll do a lot of flying and learn plenty.

How do you go about getting on a pickup team at a meet? Well, you don't wait for a team to come to you. Call the meet director before the meet and tell him that you (and maybe some others) will be arriving to jump on pickup teams. This gets the ball rolling.

Next, arrive early and let everyone know that you are available. If things don't shape up this way, get on the P.A. system and announce that a pickup team will be forming and interested swoopers should meet at a designated spot. I did this once at a meet where people were saying "the teams are all filled." Thirty-two people showed up, and we made three pickup teams. We all had fun.

Jumping at a meet beats the hell out of sitting on the ground. It may be a bit expensive, but you are assured a set number of jumps, and you'll learn a lot. Try it.

When you find an interested, partly filled team, tell them where you fly *best,* not where you like to fly. Be realistic about your abilities so the elected team captain will be able to put together a lineup that works. Every jump should be planned and practiced on the ground from exit lineup to tracking away, waveoff and dumping. A breakoff system should be decided on so everyone on the jump will know when it's time to track.

As a pickup team, you may be tempted to try to duplicate the tight, fast exits you see other teams practicing. But consider the safety factor as well. A ripcord pulled as a result of a jam-up in the door on exit won't do your team's score much good. Teams with the good fast exits have been building those exit lineups over many practice jumps, fitting each person into the stack like pieces of a puzzle. Their gear has been taken into consideration — piggybacks, or flat reserves, or ripcords installed inboard as necessary. Don't try a jammed, aggressive exit if your gear configuration won't allow for it. Better to have a spread-out exit — and fly sharper to make up for it — than a 9-man star and one man under canopy at 10,5.

This point was illustrated well at last year's Big-Z 10-man meet at Zephyrhills. There were a number of accidental reserve openings as a result of jammed doorways.

Pat Works, RWu, June 1975

So Ya Wanna Go Last, Huh?! Introduction — We like Tom Phillips who's forever riggin' up RW hardware to swoop lots. He's a floater on Jerry Bird's All Stars.

"Are you kidding me, THAT turkey?..." "I saw him lose his grip on a three-man..." "No, he's good..." "Well then, tell him if he goes below to stay out from underneath it..." "He *can* track, can't he?"

So the guy manifesting sticks his neck out and you get to go last for the first time, the object being to get in as smoothly and swiftly as possible without everyone else waiting for the guy who went out last.

Wherever you are on a ten-man Beech, or any aircraft for that matter, you are only behind the guy in front of you. Whatever your slot, from three to thirty, you'll find yourself in the same position every time, right behind the guy in front of you. With a hot exit, theoretically (variable: you), most people will cop to being able to get into a star two seconds behind "the guy in front of you." OK... far out... so what do we have now?

Try this. Do you know two guys that make a three-second pin and eight other ego trips who would verbally agree to the "two seconds behind the guy in front of you" gig?? Congratulations, man, you guys just qualified for a nineteen-second flat on paper. Count it up. So why doesn't it happen more often in the sky? Good question.

Original excuses are good jump stories, but not everyone is into competitive RW. That's what I'm talking about. The first time most people try to clean up their act a little is usually because everyone wants to go faster. That is, they have to... "the guy behind me," etc. "No, man, I jump for the fun of it." Far out, may all your stars be fun. Wanna spend $40 to $50 this weekend on some practice "fun" jumps? This is what some peoples' heads are into, and at this point the sport takes on the aspect of Team Relative Work.

"Fun jump" is a deceptive phrase. On the ground after the jump, OK, that's what it's all about. If you fly with people who dig a full-tilt boogie, fun is faster and BIGGER. This isn't confined to stars, either. Try a two-five or three-five accuracy stack from a Twin-Beech sometime. It'll blow your mind. It's the same trip as freefall. You can blow it really easily with a case of "heads-up-ass" flying. Accuracy is RW with the ground. Try it, together.

A great many jumpers would never admit to being competitive, yet all admit a desire to improve. Take your better-than-average demo jumper. If he puts it all on the line for $$$, then he is selling a commodity to the public and should do a professional job. If you think you spend enough time and money "doing your thing" on the weekend to justify wanting to be in the air with people you consider as good as or better than yourself, then you are there.

I had the opportunity to talk and get high with a lot of RW types this summer, from all over the country. Everyone wanted to spread the word..."RW." When the smoke had cleared, all agreed that "consistent" was the key word. Consistent WHAT, though? That wasn't everyone's problem. "How do you guys do it?" was a hot topic.

One of the nice things about manifesting a load yourself is having more of an opportunity to do it YOUR way, right or wrong. What happened at the World Meet is a good example of trying to organize a successful large-star attempt. We had 26 to 30 good RW types and the use of three Huey choppers. Well, the first couple of tries fell short of a record, generated some new excuses and a couple of good jump stories. Everyone gathered in the hangar, and Bird stood up and the skull-session began. Traffic jam, people in the back of the load in a hurry, bad grips, bad flying, etc. The speed merchants were told to cool it, and everyone shook their heads and mumbled yea, do it, go team, kill.

We had only one more try, nine in each chopper, 14,500 ft. and twenty-six RW types with Carl Boenish taking flicks. At about four-five, after a lost grip and a reform at a 25, we held a 26-man long enough to get a nice picture and another "biggest yet" became history. We put our gear down and watched ourselves on video rerun. That was hot. To my knowledge, it was the first time a record star had ever been made during or after a parachute meet. Good aircraft support, good organizing, better-than-average flying, and a 100 percent effort were involved. The right people were doing the right thing at the right time...Right On!

It is a lot easier to agree to a method than it is to motivate someone to actually do anything but talk about enlightenment. What it all boils down to is a systematic revolution. Any group with enough desire can be in the "head count" at national level. The rules of the game invite participation. About a dozen represented YOU at last year's Nationals. We talked about who should be able to come to the 10-man Nationals, and decided that two 10-mans witnessed by a Conference Director or National Director, with a time factor, was cool, with a registration fee to sweeten the stash for the winner. So the team from Bum Spot, S.C. doesn't have anything to beat but a stopwatch in order to come to the Nationals. Do this and talk with people, and you'll understand that this sport is overdue for an expansion and knowledge on a level that can be considered a true revolution.

Come and listen, come and talk. Be ready to work, relative, of course, to where your head is at.

Tom Phillips, RWu, March 1973

How to Put Together a 4-Man Relative Work Team!

"Get Your Head Out of Your Ass and Get Started." Getting started is sometimes the hardest part. Getting started in 4-man RW requires one of the biggest commitments a skydiver can make. Four people who thought they were the most wonderful, free-fallen, swoopen, dyn-o-MITE, sonofabitchen skydivers ever to scratch their crotch will jump together and probably fubar it up on the first few jumps.

It's not as easy as it looks. It's sometimes as hard on the body as it is on the ego, but with perseverence even a 1000-jump expert can learn to do what is ultimately the most difficult form of competitive RW today — 4-man sequential RW for time.

In choosing a team, the most important thing is to get 4 or 5 (one alternate) toads who can fall together without much effort. That is, they must instinctively fall relative to one another. This does not mean that all four have to be the same size. With the development of bell jumpsuits, mini-pigs, flat conventional reserves and other innovative equipment, size and weight don't make much difference any more. There are some limits on weight difference between team members, but the ability to fall relative to the other toads in the air is indispensable.

It is also good when teaming up to choose people you like and think you can get along with. Four-man RW is like marriage (it's hard on the nerves) and unless you have a deep respect for the other members' humanity and ability, your team can easily fall apart from the inside or you may wish it would. Everyone must be willing to "de-personalize" themselves for the team. You may go out tenth on a 10-man jump and think you're the best flyer around, but if the position you'd do best on the 4-man is first, then that's where you should go. With enough "de-personalization" and enough talent, victory is assured.

There is another way — and some teams follow this alternate plan. First: Get the meanest bastard on the DZ. We can call him Ass Hole. A.H. proclaims himself captain of the team by virtue of his temperament. Nobody argues. Second: Get the biggest fellow jumper — call him Happy. A.H. tells Happy he is going out base by virtue of his size. Happy agrees — what else? Third: Get the greatest ego on the DZ and let him go 4th. Put a star on his helmet and call him Dude. Then get another person (or a girl) who is easy-going and defenseless and can bounce off all the bullshit that is going to be coming down with this star-studded conglomeration of mis-matched, ill-fitted heterosexuals. You can call this last person Crazy.

This may seem absurd, but in the very political ways that teams evolve while everyone is maneuvering for position, RW teams sometimes do get together in just this way — or in other ways that are equally as nonsensical.

There is, of course, the question of team captain. Really, it doesn't matter who the team captain is on a 4-man team if the team is a conglomerate rather than four individuals, because the attributes of a good team captain should be practiced by everyone on the team. However, every team needs a captain (if for no other reason than to answer the P.A. system at meets and take care of paperwork and other logistics.)

What are the important attributes of a team captain? Basically he is a servant of the team, not the other way around. He must anticipate everything from personal problems to when to get on the airplane. Most of all, he must be a winner, personally and morally.

The biggest service he will perform is giving members of his team the confidence that they are the best skydivers in the world in any given position. He must instill this confidence without saying it directly; he must believe it; he must be sincere because between intuitive people there is no insincerity. If the captain makes a teammate believe that the only reason he's on the team in the first place is because the captain's a good guy, and that one mistake will oust him, then he might as well save his magnanimity. A certain amount of pressure is good, but lack of confidence in his team members is not the right kind of pressure.

This is all you need to start except for one more quality. Desire. Unless you want to win, you won't. The desire to be a winner must come from way down deep. At the risk of over-emphasizing the competitive aspect, it should be reaffirmed that competition is winning and losing. There are many losers — anyone can join that club. There is only one winner — a very exclusive group.

With all due respect to desire and the will to succeed, when it comes right down to the wire it is *ability* that wins.

Everyone has heard the old drone "Just give me somebody with real desire and I'll make a relative worker out of him; I don't need no Skygod." That is the most fragrant form of bullshit. Everyone knows a jumper who has a lot of desire, good intentions and a multitude of practice jumps that do him no good.

If given the choice between the good jumper and the sincere jumper with desire, *all other things being equal,* take the good jumper. With enough desire a person will succeed eventually, but everyone develops at different rates. RW is more difficult for some than others. The "sincere" fellow may have more fun making jumps away from a serious team. He may develop ability faster without the pressure of a team.

Marc Cohen, RWu, June 1973

About Evolving 4-Man RW Team Competition (1972). Four-man RW is an exciting thing to do. It requires an intensity of thought and quickness of reflexes not found in 10-man stars. It is no longer "mass style" as some idiot reported.

Unlike 10-man RW which evolved from the sport, 4-man RW was "invented" by USPA to satiate those of us who dig RW. Lots of brainy people spent many months drawing pictures and writing letters to create this mess. Like Ford's Edsel, it had problems. Like, up 'til now, you had to practice out of a Cessna 180 series because the exit was all-important. (And we all know that circus exits do not mesh with the realities of RW.) Now, forward-looking members of the USPA Competition Committee have done a far-out thing: they asked the people who do RW how to fix their Edsel. The RW answer was to chop it into a Pinto:

"Recommended changes to Part 51, four-man relative team event." A meeting of some 35 relative workers was called by Ted Webster on

18 June, 1972. The following recommendations are made as a result of that meeting. Bill Smith's proposal was accepted almost in its entirety:
"We propose that a change be made in the national 4-man relative work rules to overcome the problem of different exits from different aircraft. We submit that a 4-man star be used as a "base" for each series of maneuvers. When the star is broken off, the stopwatch would start. To provide separation each jumper would break off, back loop and then start the first series of maneuvers. No time limit would be placed on the performance of the basic star. Thus it would not matter what type of aircraft a team was practicing with, and each team could come to the Nationals on an equal basis."

Now you can practice this fun event out of *any* type of aircraft. Since there is now no advantage to an acrobatic exit, real aerobatic RW will determine scores. Your ability is now more important than timing an exit.

RWu, July 1972

About 10-man Team Competition (1972).

"Recommendations to establish a USPA Part 53: A National Ten-Man RW Event." A meeting of large-star relative workers was hosted by Jerry Bird on 18 June, 1972 in Tahlequah following the first National 10-man Star Team Championships.

"...it is the intent to establish a freefall event which will present the opportunity to evaluate the relative work ability and demonstrate the sportsmanship of ten-man teams. ...It is recognized that alternate formations will probably be incorporated into the event. ...The ten-man championships shall be held concurrently with the style/accuracy and 4-man championships. (RW SHALL NOT BE SUBJECTED TO THE UNREASONABLE DELAYS AND 2ND CLASS SCHEDULING CURRENTLY EXPERIENCED.)

...Eligibility: To qualify for the National Championships a team must perform two consecutive ten-man stars for a minimum average of 40 seconds under the direction of a Conference Director...a $100 qualification fee shall be collected and earmarked for the U.S. Ten-Man Team Fund. ...Teams consist of 12 members...any 10 may jump...only four substitutions (new people) allowed. ...No weird exits. ...The overall individual relative work champion shall be recognized...for scores in both 4 and 10-man RW."

RWu, July 1972

My Kinda Star*
Far above an ocean,
Far above tall trees,
Far above creation,
In a world of open seas.

A star consisting of people,
A star consisting of love,
A star consisting of brotherhood,
Is a star from far above.

If you can feel a precious love
For all those in company,
Then you can build a star with them.
Just try it — then you'll see.

*Written by Estelena Fulp, 7 jumps, in Crawfordsville, Ind.
RWu, December 1974

RW Questions with Answers by USPA (1972). I have spent some time talking to people about the 10-man National Event. Overall reaction was positive. Most jumpers believe that this will open the door to stronger relations between all parachutists. Without going into detail, I will list some of the negatives, with response by USPA spokesmen.

Q. *Most jumpers with whom I come in contact do not do style and accuracy. There is some question about the applicability and relevance of the USPA license system to relative workers, since it is based on style and accuracy ability.*

USPA. "The main reason, Pat, that I seem to hear about this licensing system is that just because a person has a license does not make them a good relative worker. In all honesty and reality, the exact same is true of style and accuracy people. Just because a jumper has a license doesn't mean he can turn a 6-second series or bang out 5 or 10 consecutive dead centers.

"It is much the same as just because a person has a driver's license, it does not mean that this person will be a good driver. It is something that is required by each state and we follow it whether we like it or not.

"The same, I am sure, is true of the USPA licensing system. Perhaps someday it will be revised but I must admit that I doubt it will be done before the 1972 National Championships."

Q. *Some years ago style and accuracy meets were a lot of fun. For some reason, this fun aspect was lost. There is a very real fear that USPA may "organize" the fun out of relative work. Many jumpers feel it is imperative that the relative work teams at the Nationals determine their own destiny with minimal help from the national organization.*

USPA. "I couldn't agree with you more on that 'some years ago the style and accuracy meets were a lot of fun.' I think the main reason they are not so much fun anymore is that the days of a guy lucking into a victory spot are over. To do well in style or accuracy competition these days takes a lot of practice. The same, I believe, is and will be true of 10-Man Star Relative Work. Once something becomes competitive, those who aren't quite so good at it start to lose a little bit of interest — and some of the fun goes out of it.

"There are already some who are disappointed that 10-man relative work is becoming so competitive. This, however, is human nature and I'm afraid there is not too much we can do about it.

"In regard to USPA 'organizing' the fun out of relative work, I believe we have this potential problem beaten...it is the relative workers and the relative workers alone, under the guidance of Skratch Garrison, who are making up the rules and regulations for 10-man competition. In my meeting with Skratch, I pointed out to him that we ought to get as detailed as possible in the rules and make them absolutely water-tight so they will be accepted, in total, by the USPA Board as a USPA Part.

"If Skratch and his committee do their job correctly (which I am sure they will), the rules and regulations will be accepted in total. Then this particular USPA Part for large star relative work will have been written by large-star relative workers."

Q. *The 10-Man National Event will be a test situation for both USPA and relative workers. Obviously, USPA may later decide to again ignore large-star relative work, or relative workers could decide to operate without USPA. It is a two-way street. There should be understanding on both sides that a major split in the organization could be detrimental to both.*

USPA. "The 10-Man National Event will be a test situation for both USPA and relative workers. I couldn't agree with you more. However, I am not really worried. I have the utmost confidence that if we all use common sense and are willing to bend a little bit here and there (that's

both sides), then we will have a most successful 10-Man
Championships at the Nationals. If everyone comes to the Nationals
(staff, organizers, competitors) looking for a well-run Championships
and outstanding display of skill, a real desire to see the
Championships a success, *and* have an enjoyable time, I can guarantee
you that they will get it."
–*RWu, May 1972*

**A World Championships in Relative Work! What Does It All
Mean??** (1973) OK, now adjust your ego to the fact that you are now an
athlete of Olympic calibre. Straighten your shoulders and condescend
to explain to your short-sighted friends that "your crazy hobby" is now
a major world sporting event.

In one short year our thing of precise, beautiful, ecstatic involvement
with other people in a form of three-dimensional aerial ballet, with the
wind providing the symphonic score orchestrated by the clouds, has
been viewed by le monde. And that king that governs all of the world's
air realized, accepted and rejoiced with us in the newest of
International art-forms — freefall relative work.

After the big FAI meeting in Paris came the USPA Board of
Directors meeting in Florida. A heavy thing came across at both
meetings — freefall RW is, in fact, a major air sport and is recognized
as such. And the big organizations that control all air sports want very
much what we want... RW to continue to grow smoothly into the
significant athletic event that it is, with fun and freefall for all. If this is
to happen we must continue to work together as an International
Union of Freefallers. We are all just beginning; let's begin together.
Make lotsa RW jumps. Communicate your feelings on what you're
doing and don't delegate the future of your favorite activity to some
paper-pusher who's more interested in the glory of piles of paper than
making RW jumps.

We're gonna have a World Cup RW meet. Problems can be
numerous.

Rod Murphy, the Henry Kissinger of the FAI's RW Committee,
made a visit to give us a positive briefing on the international aspects of
relative work competition. The FAI's RW Committee is an
international group who are watching and trying to not have just a few
skydivers or individual countries who, however well meaning, might
set RW off on a weird track that'd take YEARS to correct so it reflects

what we RW'ers want to do.

Rod was instrumental in the RW competition proposal made in Paris to the FAI-CIP group. He's from South Africa, and here's what he has to say: "The first RW World Championships could be an athletic event or a political event, so we've got to plan ahead. RW people must realize that on a world-wide basis things happen slowly. For example, the current 10-man star rules must be translated into something like 29 languages. That means that each word in the rules will have a different meaning and interpretation to all readers. Plans must be made and presented at FAI meetings. Misplanning, or poor presentation of a plan, could delay adoption of a proposal by an easy two years."

Thus the FAI RW Committee has a problem: the USA Ten-man rules won't do for a world meet where things must be worded like a peace treaty. Translation and politics, coupled with poor communication and differing goals, lead to problems and protests. Protests lead to ill will and delays. Twenty-nine nations can't all think the same, points out Rod, and some countries have a different boogie than the U.S.A. Think about it. If you represented your country in a world meet and were defeated and had to return home where defeat means disgrace and perhaps loss of job or housing, you'd make damn sure you got the best shake you could possibly get. Including protesting for the sake of protesting.

It looks like the World Cup could be a rotten banana mess if every country doesn't give a bit. Let's hope we can let the sport grow; let positive things help the growth.

"What are the rules for *judging* the meet?" asks Rod. "We need international calibre judges. Where're we gonna get them? In 30 years the FAI hasn't produced competent judges. Where are we gonna get good RW judges? Some RW people don't want to be judged by style judges, and the FAI won't accept separate classes of judges."

Rod suggests we invite style judges to RW meets and teach 'em to judge RW. They are experienced and tend to be professional, because after all, judging is a discipline. It's hard to be a good judge when your best effort only garners curses.

The point is, we need judges. And we could use some intelligent articles on HOW to judge an RW meet. For instance, in judging RW the angle of observation on a 10-man star is critical. What are the limits of this angle?

A good start in this direction was the motion at the Paris meeting which was approved by USPA's Board that up to three foreign judges be invited to participate in the U.S. Nationals each year. This should improve the level of international judging.

Remember, the FAI is BIG. Its presidents, vice presidents, committee heads are often Kings, Princes, Dictators, Prime Ministers who banded together in the world FAI as a formal organization to defend the use of airspace for sport. As a part of FAI we are also big and have the power and influence of great men to back our activities. If we act deliberately and *in unison.*

Pat Works, RWu, March 1973

Here's What Eilif Ness, Norway, Has To Say About the FAI-CIP* RW Committee: He's chairman of the committee which will arrange RW training meets, gather information on technical developments, and make suggestions to further international relative work competition.

"From now on it is up to the Relative Workers of every nation to work within their own national organization to develop teams for international competition...and work to have their national Relative Work Teams sent to the different world meets. ...I am not quite sure that the grass roots jumpers in the different countries really appreciate the enormous importance of the decisions that have been made by the FAI, and the responsibilities that are put on them as a result of these decisions. It is now up to the Relative Work jumpers to prove that the work has not been wasted."

*FAI (Federation Aeronautique Internationale) — (The official international group responsible for all aviation-related activities. CIP is the parachuting arm of this body.)

RWu, March 1973

RW Expansion: (1973). No doubt those of us who have achieved experience competitively or non-competitively in this sport have mulled over the issue concerning standards of competition.

Accuracy is rather basic (though judging a downwind stab can lead to controversy when the first three slots are separated by no more than the diameter of the judge's eye). Style, that lonesome series of overshot flat turns and questionable backloops, seems to leave a lot to be desired by any given number of jumpers one might encounter.

Now we have a relatively new form of competition thanks to countless individuals who prefer the company of a fellow jumper while losing altitude as well as the ride to exit point. Once the first few hook-ups were a success, it was only a matter of time before ideas such as multi-plex star formations — snowflakes, caterpillars, skirmish lines and other strangely asymmetrical patterns fabricated by a crew of novelty-seeking skydivers — were conceived.

So we have the three: Accuracy — a break-neck lunge at the little disc hoping to bury it with whatever portion of the body strikes first or maneuvering a half a thousand dollar ram-air backed by another $500 worth of practice jumps to the disc enough times in succession to win hands down — yielding a plastic trophy and/or 25 big ones which is probably spent on a few cases of Budweiser for that evening.

Style is something else again. High velocity acrobatics is indeed a science and an art and anyone achieving a clean nine-second series can certainly beam with self-accomplishment from within. But to convince the majority of today's sport parachutists that to climb to 6500 ft., exit, dive, crank, loop and pull is the epitome of fulfillment and excitement would be comparable to persuading Bill Ottley he'll be reincarnated as a bear rug with 20/20 vision.

In April of '66 I encountered what seemed to me the most awe-inspiring event ever to unfold in the challenging sky above. Having never witnessed a live parachute jump, not to mention freefalling human beings, I was now in the position (at Pop's place, Clewiston, Fla.) to squint into the glaring blue and see two dudes not only in free flight but joined together performing loops. This may seem a bit much to today's blase jumper, but I can't apologize for feeling it was out of sight. Mind made up, 35 dollars was thrust into the instructors' ravenous palm. I would learn to do loops in the sky. Welcome new life. Adios, past...

Ask any novice air-diver who has been exposed to relative work what he's up to, where his head's at. Stars, big stars, small stars, funny stars. Stars slow, fast, disorganized or maybe even round. RW seems to be where it's at for a great deal of us.

Now, just who sets down the rules and regulations for parachuting competition? Why is the disc so many centimeters in diameter? Who concocted the maneuvers in a series? Why a certain size of star or optional altitudes at RW meets? What is really grounds for a rejump? We are merely scratching the surface of formation freefall. We can set the rules as well as the pace. The large number of people involved in RW competitively will add strength to our plea for recognition. We are growing rapidly. In 1970 Z-Hills registered seven teams for large-star heats. In 1971 it doubled; this year thirty 10-man teams were manifested to race the clock. Great...yet this figure represents roughly 2 per cent of the nation's jumpers; included in this minority were a number of our world's greatest talent and some very hot contenders.

Toss this concept around a bit. Ten-man stars seem to be the magic number in elapsed-time star heats. There is absolutely nothing adverse concerning 10-man competition, except a high ceiling is a must as is multi-engine aircraft. Finances play a major role. And of course, ten willing individuals who will coexist as a unit relatively peacefully. Our skills whetted in the past few years, we can perform 10-mans in the vicinity of plus or minus 25 seconds after exit, thanks to Beechcrafts, Lodestars, large-door DC-3's and other multis. Consider the potentially competitive relative workers in remote areas who froth at the mouth and suffer severe anxiety when a '172 or '180 and a 2000-ft. grass strip is their lot. Ten-mans are virtually impossible for them.

Our awards are now based on 8-man star formations. We are receiving honorable mention for our feats with patches for day, night, low order, eighth slot or better Starcrests. Medallions and numbers all denote our proficiency with seven other high-altitude people. Would eight-man star competition be more desirable as a national standard? It could alleviate some problems we are confronted with, and also boost our strength by increasing the number of competitive teams.

Naturally eight-man stars are performed from a lower altitude — this parallels less cash output. Also, if the ceiling should drop from the customary 10 or 12,000 ft., the competition could continue, perhaps from 7200 ft. or lower. Competitive 8-man stars should be completed at just a shade past terminal velocity. Competitive 8-man stars would allow multitudes of jumpers with only small aircraft availability and limited finances to practice and participate.

There will be various pros· and cons concerning this issue. This concept is merely a thought towards a brighter future for relative workers who indulge more than superficially. The aim here is not to abase style or accuracy. After all, they are the competitive forerunners. Promotion and growth of RW is the issue. Opinions of one and all who take interest are sought. Express yourself; you are the sport.

Comment by Bill Newell, SCR-3... "I think it's a hot idea. The only reason it's 10-man now is 'cause 10 people fill up a Beech. But don't make it either 8-mans or 10-man—let's have both."

RWunderground comment... We like the idea of both 8 and 10-mans. The Scrambles *are* 8-man events. Both should be encouraged for competition.
R.W. "Flash" Gordon, RWu, January 1973

Defining Free Fall Relative Work (1973). This summer the Board of Directors meeting at the Nationals in Tahlequah will probably be the site of heavy decision-making concerning the future of *your* sport: Free Fall Relative Work.

Decisions made by competitors there could seriously weaken or strengthen freefall relative work. It's kind of like setting rules and restrictions on the growth of a kitten. With or without the rules and restrictions that kitten *will* become a cat (unless it dies first). The rules could help it to be a nice-type cat or a spitting monster.

Here are some things to think about before making decisions about RW:

I. What *is* Relative Work? It is strictly 10-man speed stars? Does it include sequential maneuvers?

II. Are RW competitors the only people who do "real" RW? What about the non-competitors?—how can we answer to their wants and needs?

III. If competence at RW is rated strictly by ability to make speed-stars could we eventually have the same mess we got into when competence at parachuting was (is) defined by "skill at style and accuracy"? A large majority of jumpers won't compete in style and accuracy because they don't enjoy the hair-splitting that these events have degenerated into.

IV. Is there any real need to alter the basic 10-man (speed star) event? Should we let it alone?

V. Should there be provisions made for other types of 10-man competitive events?

VI. Can you compete in RW occasionally and have fun with RW, too?

VII. What about judges? We must have more and better judges. How?

VIII. Who should "run" RW? Are you going to delegate your vote to a non-RW participant to handle for you? Does your Conference Director do RW?

IX. Should SCR rather than a C license be required to enter 10-man RW events at the Nationals?

X. Should there be the option for teams that want to make competition jumps from 8500 ft.? Teams that can do it consistently in under 25 seconds sure don't need 40-50 seconds of freefall.

XI. Will aircraft judges be necessary in competition? Some people have pointed out that there are teams which need to pay more attention to the rule banning "circus exits".

RWu, June 1973

Yesterday Should Never Have Quit. From Capt. Weird: "I'm somewhere where I can't jump...and I miss it very much. Also all the good people I've jumped with...I promise myself to return to the sport and people I love...My love to the (past) and original Humboldt Hummers...

"Watch the Beeches fly over,

Laying on a mountain, surrounded by clover.

Thinking of times when we were high.

Think of the times I used to fly,

To ride the floor, with ten more.

One is the cameraman, next to the door.

From countdown to exit it's just one breath.

With a life like that, there is no death. ***

Yesterday should never have quit."

RWu, June 1975

Controversies On RW Meets Of The Future (Circa 1973). *Ed. Note:* We get lotsa mail about RW. Last issue we included some ideas sent in by jumpers around the country on the future of RW competition. These reflected a desire for sequential 10-man RW, maneuvers in addition to round stars, junior and senior classes, etc.

Since then we've received several letters sayin' "Keep it round 10-mans." We are printing one from Bob Skinner and our reply, along with selections from Jack Miles and an open thing from Steve McCluer. These seem the most representative of "the other point of view." * * *

Dear RWunderground and Pat,

I truly enjoyed your articles and suggestions toward expanding sequential RW into the world of RW competition... Unfortunately the suggestions did not go over to the majority of people I've talked to on the subject. Maybe it's adverse to what we now know as speed RW... I don't know what the real reasons are but I can forward to you my impressions of the matter and a possible course of action.

I think we have to remember that 10-Man Star Competition has only been in the Nationals for one year and that it really hasn't been accepted by the old guard of the parachute community. I personally was very demoralized last year; not from the performance of our team which was really poor, but from the complete lack of organization on the part of the people responsible to make the meet successful... I seriously question the ability of the organization to run just a pure 10-Man Competition in a manner that shows the respect our part of the sport deserves. Until they can prove their concern I'd vote for straight speed competition.

Also... we must consider the jumpers in other countries that have very recently transcended into relative work competition. Until a couple of World Competitions have been successfully completed, it seems fruitless to expand the type of RW we have been used to...

Another point is the ability to judge what's going on. I still see wide variations between judges. Videotape, of course, is the answer, but will it be functional as we need it to be?

On the other hand, sequential RW appears to be the long run direction, at least for a separate class of competition or for determining an overall RW championship team. To this I see great advantages, but only after our meet organizers can hold up their end. I do wish we could hold a separate Nationals at really nice places and have the paid admission support the teams which earned the right to participate. RW really is a spectators' sport, especially if the competition was held from 8500 to 9500 ft.

The establishment of classes is also an excellent idea. Very few people have even been in a 10-man star which was formed in 25 seconds or less, but they have to compete with teams that make it a habit. It might be advisable to establish classes, but then what's the criteria for a team to jump in what class?—because they want to, length of time the team has been together, previous competition standings, or what?

In summary I feel that 10-Man Speed Competition still has years left before National or World Competition rules should be changed. It's taken your sincere efforts to get our type of jumping into the Nationals, and everyone does appreciate the efforts which have been made. However, I think our efforts could be much better spent organizing and promoting a separate RW National and World Competition than changing the basis on which we obtained our identity. This is not saying that experimentation could not be made at local meets to prove or disprove the feasibility of sequential RW; in fact, it would be a lot of fun. But let's take a real deep look around us before we attempt to integrate changes into the National and International level of 10-Man Star Competition.

    Bob Skinner (Former member of the Downers A-1)
    D-45, SCS-263   * * *

Dear Bob Skinner:

Hey guy, loved your letter. It's concise and well written. I'm taking the liberty of sending it to USPA and the FAI International RW Committee.

On the 10-man thing, I think your letter clears things up a bit. Most everyone agrees that, ultimately, round ten-mans won't be the total RW picture, although they'll always play a big part. The question was: how to change 'em and when?

As you pointed out, the answer seems to be to change things when RW *participants* want things changed...and not 'til then. Anyway, the really important thing is to not make hard 'n fast "rules" about what RW is or isn't but just to let RW be what is good for RW. At one time folks thought style and accuracy showed your skill at parachuting. After a while though, all it showed was your skill at style and accuracy. Unfortunately some paper pushin' asshole made it an inflexible rule that skill at parachuting is defined by skill at style and accuracy. And so it stayed that way til everybody said "screwit" and did their thing which is currently 10-man RW. RW could petrify into a ritual, too.

But I sure hope it doesn't 'cauz then it wouldn't be as much fun.

    Pat Works
    SCS-1   * * *

Here's a reader who opposes the views expressed in our last issue. Jack Miles, SCR-570, SCS-44, writes (we're excerpting from his 11-page comments due to space):

"The bulk of RW teams cannot handle making 10-mans, let alone fast ones or sequential maneuvers..." and "...the people that are shouting loudest for alternate maneuvers can barely handle 10-man stars of any speed." ...(They are just) "Turkeys & Toads..."

Further, there shouldn't ever be both 8-man and 10-man events... "because of the chaos created at Z-Hills caused by having two altitudes." (Teams in that competition could opt to jump from either 10.5 or 12.5.) "I say if you can do an 8-man but not a 10, then stay home til you can, or move to Elsinore if you are really serious about RW!"

Jack continues to say that anybody who really wants to do RW can get a 10-place plane. "Buy, lease, rent, steal, etc. It just depends on how serious you are!" He believes that the only reason that there are 8-man SCR Scrambles is because "so few 8-mans are made... Look at the last (Calif.) Scrambles results! Big deal." He also feels that no large stars should be attempted during any meet.

"If promotion and growth of RW is the issue as you say it is, then the propositions put forth in that article should be put down the porcelain facility where they belong."

"In short," he concludes, "the basic premise is OK, *BUT* it is a few years in the future... I think a lot of people in RW should concentrate on getting their act together in the air rather than running their mouths on the ground..." People want alternate maneuvers, Jack thinks, "only because they can't beat a speed-star team any other way; I'm not alone in these opinions."

Jack Miles   *   *   *

An Open Letter
TO WHOM IT MAY CONCERN:

My proxy "vote" or statement is as follows: I do not believe, as some alarmists would like to have me believe, that the future of 10-man star relative work "is in grave danger."

I attended several meetings this summer held by relative workers at the Nationals. It was almost unanimous among those present that large star relative work was over-due in getting the attention it deserves. The policy of USPA has been, if not hostile, at least indifferent. Now it seems to be in a state of benevolent patronization (i.e., humoring us). It was the intention of Pat Works in organizing the Relative Work Council, which really does not exist, to voice the current feelings of relative workers across the United States. The purpose of the RW Underground is to act as a clearing house of ideas submitted by various readers. It is the only voice of relative work in America. It does not create policy, it simply voices it. As a voice of the largest segment of jumpers in the country (i.e., relative workers), it is not a voice that can be ignored by USPA. It is a means to get an otherwise indifferent system to work for us.

The recent article in RW Underground has been taken as the gospel, the "New Law." It is not. It simply expressed an opinion held by many that relative work is better than anything else because it is so versatile. If you shoot accuracy, all you can do is ride a canopy and try to get dead centers. If you turn style, all you can do is figure 8-back loop-figure 8-back loop...and nothing else. If you do *anything* in free-fall with more than one person you are doing relative work, whether it be two-man, four-man, or ten-man.

Style used to be the epitome of freefall. Now it has stagnated into a dull routine. Relative workers in every state of the country are unanimous—they do *not* want relative work to become a routine.

To the charge that the RW Council is going to do away with ten-man stars, I say that is a lot of bull shit. In the first place, you *are* the RW Council...at least you would be if you would write a letter or express some kind of opinion where somebody can hear it and do something constructive with it instead of whining and bitching among yourselves. But that is off the track. The point is that a great many people want to see RW remain versatile. Most of the "big shots" at Elsinore consider themselves to be hot shot relative workers but a lot of them look pretty sick when they have to do anything other than make a circle...so maybe they aren't relative workers in the truest sense—they're just star makers. I doubt very much if even USPA would be stupid enough to do away with ten-man stars. What they *would* do is add another event in which more than just stars are made.

Look at it this way. In "conventional" jumping you could enter the Nationals and compete in just one event, either style or accuracy, but you could not get overall. The same could be true of relative work—if you want to, you could enter just the ten-man star competition and not the whole thing...but you could *not* win overall. USPA has already expressed a desire to have an overall relative work award. It is up to you to decide how it should be run ... but Goddamn it, don't sit around crying because that ain't gonna help a thing!

I suggest you write your indignant letter and your petition or whatever you have in mind and send it to the RW Underground. They're on your side. *They are not going to take away your right to make ten-man stars.* By the same token, please don't take away the right of others to do something else and to compete in it. Dig?

Steve McCluer, "Father Farkle"

* * *

Now it's MY turn:

I know I'm repeating myself, but I still say that since RW is a sport and an expression of beauty I don't believe we should allow ourselves to be stuck in a mold of something that only some participants are into doing.

If we lock into 10-mans and make it "official," USPA and FAI will put it all on paper and it'll be "decided" for us.

But there may later be a larger group of RW'ers who'll continue to do their own thing and have fun. Look at the popularity of RW festivals. Look at the unanimous vote of the competitors at Z-Hills to add other types of RW to competition rounds.

Where will we be then? Right where we were in 1967 with style and accuracy when most of us let USPA and a small group of "serious" competitors take our sport away from us.

We aren't saying to *stop* 10-man. They're too much fun. We ARE saying that 10-mans probably aren't the ultimate form of RW. And we ask that we do not make lots of rules about "what is RW" cause it'll all change in a year no matter who writes it down anyway. We want to promote and further RW.

Pat Works

RWu, March 1973

Moon-gazing;
Looking at it, it clouds over;
not looking, it becomes clear.

Chora
1729

Lao Tzu on RW:
Those who would take over RW
And shape it to their will
Never, I notice, succeed.
RW is like a vessel so sacred
That at the mere approach of the profane
It is marred
And when they reach out their fingers it is gone.
For a time in the world some are skygods
And some are turkeys.
For a time in the world some push aboard
And some are tipped out.
At no time in the world will a man who is sane
Over-reach himself,
Over-spend himself,
Over-rate himself.
>Adapted from Lao Tzu, 500 B.C.

The Third Alternative. A "non-competitive" skydiving event tends to draw more people and create more general enthusiasm than does a traditional parachute meet. Witness the 1976 Nationals where over 1,000 skydivers showed up to boogie, while less than half that many competed.

This is NOT to say that non-competitive jumping is "better" than competitive-style parachute meets. However, anyone who has been deeply involved in both types of jumping will agree that "fun" meets or boogies are very real and exciting. Note the number of hard-core, non-serious teams at the Z-Hills Turkey Meet every year. Although the total number of teams climbs every year, there are seldom more than five hard-core "serious" teams. In fact, good pick-up teams always seem to place in the top five!

What does all this say? It says, loud and clear, that skydivers like fun and challenge more than anything else you're selling. Fun meets attract more jumpers than serious ones. It's not just the organization, but the type of jumping that wins out.

Serious teams may be the best way to win meets ... but serious team jumps are not for everyone the best way to have fun. I base that observation on more than 15 years of successful team jumping and watching others team jump.

Think about it...the Nationals are over. Everyone unwinds. Some quit jumping. Most team members have a hard time adjusting to the slower "fun" jumps. Weird formations throw everyone's RW act into the street; we are all more even when attempting something new.

Importantly, if the level of jumping has exceeded the judges' ability to call and if skill in the air has exceeded our ability to write rules...if flight has become generally perfect so that a 6-jump meet is hardly more than a warm-up that says nothing much about skill but rather shouts about luck and the judges so that meets are won and lost based not on skill but on happenstance...then, oh then, you begin to see the point of boogies.

Jumpers who don't quit the sport in disgust band together with others who share their ideas about perfection of flight for informal fun meets designed to test individual skill, foster group learning...and be fun.

A while back, relative work was an alternative to style and accuracy for a large group of skydivers whose patience with the old order had grown thin. Today, we see alternatives to even the new so-called "advanced" forms of relative work competition.

At Elsinore, Calif., on Labor Day 1977, a freefall meet was held that was an alternative to traditional RW competition. It was called "The Third Alternative". The meet was an original idea of Bret Leininger, and hosted by Elsinore team "Enough Chaos". Four 10-person teams were invited along with three of their peers as judges. I participated as titular meet director and jumped with Chaos. Here's what came down at the meet...

The four teams were formed by relative workers from Pope Valley, Elsinore and Arizona. All four would have scored high, if scores had been kept. Everyone "won"...including the "judges" who were Jerry Bird, from Utah, Al Krueger, from southern Calif., and M.J. Haught, from northern California.

The rules were simple. Three teams brought a dive and showed the other teams how to do it. The meet consisted of everyone doing all the dives — their own and those of the other teams. The judges, or evaluators, were all air judges. Each one watched each team attempt the same dive. At the end of the "meet" each judge told the assembled competitors how they saw each team perform their assigned jump, and how they thought the dive went compared to the other teams' attempts at the same dive.

For example, here is the entire organization of the "meet":

I. *The Teams*   *The Dive*
   Pope Valley (PV)   "Aggregation" (No. 1)
   Enough Chaos (EC)   "Green Light" (No. 2)
   Arizona (Az)   "Casa Gram" (No. 3)
   Lurking (Lk)   (Performed dives 1, 2 & 3)

II. *The Manifest* (who performs which dive on what round) DC-3 exit order

   Load 1 PV does No. 1; EC does No. 3; Az does No. 2 (Lk stands down)

   Load 2 PV does No. 3; EC does No. 2; Lk does No. 1 (Az stands down)

   Load 3 EC does No. 1; Az does No. 3; Lk does No. 2 (PV stands down)

   Load 4 PV does No. 2; Az does No. 1; Lk does No. 3 (EC stands down)

III. *Judges*

   Al Krueger watched dive No. 1, "Aggregation"

   M.J. Haught watched dive No. 2, "Green Light"

   Jerry Bird watched dive No. 3, "Casa Gram"

Bret Leininger spent many energetic hours putting the meet together. At the "Victory Banquet" after the meet, everyone was treated to roast turkey, stuffing, Caesar salad and beer. For dessert there were 18 *different* flavors of ice cream and sundae toppings. The judges reported on the jumps, and accompanying each report there were several bottles of ice cold champagne. Corks flew and the bubbly flowed with the telling of the jumps. It was a very mellow and happy scene.

Here's how the dives went:

Dive No. 3 ("Casa Gram") involved six separate sequences (see illustration). The starting, or base, formation was a 10-person donut-flake. The sequence progressed like this:

   a) *donut-flake* (breaks into stairsteps)
   b) *five 2-man stairsteps* (redocking into)
   c) *10-man slot-flake* (grip changes into)
   d) *10-man wedge, opposed* (breaks into)
   e) *4-man opposed diamond with two flanking 3-man wedges* which redock into
   f) *10-wedge, facing*
   ... which tracks off into the sun.

CASA GRAM

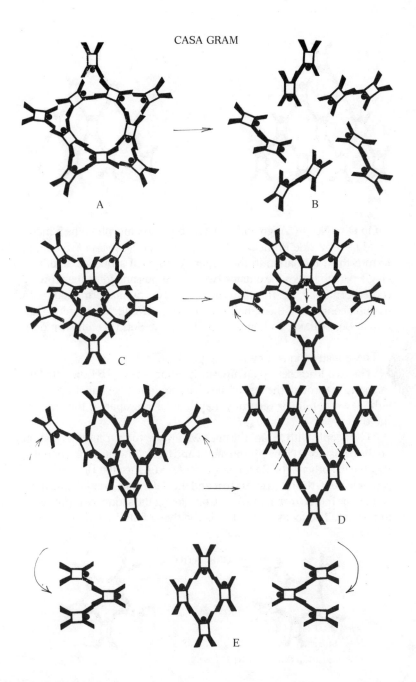

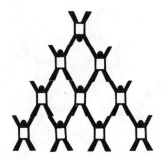
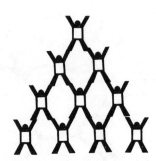

F

On Dive No. 1 ("Aggregation"), two 5-person murphy-type 5-mans build side by side in the air. Then *one* person leaves *each* 5-man to form a third formation in the center. With each sequence, another single person leaves the outside two formations and joins the growing center formation. So, this dive starts with two 5-man formations with nothing connecting them, and progresses to two lurkers flanking an 8-man donut-flake, ending with a 10-man in-out. (See illustration!)

These instructions go with "Aggregation":
"The two leads set up on aircraft heading, about 15 ft. apart. The formations through the rest of the dive should not get out of position, either horizontally or vertically. Level and 15 ft. apart is the order of the day.

"The people with *'s are the ones who move to the center formation on the transition. The 5-person in-out and the following 4-man donuts fly on each other. The 2-man stays centered. Once the Bipole in the center is built, the focus shifts to it and the outer formations fly on the center one for the rest of the dive. Completing the sequence is not very important. The focus of the dive is the flying both in and out of the formations."

AGGREGATION

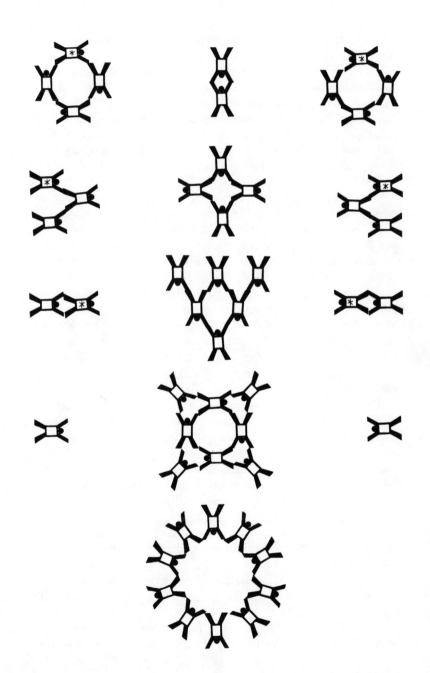

Whew! Hot skydive!! Here are some of the comments air judge Al "Capt. Hook" Krueger made about it:

"I watched Pope Valley do their own dive on my first jump...fine base formations...on first sequence left donut was higher and the formation had to go down to make the next sequence. Very close to completing the 6-wedge (flanked by two 2-man cats) when this air judge got scared and left. Probably the most thoughtful, imaginative and heads-up flying I've been in the air with. This team had not "over-practiced" and had their own struggles when things didn't go smoothly.

"On my second jump I watched Lurking perform the same dive. Very clean and concise and for a first-time team they seemed well-practiced. However, they didn't have the experience in simultaneous formations, and as a result, the formations were rather far apart...discipline and persistence were both evident...Gosh, being an air judge is a great experience!

"I watched Chaos on my third dive...they went nearly as far as the others. However, they were more chaotic. They over-amped as a result of my dirt dive descriptions of the problems the other teams had encountered with the dive, and this caused them to put their base formations too close together...these almost stacked on top of each other at one point...They were making the 6-wedge when the air judge got scared..."

Al's concluding remarks were about the concept of the meet:

"For the future it has great possibilities — no regimentation or completions required...Don't do anything that will stifle the free exchange of ideas that have been shared here...keep it small and without restrictions. Maybe the team with its dive should bring their own judge to help the "competition" learn how to do the dive in dirt dives...I found it easier to critique the dive when I learned it..."

Finally, M.J. Haught gave her "air judge's score" in the form of a TV news show commentary. It was a great ending to really good "meet". Here is M.J.'s evaluation with authentic juicy news "tidbits" thrown in for added spice:

"Good evening and welcome to KOKE Television News. KOKE-TV is first and foremost in skydiving reporting across the nation and throughout the world.

"Court procedings against Bullet Betty Hawkins are now underway. Ms. Hawkins is charged with fraudulently representing herself as a 12-year-old in order to get children's rates on jump tickets. In defense of Bullet, the ACLU maintains that jump tickets should be sold according to the individual's weight. In retaliation, heavier weight skydivers will be staging a demonstration tomorrow. The state militia are standing by for outbreaks of violence.

"On the national scene, the Union of Bakers and Pastry Chefs is suing U.S.P.A. for the great number of donuts being made every weekend by skydivers. The bakers and pastry chefs maintain that skydive donuts are presenting a poor image to the eating public because freefall donuts are fallen instead of raised.

"In New York, an auction of rare collector's stamps made an unusual expansion of merchandise. A high bid of $6,240 purchased a 1975 issue Casa Gulch jump ticket.

"The U.S. Department of Defense is investigating reports made in the Pope Valley area of UFO's. The objects are reported to resemble the Star Ship Enterprise of Star Trek fame.

"Joe Morgan has been accepted for psychiatric care as he seems unable to cope with the realization that he and his friends *are* those people our mothers warned us about.

"This weekend, Elsinore was the site of an invitational meet that may prove to be a turning point in skydiving competition — for the meet eliminated competition. Instead, the meet encouraged creativity and innovation in skydiving and communication among divers from several drop zones.

"The dive presented by Enough Chaos dealt with no-contact flying, which is an excellent method of developing one's individual control of one's own airspace. Each person *must* do their own flying. No just hangin' on for the ride. By transitioning from a connection to triple donuts to reverse triple donuts, the divers become aware of the necessity of visual eye contact when centerpointing donuts.

"When Chaos performed the dive, they displayed the aptness of their team name. They discovered that a sliding base on a no-contact dive is more challenging than on a contact dive. But undaunted, they proceeded to complete the first set of triple donuts. In this instance, it may have been more efficient to build the beginning connection maneuver *contact,* and then, on signal, release grips, fly the connection no-contact, and then proceed to the triple donuts.

"For many of the Lurkers, no-grip flying was a new experience. Group consensus on the ground was a) it was fun, b) they had learned a lot and c) let's try that again. Again, as with Chaos, a lot of time was spent on the first maneuver and it needed to be closer in when turning to the donuts. With beautiful salvage flying, they created triple donuts from a funnel.

"The Arizona team followed the principles of grace and beauty as the precision 4-person donut-machine base set the pace for clean flying. By maintaining the flow of manuever to maneuver, they were able to complete the series and track their 10-wedge toward the peas.

"The invitational meet succeeded in stimulating excitement over new ideas. Each team will be eager to try out these new concepts on their home drop zones and pass the word on to those who could not come. Hopefully the format of this meet will be continued. Let's maintain the openminded. Let's remember that the most important goal is communication. Thank you, Chaos, for hosting this innovative meet."

Dive No. 2 ("Green Light") instructions:

a) Base formation is done without any grips.

b) The six people outside the 4-man are all lurkers. (Need to keep tight.)

c) Base four does right hand donut, lurkers do left hand donut. All turn at the same time.

d) Key for the turn needs to come from the base four. (Lurkers just react.)

e) Third maneuver, if time, would be to cog the two outside donuts. (The middle two remain where they are.)

f) Or, reverse the donuts (donut madness).

Pat Works, Parachutist, February 1978

GREEN LIGHT

NO GRIP

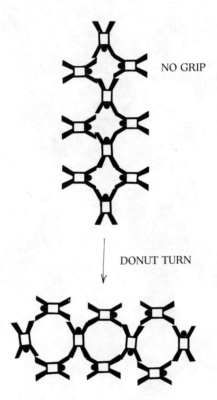

DONUT TURN

5

Specialties

Relative work is the relating of one to another in the air. It happens on the ground, too. These relationships have created a brotherhood of freefallers, and as brothers we should help each other. It's *our* sport. We must try to avoid ego-trips, politics and hassles. We should concentrate our energies on those aspects which foster the RW brotherhood. Permitting backbiting and bad vibes is like spitting in the soup we all must eat later.

Pat Works

Learning Through No-Contact Relative Work. I was flying eighth in the line-up one Sunday afternoon on another garb—excuse me, on another SCR/SCS attempt from our DZ's twin Beech. At least twenty jumps earlier I'd earned my Star Crest, and I sort of hoped for a seven star before I closed. That, of course, was too much to hope for. I closed instead on a turning, sliding 3-man. We were dive-bombed by people whose accuracy (fortunately) was worse than their relative work! My hope was rapidly turning to fear as one more 40-jump Star Crest recipient arrived nicely at wrists only to "spaz-out" while fumbling for grips and solidly take out the star. I tracked out of the funnel only to find more traffic below; the dive-bombers who went low were unloading more surprises in our faces. Canopies blossomed. I looked for a hole, brushed a cheapo, and saddled out at 1800 feet! Safe, at last!

I've spent the past fifteen months alternately participating in and (mostly) avoiding jump adventures like the one described above. I have, at least, been on both sides of the tracks.

I believe I share a desire with many to bridge the gap between the learners and the most-learned, and to reverse the trend toward greater segregation. Thus far, however, no one has suggested a way which does not impinge on the experienced jumpers by either jeopardizing their performance, or asking for too much of their available time and /or limited funds. Harness holds, organized SCR (free beer) jumps, RW seminars, magazine articles, even SCR Scrambles are not up to the task. What we need is a simple method for critiquing the learners *from the ground* on a regular, every jump basis.

I suggest formations that combine contact and "no-contact" relative work, which would make it possible to learn quickly and safely from our mistakes.

How can you expect inexperienced people to fly in a weird formation and without contact if they can't even get into stars? It should be obvious that if inexperienced RWers can't arrive and hold a position near a stable two-man base, they will undoubtedly fly poorly in any star they do break into. It is *this* poor flying that makes it difficult for learners to build stars in the first place (trying to catch a sliding, roller-coaster star).

Learning to pick out a specific position will seem strange to everyone at first. However, once accepted, it becomes quite natural. With ordered slots we increase awareness, and most importantly, reduce the likelihood of collision.

Some of the *most* fun skydives I've ever made were no-contacts. It is a great way to learn to fly, and a good way to sharpen up anybody's flying. Like anything else, you'll have to try it to know if you like it.

As soon as all participants are satisfied with their consistent performance in no-contact, and just as airplanes fly formations first at 100 feet and then 50 feet apart, we should be tightening up our formations until we "may as well" hookup. There is no reason to abandon the initial no-contact, however. By preserving it, we retain the emphasis on clean flying.

Dave Bellak, Spotter, July–August 1975.

Teaching Relative Work. We relative workers are a unique breed. We usually spend far more time promoting ourselves onto a load or in non-constructive politicking than promoting our sport. RW is an exhilarating experience which we should help others to learn . . . and to enjoy.

As editors of *RWunderground* we get a lot of mail from RW'ers all over the world. They pose questions "How to . . . ?", suggestions "What if...?", ideas, and some mighty fine thoughts about relative work and our growing world-wide fraternity of people who do it.

There has been more interest in the techniques of teaching relative work to novices than ever before. This is a good thing, a constructive step in the growth of the sport. A lot of attention has been focused on the safety factors of doing relative work. Obviously a well-trained student of *any* discipline is more likely to be a safer student.

It took those of us who've been into relative work for a while a long time to learn it because there was no one to teach us. Because it was difficult for us to master, we sometimes forget that we now have the skills to teach relative work to novices.

RW novices today will learn much faster than we did, and they won't make our mistakes. One of the quickest ways to build bigger formations is to have more qualified jumpers to build them. And one of the best ways to ensure safe relative work is to have plenty of qualified relative workers to choose from.

All we have to do is have every accomplished relative worker work with a novice, or two or three of them. The aim is to impart not only the mechanical skills required to fly the body, but also the mental attitude that releases the ecstasy of RW.

We'd like to share some of the suggestions sent us by relative workers:

The first are from Lt. Bob Iverson, SCS-456, who has some things to say to RW novices:

"Perhaps you find yourself in this situation. You've got a few relative work jumps and want more... big stars! But there aren't really any other good RW people around or maybe you're just not quite good enough to get in on the big ones. Or maybe you finally got on some big loads and bombed it...or nobody even saw ya...despair not!

"Big stars do not *necessarily* indicate that people in the star are good relative workers. The really good flyers know who's doing it and who's just hanging on...

"It's been my observation that many people asking to get on ten-man loads aren't capable of making consistent two-mans! Two-man stars can be where relative work is at. I'm talking of a two-man proficiency that's beyond the old "C" license qualification of chasing safely a flat and stable base and hooking up.

"Grab another would-be Boogie Freak and practice. Sub-terminal practice is a really good polisher if ya plan on basing biggies...it even puts finesse into those late flyers.

"Neither jumper should lose visual contact with the other. Always be aware of where the other man is. Both people are moving, *working together,* constantly adjusting for each other's idiosyncracies. Together!! Smile!

"Now...Are you good? Did you get it at sub-terminal...six seconds out? Did you bang into each other? Could you fly next to each other, not touching? Were you stable, no turns? You know the right answers—what they should be if you're going to be a good relative worker.

"If you've got two-mans licked, or think you do, try switching the exit order. Get the two-man. Backloop. Do it again. All before reaching terminal!! Send the "base" out. Give him a three to five-second headstart. Go! SWOOOOP! Can you still get him in about twenty seconds??

"Now you're talking RW—big stars and formations—16-mans and bigger! By doing two-man stars, funky ol' hookups, you know your capabilities. You know when you ask to be on the next big load whether you're good or not.

"Smooth, confident, aggressive, safe...and all those other things which go into making a good flyer. Get yourself together. Chase grapefruits if no one else is around. Really!"

Ken Coleman and Sam Brown, of Michigan, put down on paper for us the procedures they've devised to teach relative work to novices:

Altitude

5,500 ft.   Give the student a friendly, brief introduction to the art of freefall relative work. Anyone past their first 20-second delay is a good candidate. Emphasize the beauty and the things *you* like about RW. Tell him of the brotherhood he's about to join.

7,500 ft.   PHASE I. Prerequisites: enthusiasm for RW, ability to perform basic freefall maneuvers:
1. turns
2. track
3. clear (waveoff) to pull
4. ability to make unpoised, bomb-out-the-door exits.
5. ability to exit the aircraft from the reverse "pin"

	position (facing the tail, his back to the strut of a Cessna-182)
7,500 ft.	FIRST RW JUMP. The student's assignment is to concentrate on making a stable exit. He picks a heading and holds it. He thinks about relaxing; his seeing or not seeing the pin man (you) isn't as important as his relaxing and enjoying the jump. In fact, seeing the instructor should key and reinforce the student's will to relax his mind and body in order to fully enjoy his first closing, docking and entry. The instructor concentrates on doing perfectly controlled, clean airwork. Do not pin the student until after terminal is reached. Make a nice slow, clean entry if your novice is relaxed enough to allow it.
7,500 ft.	On the second jump, the student's preliminary assignment is the same as above. After this hookup, the instructor tucks up and allows the student to level the two-man out. Time permitting, the instructor next spreads out and again allows the student to level it out. The purpose of this jump is to get the novice RW'er accustomed to the idea amd mechanics of flying in contact with others. Smile.
7,500 ft.	Third jump starts just as do the first two. After the hookup the instructor raises one leg, turning the star. The student's assignment is to stop the turn and then reverse its direction.
7,500 ft.	Step four. Again, hookup after terminal velocity has been reached. After the initial hookup, the instructor backs off ten feet and lets the student try to close for a possible second two-man. Discuss floating, vertical rate of descent, reverse arch, and the necessity to pull before impact.
7,500 ft.	Graduation from student to novice! Student exits second from the pin slot. The student does as much of the relative work as possible. If successful, repeat step four, above.

* * *

Relative work is "new" — we've hardly just begun. If we start today to plant the seed for a growing tradition of friendship we'll be able to reap the many pleasures of relating to others in aerial ecstasy for a long time. Work with novices to promote your sport.

Pat & Jan Works, Parachutist, 1974

"How I yearn to throw myself into
Endless space and float above the awful abyss."
GOETHE

Behind The Viewfinder. I can remember when the only people you saw with cameras were friends of first jumpers or whuffos. I jump on several DZ's and it seems that more and more people are getting into 35mm single lens reflexes. I also can remember when rolls of film came back black. Here are a few things Inve picked up since then.

The name on the viewfinder has little influence on the quality in the final print. The most important point to make in getting a good picture is to KNOW YOUR CAMERA!

Many a great photo has been lost because the neophyte photographer had to concentrate more on his camera (focusing, film advancement, etc.) than on his subject. Practice with the camera controls until it is an overlearned experience, like eating with a fork. You don't think about it, you just do it.

The next major point is understanding light. Your light meter "lies" to you all the time and you have to know how to expose accordingly. Memorize the exposure guide that comes with the film. Daylight filming on the DZ concerns the photographer with only one real problem. This is the difference in exposure between sun and shade. Partly cloudy days are a real headache as you constantly have to adjust the exposure. Subjects in the shade are only receiving diffused reflected light from objects around them. Exposure should be increased 1, usually 2, and sometimes 3 f-stops to correct. This also holds true if you are shooting into the sun. You will be filming the shade side of your subject. Correct exposure for the shade side will wash out the background.

If the desired effect is a silhouette, take a light reading of the sky, omitting the sun in your reading. For a shot with the sun included in your viewfinder, expose by taking a light reading away from the sun using a small aperture. F-11 works best. Open up 1 f-stop and shoot another frame.

Once you become familiar with your film you can depend less on the light meter and more on your experience. The best daylight color film is Kodachrome 25. It is very slow and difficult to learn on (you'll have many out of focus and blurred shots.) Kodachrome 64 is an excellent compromise and recommended for the less experienced. High Speed

Ektachrome is also good for lower light levels or when maximum depth of field and high shutter speed is needed. Don't use color negative film unless you are doing weddings.

Black and White film is scaled like this:

Ilford Pad F, ultimate

Kodak Plus X, ok

Kodak Tri X, use only when necessary

Use a shutter speed of 1/250th for canopy shots or slow action (walking, etc.) Anything slower and you'll sacrifice to camera shake or unsharp subject. Always have your camera cocked, pre-focused with the lens cover off and set for the light you're in. Just *being ready* is vital in sports photography.

DZ photographers are dealing mainly with human interest. I see too many shutters tripped from "discreet distances". To get a good shot, walk in close, say Hi, and *Fill the Frame,* then shoot. It'll be the difference between a dramatic shot with visual impact and just another snapshot.

Carl Nelson, Freak Brothers Flyer No. 6

Your progress... "All of a sudden the progress will stop one day, and you will find yourself, as it were, stranded. Persevere. All progress proceeds by such rise and fall."

Vivekananda

"What can't be said can't be said, and it can't be whistled either."

Ram Tirtha

Boogie Mechanics. The Dirt Dive Lurk.

To learn my legs I close my fingers

To learn back-ins I do back-in Diamonds

To learn expanding-contracting attention, The Hobbit Dive

To learn altitude, The Oreo Cookie

To learn that which I thought I already knew

The Dirt Dive Lurk, which goes like this:

I get my load all dirt dived up

Then sign us up and lurk for five

Are students doing sensible things

Or should they grow more certain wings

That's all. No more. Just eavesdrop.

A very light touch indeed.

Practicing this state of Lurkfulness
Can't hope to catch them all
But it will make me more receptive
Next time someone's about to fall
And if there's something I can say
To help them out or shorten the way
To make their jump less scary
Or maybe more
That's far out too.
Lurkfulness can resonate.

Right now is time to do each our own thing
So far we've used 19/100's of our dives
And some time again when the feeling is there
We'll chip off another five or ten in the air
And start something new
There's no hurry as long as we remember
Up high is time to fly
Down low is time to go.
Sport Death is still around.
Skratch Garrison

Greg's Song
(to the tune of "Let it Snow")

Oh, the DC-3 is really climbin'...
Ready to build a 16-man diamond,
Twelve-five and we're ready to go...
Don't go low, don't go low, don't go low!

Love to jump an' there'll be no stoppin'...
And I don't mean any hop 'n poppin',
Ready-ready, three-two-one-go...
Don't go low, don't go low, don't go low!

Interlude:

F   C   G7   C
Clear the door, what a rush, exit's hot,
C   G7   C
Feels so good that it must be a sin.
C
In your dive, point your toes, there's my slot...
D7   G7   C-C7
Flare out, slow down an' you're in...

F
Well, the formation is really building'...
                        C7
Better be in—there'll be no snivelin'
          Gm
'Cause there's a camera on the load,
  C7
Don't go low, don't go low, don't go low!

Interlude:
  C   G7   C
The diamond is hot...it's beautiful...
  C   G7   C
It's on film and nobody was a geek.
C
Three-five, track away, clear and pull,
D7   G7   C-C7
Is that that my pilot chute on my feet?!

             F
You're workin' hard, yes- your mind's a-humpin'...
                    C7
The adrenalin is really pumpin'
           Gm
Then it clears, you put on quite a show...
  C7
Don't go low, don't go low, don't go low!

         F
The high speeder was so damn frightful,
                      C7
Now your canopy looks sooooo delightful!
           Gm
Imagine ME! stopped at five — "oh" — "oh"
  C7
Don't go low, don't go low, don't go low!

Greg Burrows, 1976

Thoughts on Teaching Relative Work. Everybody oughta train a few first jump students. It really makes you aware of just what you are doing up there. But, it is a lot of work to do it right, and Freefall students are a lot more fun.

I figure they are ripe when they can go do a 30 all by themselves with reasonable understanding, and they have that kind of excited, turned-on aura...slavvering at the mouth for a hookup or something. You can always tell a real freefall junkie by the way they keep coming back, and then it is easy.

Then there is another set of people who have the potential...but they are a little unsure...and jumping is putting them through a lot of changes.

For the real addicts, the best thing you can do is tell them all you know as quick as you can and get them into the mainstream of jumping while they are full of enthusiasm and their viewpoint is still fresh. For the others, you have to rap to them in the parking lot and while they are packing and just generally enthuse on them.

Jumping seems to affect people in a lot of different ways, but one of the good ones is the self-worth, confidence trip. Sounds like a karate instructor, but I think that is true of lots of these activities like rock climbing and hang gliding...where people get out and do something significant. Where...as Matt put it...you are making decisions that count.

The best kind of jumps we have found to make with these people are ones that involve the most flying. At first it has to be just you and the student, so he can concentrate on his own flying, not on what someone else might do. Then more jumps, more people, more complicated...then you have to watch over them while they go through that stage where they can do lots of things but don't yet have that overall parachuting experience to know when to have fun and when to SAVE YOURSELF!!

I have only been able to jump with a few people all the way through. But the cumulative effect of every experienced jumper making a couple jumps with this one, and maybe 5 or 10 with that one, just a couple jumps a weekend...has got to make a difference. It only takes a few jumps and pretty soon they are all afire to organize loads of their own and you can just kick back and let 'er rip. Students are a good investment...that's how you get people to jump with.

I don't have any set procedures, just try to design a jump that fits their level. In the earliest stages I have them do all the work, spotting, etc., and have them go first. It saves time, teaching them the close-in stuff first, and diving down or floating up are easier to learn if they already know what to do when they get there.

Have them go first, then dive down and set up in front of them and a little low, and let them start working. With a stable reference to work on, most people pick up the basics pretty quick...mostly consciousness-raising about being in freefall...pointing to the ground once in awhile to get them in the habit of looking...effective breakup-track-look-pull-save your ass—canopy avoidance and hazard hopping. Then some good 3-5 man jumps.

One nice thing about the sequential upsurge is the de-emphasis on size. I think all this is going to result in some pretty noticeable changes in a couple years. Those students take all this stuff they see in the movies for granted...like, well, that is what people do up there. And it is not that hard to learn if you are doing it with people who already know a little bit.

No contact flying works about as good as anything. Add some good four-man sequences, flying stairsteps and so on. Really enjoy those jumps...relaxing, sometimes try out a few things myself...

Skratch Garrison, excerpted from a letter to BT, 1975

Night SCR

"Think of the night
As the plane lifts off
With her engines singing high.
Just you, your friends, and small dim lights
In a great dark empty sky.

You hear the plane
You feel the Wind
You see the lights below
As you step into a wonderous world
That few will ever know."

Pat Works

Pre-Stars. After coming from the Gulch with nine consecutive pre-stars and six after-stars, I'm deciding pre-stars are safe and make you a better skydiver. It gives you one extra approach each jump for your money. It makes you super-aware 'cause you got to hustle. When at the end of a load, plan a pre-star; the bigger the load, the bigger the pre-star.

Some people don't approve of pre-stars, but if you're quick and know how to track, you should get there just in time to watch the man you dock on dock. There's a lot to pre-stars besides 2 to 4-man stars. You could make lines, caterpillars, and even wedges, and slide or track together in formation to the next target.

It's all a matter of awareness and not all jumpers got it. Just don't knock it till you tried it. I haven't found anyone who hasn't dug it.
R. Nelson, *Freak Brothers Flyer No. 4*

Pre-Stars? "Hey Man, You're Late..."

Well, I finally ran into another *Roger* Freak Brother named Roger Clark. He was employed by a good friend and master rigger, Bill Buchman.

I had been experimenting with pre-stars at the Gulch last winter, seeing how much time would be lost or how late I would arrive. Teaming up with Steve Gras, Mike Snoid, Clarice Garrison and Jeff Taylor, we found no loss in time, an extra rush, and one extra maneuver per jump.

As the Gulch died for the winter, I migrated back home to jump with my old friends. Here, I met Roger Clark. He was of similar height and weight and to say the least, quite an excellent skydiver. We made some swoops and, as usual, I watched his approach on entry. I found him to be "easy" for any kind of crazy ideas, so I boggled his brain by asking his participation in a pre-star. This quickly addicted Roger and soon we found ourselves in the back close enough to make some kind of hook-up. We've made lines, caterpillars, and stars with as many as five people and never arrived late. We got so into pre-stars we no longer planned them, all we had to do was look at each others position in the line up and our smiling faces would quickly snicker.

Soon it became a habit to go for each other. We could have a pre-star as quick as most people went from prop blast into their dive. The secret was the exit. The trick was to go out together, having the rear man flare out in the prop blast and blow even or over the top of the first man *or* the man who turned around. The base had to dive and clear the prop blast before he turned around so the following people knew right where he'd be. If he turned too soon, the prop blast would alter his position differently every jump, catching him in his turn. In such a case, he would get more horizontal than vertical separation making a longer time gap for the initial hook-up.

We continued this throughout the summer making the best of a skydive. When people would come down from a jump all bummed out that the jump wasn't completed or bombed, Roger and I would be happy talking about our pre-star, not caring about the blown jump.

Many fear pre-stars by themselves and others only because they have never experienced the sensation and excitement of the pre-star. I say it's only an expansion of the sport and I don't want anyone to limit this sport of ours so: "KEEP THE PRE-STARS CRANKING!"

Roger Nelson, Freak Brothers Flyer No. 5

6

Tradition...Looking Back

Relative workers are important
in that they are all
bound together in a
universal relatedness
which transcends their own
Personal experience.

B.J. Worth, RWu, March 1973

Statement of Purpose

Freefall Relative Work. We are a band of brothers, native to the air where we are united in freefall relative work.

Our goal is to promote parachuting in general and relative work in particular. RW is a beautiful, exhilarating experience which we like to share with others.

In order to do RW, you must relate to others in the air. This relatedness has created a brotherhood of freefall. As brothers we can and should help each other. Because it's *our* sport, we must try to avoid ego-trips, unhealthy politics and hassles. We must promote those aspects of our sport which foster the brotherhood for all.

Good RW promotes itself. RW is where it is today, now. It was non-created. RW just happened and grew. Being non-created, RW is transcendent over acceptance or rejection. Unfettered, it does not ossify into ritual mechanistics and so continues to grow.

If directed by a brotherhood of freefallers, this growth can strengthen us through unity in numbers. Look how many of us there are today. We are all just beginning.

Let's begin together.

Do lots of RW.   *RWu, June 1974*

In Quest of Perfection... The Traditions of Freefall Relative Work.

1. Our common welfare should come first. Personal satisfaction depends on RW unity; a Brotherhood of freefall.

2. There is no central RW authority. Our leaders are trusted servants of the sport; they do not govern.

3. Freefall relative work is democratic and unbiased. The only qualification for membership in the Brotherhood of Freefall is a desire to fly for the joy of flying.

4. Each group of RWers has but one primary purpose — to carry the ecstasy and excitement of doing freefall relative work to all parachutists who have enthusiasm for flying.

5. Each RW team or drop zone should be autonomous, except in matters affecting relative work or parachuting as a whole.

6. The Brotherhood of Freefall is designed to place principles above personalities and the perfection of flight above all else.

7. The merit badges of the Brotherhood are the SCR/SCS awards. The NSCR, 16-man and XX are higher awards.

8. Our relationships with all other parachutists who have yet to join the Brotherhood are based on attraction rather than promotion. The positive results of RW enjoyment, warmth and fellowship emit good vibes which speak louder than any promotion we could possibly do.

RWu, June, 1974

"Six rings for the star-kings under the sky,
One ring to rule them all, one ring to find them"

> *The Fellowship of the Ring*
> *J. R. TOLKIEN*

A Brief History of Ten-Man Star Competition

How It Started. 10-man Star Competition started the very same way as many famous and infamous deeds throughout history: a drunken, boastful argument between two Gentlemen.

I can remember that argument vividly. (Hell, I started it).

It was on a Wednesday evening in 1967 at the Rumbleseat Tavern. Every Relative Work jumper in Los Angeles was there to view movies of the recently made 10-man stars.

Two different teams, the "Arvin Good Guys" and "The Group" from Elsinore shared the world's 10-man star record at that time.

Bob Allen, Arvin's photographer, and myself, a member of "The

Group" were discussing the two teams' ability to make the 10-man again. Bob said "The Group's" 10-man star was luck, but Arvin could do it again anytime.

I just couldn't let a statement like that go unchallenged. The discussion turned into a lengthy argument, which ended with a $5.00 wager between Bob and me.

It was decided that the two teams would jump, attempting a 10-man star to settle the bet.

The next day I commenced drafting the first set of rules for the jump. This original draft was modified extensively by a rules committee consisting of Skratch Garrison, Carl Boenish and Jerry Bird.

In the meantime the "Old River Rats" decided they could also make 10-man stars and joined in the competition. This grudge match now started to look like an actual meet, hence a trophy was needed. I only had to make one stop to find a sponsor for this trophy—*The Rumbleseat Tavern* in Hermosa Beach. Frank Carpenter's Para-Scuba Club donated a 24-inch Perpetual Trophy to be awarded to the winning team each year. The first 10-Man Star Meet was held in November 1967 at Taft, California. Three teams entered, each making two jumps.

Arvin made the only 10-man of the meet—two perfect back-to-back 10-man stars. The rest of this story is recorded in the pages of *Skydiver* Magazine and USPA *Parachutist* Magazine.

Yes, I lost the $5.00, but I have seen a new dimension in parachuting gain International acceptance.

Garth Taggart

History of The Star Crest. An organization that has contributed a great deal to the growth of relative work around the world is the Bob Buquor Memorial Star Crest which awards for freefall relative work accomplishments.

Bill Newell founded the Star Crest in 1967. The purpose was to award everybody who had been in an 8-man at that time (about 20 people), and from then on out, some kind of recognition for it. He named the Star Crest after Bob Buquor, a freefall photographer and one of the first promoters of star-making.

Bob had been filming 3 and 4-mans at Arvin as far back as 1964. His photos helped to spark interest in building bigger stars. The first 8-man was built at Arvin on October 17, 1965 from a Howard and a

Cessna 195. Unfortunately, Bob didn't live to see the first 10-man built in 1967. He drowned in 1966 while filming freefall footage for a Hollywood movie.

That first 8-man in 1965 was quite an accomplishment. It had taken about 13 months to go from a 6-man to an 8-man. And it took another two years to build the 10-man. When that happened, two groups, Elsinore and Taft, did it within a month of each other.

The organization has grown into the many thousands, and USPA has since recognized the SCR and SCS awards as marks of achievement in relative work and a principal reason for its growth.

Certificate of Merit to Jonathan Livingston Seagull

Along with the RW Council's awards to individuals who have contributed to the growth of RW, a special Certificate of Merit was presented to Jonathan Livingston Seagull... "for outstanding service to relative work." A few weeks later brought a note from author Richard Bach: "Many thanks... on behalf of Jonathan Seagull... you know him well."

RWu, January, 1973

Recollections of Summer of '70... Southern California-style

Relative work and life in Southern California — the summer of Ted Webster's 10-man Sweepstakes Meet — some things are different, some things remain the same.

Gear was heavy. The standard relative work rig was a Para-Commander in a Pioneer 3-pin with a 26' Navy or Security conical (the only sport reserve available). We had three hogbacks on our team. It was generally felt at the time they were okay for big guys, but conventional was better for most people. I had the lightest rig on the DZ, a step-in with rocket jet fittings instead of capewells, 26' Navy, Pioneer 28' 1.6 main. It weighed about 27 lbs.

Jumpsuits had turned the corner. Although they didn't look that different except for color, it was hard for someone with a Pioneer jumpsuit to keep up with a bunch of people in Ward-Vene suits.

We had Beeches and could put almost any number up by flying formation with the Cessna or Howards.

Relative work, of course, was not near the size it is today. Max Kelly and I had the highest SCR numbers on our team; he's 235, I'm 183. The numbers were up to about 500 or so at that time. There had only been a handful of stars eight or bigger outside California.

Ted Webster's Sweepstakes...it was the biggest RW meet ever...'course competition had only been going on since 1967. Initially, there had been no plans for a meet.

Ron Bluff, who ended up as "team leader" (a weird title for a weird job), Jerry Bird and Ted Webster (who was putting up the bucks) evolved a plan at the end of 1969 to demonstrate RW at the World Meet in Bled, Yugoslavia, the following September. A team was picked, half from Taft, half from Elsinore, as a representative group from Southern California.

However, the hideous long and agonizing howl that arose from those not lucky enough to be picked changed the best-laid plans of Bird and men. A competition was forced by the incessant demands for fair play, so instead of practicing all the things we'd daydreamt about — formations, etc. — we began practicing for 10-man speed stars. All the people who'd done the yelling were already far behind; while they scrambled teams together, we practiced.

Looking back through my logs, I find that what I remembered as a long and arduous training period was remarkably relaxed considering the stakes involved. The All-Stars only made thirty jumps in the two-and-a-half months before that 1970 meet. In contrast, "Terminal Chaos" made the same number of jumps in the two and a half *weeks* before the 1977 Nationals.

Also in looking back, I found that half the fun jumps we were making then were formations, mostly snowflakes, but we built the first Murphy — an eight-man with me in backwards — that summer, too. How did we get side-tracked to circles? The very competition we wanted did the trick, I believe.

Hal Hurley and Ron Bluff picked the Elsinore people: me, Max Kelly, Mike Milts, Ray Cottingham and Stan Troeller. Jerry Bird was Captain and he picked the Taft people: Donna Wardean, Sam Alexander, Dick Gernand, plus Bob Feuling from San Diego and Russ Benefiel from Elsinore. It was a compatible group; we meshed at once into a team.

Personally, it was a weird situation. Our main competition was the Arvin Good Guys, and I lived at the beach in Malibu with two of them. The only other team with a chance was Dirty Ed's, and I was going with his ex-wife, a situation he considered intolerable. I had no trouble getting up for the meet.

It was pretty funny at the beach. We were practicing at Elsinore, and the Arvin team at Taft. I'd usually get home first. I'd be slumped in the living room relaxing from the weekend when they'd come in. Ron Richards, the Arvin team captain, would be the first in the house—

"How'd you guys do?" I'd ask.

"Great! great—how 'bout you guys?"

"Oh, OK. Tens in the thirties..."

"Well, shit! We're doin' *that* good!" He'd smirk and go off to his room.

Then Terry would come in, and I'd ask him.

"We're doing fine," he'd say. "We're working on some stuff, but it's looking good."

Then Debby, Terry's lady friend, would come in. While Terry fiddled around the kitchen opening wine, I'd ease up to Debby and quietly ask how they did.

"Terrible!" she'd say. "They funnelled two, and had someone low on one jump!"

It was all I could do to keep from cracking up.

We were confident—so much so that with the meet set for the 18th of July, Jerry gave us the 4th of July weekend off! (Can you imagine that happening today?)

While we were gone the psychological warfare escalated. Webster put out word that wives would also be allowed to go. A couple of the Arvin guys got married. None of *us* went that far, rightly figuring that Ted would let us take our old ladies.

Then Jerry Bird started the rumor that we had already gone down and gotten our passports. When Terry and Ron confronted me about that, I just smiled my best Sphinx grin and said nothing. Richards almost went into shock.

The morning of the meet JB handed out little orange buttons that said "Better 'cause we want to be." He'd picked them up from Hertz or Avis or somebody, and we all wore them, ladies' auxiliary included, so they were everywhere. It was the kind of thing that made Ron Richards physically ill, which was exactly what Jerry wanted.

Ron did have something up his sleeve, however. There had been whispers and stuff about some Arvin secret weapon, and to Ron Richards goes the credit for changing the first part of RW forever. He had invented the floater.

Brian Williams in 1970—a little bitty, good-looking dude, SCR number eight. (If you had totalled the SCR numbers of the Arvin team, it would have been under a hundred!) Brian had a big foam-filled jumpsuit and launched *in front* of the base/pin. He came in about eighth, if I remember right. It was startling to us, but not really scary as we got to watch them Friday. Their time was not as good as ours. (It did take a couple of years to work the kinks out of the idea.)

Our Friday practice jump was a low-30's eleven-man, a by now almost automatic performance, and we dispersed to get ready for the next morning. We were staying at a place up in the Sedcos that was secluded, had a pool and a fine view of Elsinore's DZ.

The morning of the meet—the floater tactic and Dirty Ed's team's week of practice made Hurley nervous, but he's the only one I recall feeling that way. The rest of us were cocky.

We were the first to jump, and had a 32. Bird said to turn it up a bit.

Dirty Ed's team overamped and took themselves out. On the way to a sub-30 they broke into a line and took about 45 seconds to close it. They had no chance after that, and bit themselves to death like sharks in a feeding frenzy fixing the blame (the second most important part of relative work).

Arvin had about a 37 or so, if I recall right. Still a chance, theoretically, but we got faster (averaging about 30 seconds) and they dropped eight to ten seconds a dive on us, so the meet was never in doubt. We just cruised along doing our thing and let the other guys break up chasing us. It's JB's favorite tactic and it has served him remarkably well over the years.

We got a blue ribbon—and jumpsuits, helmets, 20 practice jumps, kitbags, boots, jackets, patches, and a free trip, expenses paid, to Yugoslavia (with our girl friends).

The next jump we made after the meet was a team photo twelve snowflake, the second twelve-formation made (the first was also a snowflake—August 3, 1969!)

The weekend after that we jumped into team training for the style and accuracy people being held that year at Marana, Arizona, site of the '68 and '69 Nationals. We made a 10-man with smoke from fifteen-grand. I remember we were *extremely* dingy from hypoxia—Sam Alexander went base and it took us 15 seconds to get him to go. I rolled lazily through the prop blast jerking on my smoke lanyard—everyone was kind of drifting for the first 15 seconds or so. We thought it was sloppy but it was the first star most people on the ground had seen, so demo-wise the jump was a success.

We also took a load up in one of the Cessna 207's they were using for training and made a nice six of six. Mike Schultz was on the load, along with Clayton Schoepple (overall champ that year) and Gloria Porter (women's accuracy champ and a real fox). It was Gloria's first star bigger than a two-man, and she had almost a thousand jumps. That would be hard to imagine today.

The next weekend we broke the 20-man barrier. It *was* a barrier — we'd been working on it for six months. The first one was clean and smooth, breaking for altitude. We backed it up with a 21. In the pictures, half the jumpsuits are team red-white-blues.

A few more practice jumps and we departed for Europe as the first United States Freefall Exhibition Team.

Yugoslavia in September has weather rather resembling the Midwest — clear in the morning, clouds forming in the afternoon. Consequently we had constant cloud problems and made many low altitude (4000 ft.) four and six-man dives. The altitude meant that we just had to take it off the bottom, so me and Stan and Max took it to the streets. The people running the meet didn't hassle us, figuring we were professionals and did this for a living.

The best one was when the organizers approached JB and asked us to demonstrate the four-man-backloop formation then being proposed for RW competition. Jerry looked up at the clouds and picked me, Max, Stan and Dick Gernand. Dick's only problem was that he was jumping an old Irwin Deatha-Two-Paranoid, the forerunner of the Paradactyl. It was not the ideal low pull rig.

We got about six-grand, built the four-man quickly, then made a discovery that has haunted sequential since — namely, caterpillars are *hard* to build. We got it about 1500 ft. and Dick's eyes were bugged out six inches as he let his OSI'ed wing out about 1200. I was open about half that.

At the closing ceremonies we could only get eight-five. The clouds were broken, spotting would have been a snap, but the Russian pilots would not go above the deck (as a matter of fact, they did go above it but came down!) which really infuriated us. Stanley dumped his smoke in the door, then Mike and I, then Ron, and Donna, standing up right next to the pilots, popped hers, too. The airplane was emanating a solid red cloud of smoke and Russian expletives as we exited. We landed, got on the bus, and hauled ass.

It's funny looking back now—if you'd asked those people on that bus if they'd do it again, they'd have reassured you they were going to keep jumping. Five years later when the next USFET was formed, only me, Max and Ray were left from the original, and only five of the twelve were still jumping. At least, they're all still alive.

Joe Morgan

"Most men are content to stay at home
With their loved ones by their side,
And there was a time when I could sit
On the beach and watch the tide.

But I glimpsed the Gates of Heaven
One morning high in the sky,
And since that day happiness is—
To strap on a chute and fly.

...Tell me how in the name of God
I could ever stay earth bound,
Turning my back on the peace of mind
And happiness I've found?

So if it seems I have no thoughts
For my family or my friends,
Just keep in mind I've found my star
And I'll chase it till the end."

from Charlie Straightarrow

The History of Relative Work. The first parachute jump in history was on October 22, 1797 in Paris; the first freefall jump on April 28, 1919 at McCook Field, Ohio; the first world championships in August, 1951 in Bled; the first style program on a World Parachute Cup meet in August, 1958 in Bratislava, Czechoslovakia.

The first relative jump in history happened when...? I don't know exactly. It is sure that on July 16, 1958, RW—in the form of a baton pass—made its U.S. debut, when Charlie Hilliard and Steve Snyder accomplished the feat over Fort Bragg, North Carolina.

I can't say if there wasn't a previous hook-up or a baton pass in another country, especially an eastern one. It is certain that stars began in the early sixties, most of the RW pioneers jumping at the

197

Arvin DZ at that time. Pretty soon Southern California star-builders were getting it together. In the fall of 1964 the first six-man star was made, filmed by Bob Buquor. "Wild Willie" Newell (now administrator of the SCR/SCS program) was in it. The first 8-man followed in October 1965 at Taft, California. It was formed by the "Arvin Good Guys" and filmed by Buquor.

Eight Became Ten. Although star-building and the SCR program (SCR = Star Crest Recipient, created in 1967 by Bill Newell) initially focused on 8-man formations, this gradually changed to ten people as a basic unit — for the simple reason that the almost-always available Beech D-18's carried ten people legally, with one or two more often able to squeeze in.

The first 10-man formation in skydiving history was achieved July 2, 1967 at Taft, north of Los Angeles, filmed by Luis Melendez and organized by Jerry Bird. The jumpers were Gary Young, John Rinard, Clark Fischer, Jim Dann, Jerry Bird, Bill Stage, Terry Ward, Bill Newell, Brian Williams and Paul Gorman (87 jumps!). Within three weeks another group, based south of Los Angeles at Elsinore, put together a second 10-man.

November 5, 1967 marked another significant day in the history of RW. The first USPA-sanctioned RW-competition was held at Taft. Garth Taggart wrote the rules, assisted by Jerry Bird, Skratch Garrison, Bob Allen (Taft cameraman) and Carl Boenish (Elsinore cameraman). This set of rules lasted until 1971 when they were only modified and finalized by Skratch Garrison. The Taft team won the competition with two 10-man stars in 45 and 50 seconds. Elsinore bombed the 4-man base on their second jump and ended with 12 points.

Late in 1969 and early in 1970, the focus for relative workers switched to Elsinore. There were lots of people, the right aircraft — and enough of them — and they had an enormous dry lake bed to compensate for bad spots. Here's where Carl Boenish filmed the first of the great RW movies, *Sky Capers,* and later began *Masters of the Sky.*

RW on a WPC. In 1968 USPA sanctioned a 10-man team (the Arvin Good Guys) to go to the IXth World Championships in Graz, Austria, and display large-star RW to the world. Because of organizational and financial problems the team was unable to attend.

But finally at the conclusion of the Xth World Meet in Bled, the world knew what the U.S. jumpers meant when saying Relative Work. It resulted from the energies of Southern Californian Ted Webster, who hosted the first and only "Webster Sweepstakes," offering as first prize a trip to Bled. Jerry Bird and his team won the competition and put on a demonstration at the WPC that was not to be surpassed until the XIth World Parachute Championships in Tahlequah, Oklahoma. "We talked RW, showed RW movies, especially Boenish's *Masters of the Sky,* which had never been shown publicly until then," said Jerry Bird. "We did stars and snowflakes. Jumpers from all over the world saw RW done for the first time."

Some Firsts. Before that demonstration some big firsts had already been done. The first 12-man was built high over Taft by Jerry Bird's team early in 1968, the first 16-man in April 1969 and the first 18-man on December 7, 1969 by the Jerry Bird "All Stars" and the "Arvin Good Guys."

The first 8-girl star (it was exceptionally not organized by J.B.) was built at the end of July, 1969 at Elsinore. The girls taking part were: Jean Schultz (88), Laura MacKenzie (651), Ann Gardiner (440, now wife of Curt Curtis), Diane Bird (174, now Diane Kelly), Luena Garrison (279), Linda Padgett (525), Patty Croceito (395) and Sheila Scott (197, now wife of Ned Luker).

Some weeks before the WPC at Bled the "Golden Twenties" began. A 20-man star was formed over Elsinore in August, 1970, and held for seven seconds. A second jump was made with the same group and a momentary 21-man star was formed but held only 1.1 seconds.

The first 24-man was achieved in Perris Valley in January, 1972 and reproduced on many wall posters. At the end of the XIth WPC (accuracy and style) at Tahlequah, Oklahoma, in August 1972, this series was momentarily crowned by the 26-person star (25 men and one woman). Most of those big stars have been "Jerry Bird Productions."

When Jerry Bird participated in the 2nd RW-World Cup in Pretoria, South Africa, August 1974, he pushed the official FAI-record mark of a 10-man speed star from 16.7 seconds (achieved by Russian jumpers on March 15, 1974) down to a sensational 12.76 seconds. Captain Hook's Sky Pirates, the All Stars and other jumpers put together a 28-man FAI world record star in Ontario, California on August 25th. On July 14, 1975, 32 parachutists formed a star and held it longer than 5 seconds over Tahlequah, Oklahoma.

On November 30, 1974, at Casa Grande, Arizona, a 16-woman world record star was built.

The fastest 10-woman star was built in 34.2 seconds over Issaquah, Washington, on August 3, 1975.

In 1975, the largest star in Europe was achieved by 28 French jumpers at the Paris Air Show.

Competition Scene. RW as part of national championships quite naturally started in the USA. It began in 1970 with the 4-man event; the 10-man event followed in 1972. Many RW competitions have been run since then, including the world's largest parachute meet ever held at Zephyrhills, Florida. The first annual 10-man star meet at Z-Hills was an ambitious undertaking over Thanksgiving Weekend in 1969. A total of five 10-man teams showed up; in 1974, 520 jumpers had registered to compete on 52 teams.

After the big RW show by the United States Freefall Exhibition Team in Bled, the rest of the world awoke in the early seventies — though there had already been a few RW jumps done before. The Russians, for example, showed a film in Bled with some RW — a caterpillar.

In Australia and New Zealand RW started even earlier. The first international RW meet took place in January, 1972 at Masterton, New Zealand.

Seven teams from the USA, Canada, Australia and New Zealand participated. The meet was won by the "Flying Farkle Family" (USA); their average time was 26.46 seconds for five jumps; their fastest star scored 23.2 seconds.

Australia, Canada, France, Great Britain, Germany, South Africa and the USA sent teams to the first FAI-recognized World Cup in RW at Fort Bragg, North Carolina in 1973. The US teams won both events. France (2), Germany (3), Great Britain (4), Australia (5) and Canada (6) followed in the 10-man event. Germany (2), South Africa (3), France (4), Canada (5) and Australia (6) followed in the 4-man event. The average time of the 10-man winner, the "Columbine Turkey Farm" (USA), was 19.78 seconds; the fastest time was 17.3 seconds. The fastest time of the winning "Greene County" team in the 4-man event was 5.6 seconds, their average 6.33 seconds.

At Easter, 1974, the first European 10-man competition was organized through German-Austrian cooperation at Innsbruck (Austria). There were 10 teams from five countries. The "Icarius

Group" of France won the meet, "Endrust Skydivers" (GB) placed second, the Scandinavian "Viking RW Team" third, and "Walter's Vögel" (Germany) fourth. "Icarius Group" averaged 27.9 seconds in three jumps.

The 2nd RW World Cup was hosted by South Africa in 1974. The winner out of 12 participating nations was once again Jerry Bird, this time with his "Wings of Orange" in an average time of 18.77 seconds. The world record of 12.76 seconds was set up before the competition started. France placed second, Germany third.

The 4-man event was won by the "Rainbow Flyers." They totalled 42.99 seconds in six jumps which means an average of 7.17 seconds; their fastest formation was the diamond in 6.42 seconds. France and South Africa followed in places two and three.

The "Wings of Orange" won the second European 10-man competition, held at La Ferte Gaucher (France) some days after the World Cup. Five nations participated.

RW at the CIP. At the 1969 CIP meeting (International Parachuting Committee) "Proposals for new tests to be included in the programmes of future World Championships" was a point on the agenda and was discussed during the meeting. The US-delegate (Charles MacCrone) announced a new display with the method of marking. The word Relative Work was used the first time at the CIP. In 1971 the US-delegate (Norman Heaton; MacCrone was elected President in 1970) proposed to maintain in 1972 the same events as at Bled and to leave the discussion of the 1974 XIIth WPC programme for the next meeting. At the same meeting he announced a detailed proposal about a new category of (RW) records at the next meeting.

In November 1971 a CIP working group, consisting of Franz Lorber (Austria) as Chairman, Marc Schneebeli (CH), Ivan Lisov (USSR) and Uwe Beckmann (Germany) submitted a proposal for parachuting records, providing baton relay jumps and star-jumps as record categories. "We specially ask those countries which do have some experience with RW to complete the regulations concerning RW records," the group wrote in its proposal. There were no comments but at the meeting in February 1972, most of the delegates felt that the rules were incomplete. So the principle on RW records was adopted and a new working group—consisting of Eilif Ness (Norway), Rod Murphy (South Africa), Bert Wijnands (Netherlands), Norman Heaton (USA) and Gregor Ivascenko (Yugoslavia)—was charged with the task of studying the technical application of these records.

During the same meeting a proposal of the Dutch delegate Wijnands was adopted to include a RW event as a fourth event in the 1974 World Parachute Cup.

In 1973 the above-mentioned working group proposed the actually existing record rules, which were adopted. The originally adopted proposal to include a RW event as a fourth event to a "classic WPC" was modified in such a way that an extra WPC/RW consisting of two events (10-man event and 4-man event) would be organized between the "regular" WPC's. All delegates were in favor, with two abstentions—USSR and CSSR.

The rules for these events—largely based on the existing US rules—were adopted at the same meeting. At this 1973 CIP meeting, Eilif Ness (Norway) was appointed permanent president of the international RW working group of the CIP. France, the USA and Israel offered to host a first World Cup in RW the same year. France was the successful bidder but withdrew its bid in April because of internal difficulties. The First World Cup was offered to and accepted by the USA.

One year later, 1974, there was only one bid to host the 2nd World Cup. It came from South Africa. There were no objections. But there were two bids to host the 1st World Parachuting Championships/RW, one from the USA and one from the Federal Republic of Germany. Germany won it. The rules were adopted in 1975.

Uwe Beckmann, Sportspringer, 1975.

About Your SCR & SCS — A History of the Star Crest. In relative work there are three merit badges recognized around the globe as proof of relative work proficiency. These are the Bob Buquor Memorial Star Crests — SCR, SCS and NSCR. They are awards of skill and merit, recognizing a parachutist as an accomplished relative worker, combining reliability, enthusiasm, skill and teamwork. According to a recent jumper survey, more skydivers have SCR's and SCS's than any other parachuting merit award.

Bill Newell initiated the BBMSC in 1967 as a memorial to the late Robert H. Buquor who played a major role in the origin of star formation RW. As Bill describes the goals of the BBMSC: "We are striving to keep the original ideals upon which we were founded alive for today's skydivers as well as for the pioneers of yesterday. That basically boils down to making lots of far-out skydives with dynamite people and having a groovy time... It is to Bob's driving enthusiasm for relative work that the SCR membership is dedicated. We hope you will carry on his love and dedication to the art of flying by trying to help others enjoy the sport as much as you do."

The following is a condensation of a 1973 interview in which Bill describes the Star Crest's history and organization:

Q: What prompted the founding of the Star Crest?

Newell: Well, there were about 20 people at that time, before 1967, who had been in 8-mans, and that was all. It was a pretty difficult thing to do, so I figured that I'd like to have everybody who was in an 8-man at that time, and from then on out, receive some kind of award for it — some kind of recognition.

Q: And it began with the 8-man star built by the Arvin Good Guys?

Newell: Right, with the Arvin Good Guys. The very first 8-man was made on October 17th, 1965 in Arvin, California at about 3:00 in the afternoon. We used Walt Mercer's Howard and a Cessna 195 flown by Dave Keaggy. The entrance order in the star was the same as the exit order. Gary Young was base and Al Paradouski was pin. I came in third and Mitch Poteet was fourth; Bill Stage, fifth; Jim Dann, sixth; Don Henderson, seventh and Brian Williams was the eighth one in. We had it at about 5500 feet after exiting at 12,500.

Q: Did you guys think about making a larger star at that time?

Newell: As soon as we hit the ground we were hollering for a 10-man.

Q: Did you go for a 10-man?

Newell: Yeah — we tried. The closest we ever got was a 10-man for about 2 seconds. Bob Buquor came in last and it crumbled.

Q: It occurs to some that since most of the competition is done by 10-man star teams, you would base the Star Crest program on 10-mans rather than 8-mans.

Newell: I began the Star Crest before that kind of competition got started. Actually, the one thing that prompted 10-man star competition more than anything was the closeness in the making of the first two 10-mans between the Arvin Good Guys and the Elsinore group. We (the Arvin Good Guys) got our first 10-man July 2, 1967 and Elsinore got their first one on August 5th. So then it was like, "Well, who's the best?" In November that same year we had our first meet to see who could swing the most 10-mans. Time wasn't a big factor then; it was just getting 10-mans.

Q: Let's talk about Bob Buquor a little bit. What kind of a guy was he and what do you remember best about him?

Newell: Bob Buquor was filming 3 and 4-man stars in Arvin as far back as 1964. I met him in March of that year just after they'd gotten their first 4-man star. I forgot just who was on it; I'm pretty sure Mitch Poteet and Don Henderson were in on it. The best thing I remember about Bob was that he was one of the first guys at the drop zone to treat me nice. He'd go out of his way to come up to me and say, "Hi, how're you doing? How's the jumping going?" I had only about 50 jumps; it was still a bit hairy. I was at a strange drop zone and he was one of the first ones to make me feel at home. He had a zany, outgoing personality.

Q: Wasn't he one of the first paraphotographers in the sport?

Newell: One of the first three or four. I always considered Bob one of the best photographers, even when he wasn't filming stars. He was definitely a damn-good relative worker.

Q: What became of Buquor?

Newell: Bob Buquor filmed around Arvin most of the time. He was in on the Rod Pack jump, when Pack jumped without a parachute. Doyle Fields did the movies on that and Bob shot the stills for *Life Magazine.* He filmed a lot of movies and also was sent to Germany in 1964 by ABC to film the World Meet. He was about the best around at that time, I thought, especially for stills. Stills were his specialty.

He lived in Pacoima in a trailer house. I understand he came from Texas and that he was raised in California. He made his first jump in Elsinore in '58. Tony Lemus got him interested in it. Bob died in July 1966 off Malibu Beach. He had over 990 jumps. He drowned while filming for a movie called "Don't Make Waves" starring Tony Curtis, Claudette Cardinale, and Sharon Tate. I was working with him at the time, packing parachutes under Gary Mills. Jim Dann was the stunt man and we were all working for Leigh Hunt. Actually, he wasn't supposed to hit the water. He was supposed to hit the beach, but the spot was off. He went down with about 40 pounds of batteries and camera gear. He hit the water and went straight to the bottom, in 30 feet of water. He had his helmet in his hands.

Bob was a good cameraman but he had a hard time getting some of his pictures published in the parachuting magazines. He tried to get them to print our names and do a little spiel on what we were doing, but most of the time the subtitles would read, "A Star Over Arvin" by Bob Buquor, and things of that nature. So when he got killed I didn't think he'd been properly recognized for the good work that he'd done up to that time. It seemed logical to honor him with the Star Crest.

Q: What was he filming for, his own fun or for commercial reasons?

Newell: Just more or less for unusual photography he could send to the magazines, and to see if we could get something together in the air more than just plain grab ass or zapping each other. Bob Buquor was doing so much star filming it soon became his thing, his baby. Nobody was pushing star work that much at other drop zones. So actually Bob Buquor was the one who started star work, as far as I know, and there was nobody else besides us doing it at the time.

We just started adding more guys and got bigger and better stars over a period of time. But in those days it took a long time to add another man to a star. From the first four to the first five-man it took something like six weeks. From the first five to the first six it took about two or three months. And from six to eight it took about thirteen months. From eight to ten took two years.

Q: When was the next record that beat your October 1965 8-man?

Newell: That was a 9-man with Donna Wardean as the first girl in anything over a 7-man, June 11th, 1967 at Taft.

Q: How did you get the design for the patch? Was it your own design?

Newell: Yes. I just thought it up and drew it on a piece of paper. I used a shot glass for the center target, a coffee cup for the outer perimeter and an old wooden ruler. It was crude and I had my boss straighten it out for me. He drew it to a scale of four inches. The original idea came from an inspiration of seeing the movie "Blue Max" where the top "aces" received a far-out thing for being super good. The idea of the design came easily for such a complicated-looking design. I just pictured the little smiling "minute man" they used to advertise in the 76 gas stations, stuck 8 of them holding hands in a circle with crosshairs in the center to make a distinctive-looking target.

Q: What did you do to have emblems made?

Newell: Well, first I took it to a bowling shirt outfit in Bakersfield and tried to have them do it. But it was a sewing machine job and it looked lousy. So I contacted the National Emblem Co. in Los Angeles and they told me that in order to have a patch made I'd have to put in a whole order. I couldn't have just one or two. So I had to buy an order of 80 patches even though there were only 20 people who qualified for them at the time. The thing was, I didn't have any money. So I wrote everybody a letter — all 20 of them — saying, "You're one of the first twenty persons in the world to have ever been in an 8-man star and I'm thinking about getting patches made and issuing numbers and I request that you donate $7.00 for four patches." I had to sell everybody four patches to have enough money for the order. And everybody went for it.

Q: Can you describe the awards you have in effect at this time and what one must do to obtain them?

Newell: Well, the Star Crest Recipient (SCR) was started in March 1967 for anyone hooked up in a flat, round, and stable star formation for a period of five sec., or 1000 feet. This was fine for awhile until it became apparent that jumpers were getting better and that wasn't where it was going to end. Then we started getting gripes from SCR holders who earned their Crest by doing a little more flying, that some toads with pals in the "in group" were just being thrown out and allowed to wallow on a big mattress of air while their friends came in and hooked up around them, thus GIVING them their 8-man. I didn't see it this way because it takes a certain amount of talent to wallow on a big mattress of air. And without our baseman on the first 8-man, we would have put our second man out to hook up with no one and still be grooving on 7-mans.

But I could see that the other cats had a good point, too, so to be fair to both parties I initiated the SCS Award (Star Crest Solo) to give the super flyers a chance to prove their worth over the less-talented RW type. This award was retroactive and was started the same day the SCR's reached 800, July 10, 1971. Thought we pleased everyone? Guess again. Then we received a barrage of bitches from jumpers who had met the SCS requirements (enter as 8th or later and hang on for 5 sec.) before we started the award and didn't want to re-do it for their SCS number. But on the whole it's been good for everyone and has worked out fine. It's even made lard asses lose weight and paper butts tuck up for their chunky pals. Hence, more real teamwork.

Q: And the Night Star Crest Recipient; how did that come about?

Newell: Ted Webster more or less got that going for the guys by phoning me after they made a 9-man at night at Elsinore October 2, 1971. It was the first star over a 6-man that was ever made at night and they did it at 9:00 p.m. Ted wanted to know if it was OK to get some patches made up with the Star Crest design on it for the jump. I told him that I thought it was so far out that they did it that we should just add Night Star to the existing SCR & SCS. We agreed and that's how the NSCR got started. I might add that in order to be eligible for the NSCR as we award it, the Star should be 2 hours after sunset or 2 hours before dawn.

Q: What about people from foreign countries — do they qualify the same as U.S. jumpers do?

Newell: It's the same for people all over the world. All you have to do to join the Star Crest is prove you've been in an 8-man star for 5 sec. I didn't plan it to go international. When I started getting applications from Australia, South Africa, Europe and other places, I didn't see any reason not to list them.

Q: Do you forsee a time when relative work meets will be limited to holders of SCR numbers?

Newell: I'd hate to see that because if a person doesn't want to send in for his patch he shouldn't have to. A person should do it because he *wants* to. If they say in the future that no one can jump in a meet unless he has an SCR, that's not too cool. They may request that he be SCR-qualified for safety reasons. At meets like Scrambles where it's all set up for that sort of thing, it's fine.

Q: How about the WSCR; what is your connection with this group?

Newell: No connection. I had been approached several times over the years to start a Women's SCR, but frankly I cannot see how it ties in with our format. It could even be misconstrued as discriminating against the boys. We're not concerned with what one's gender is; our rules simply state that you have to be in an 8-man or better star for 5 seconds; and just function in the air as a good flying human being.

Q: What about giving out patches for large stars. Do you have any plans to do that?

Newell: We handle patches for 16, 24 and military 10-man stars, but we don't list them or give numbers for them. Jumpers have to send in proof of these stars to purchase the emblems and we do file away the applications in case there's any question. People like patches for getting into large stars, and jumpers make their own large-star patches to whatever fits their fancy.

The Star Crest program promotes itself. I think this is the way it should be handled. If we tried to commercialize the Star Crest, I think it would kill it. Our plans are for growth. We're trying to make ourselves stronger so we can operate more efficiently. We are a non-profit organization for the advancement of relative work skydiving. We're going to try to keep on doing what we've been doing and improve with time. As jumpers require more, we'll try to keep up with their needs and demands.

Star Crest Magazine, October 1975 and January 1976

Merit Badges. The USPA licenses (A thru D) and ratings (jumpmasters, I/E, etc.) are obviously required to establish, promote and maintain a degree of safety in parachuting in general, and filling out paperwork specifically.

Of course, these licenses have nothing to do with parachuting skill (just as having a driver's license doesn't insure that you are a good driver.)

In RW there are two merit badges recognized by all participants both here and abroad as proof of RW proficiency. These are the Bob Buquor Memorial Starcrests: the SCR and SCS.

An SCR receipient has:

"Participated in a Free Fall Star Formation involving eight or more skydivers in a completed circle held together for a minimum time of 5 seconds or 1000 feet."

This one *may* have been "given" you. Even so, those who gave it had to be real RWers who wanted to relate with you. Either way, it's meaningful.

The SCS must be earned. "...By entering into this star formation as 8th or after..." The SCS proves a degree of skill at flying both early *and* late. This is important at a big star attempt, and SCR Scrambles, or when you are visiting another RW drop zone. This way, when the Starmaster or manifestor sizes up your skill by eyeball, he can temper the fact that you're 5'6", weigh 210 lbs. and are called "Bowling Ball" by your friends with the fact that you are an SCS recipient, and thus can fly.

There are currently a whole mess of offspring to the SCR: Night SCR, All-Girl SCR, Teen SCR, International SCR, All-College SCR, All-Military SCR, All-red-jumpsuit SCR, Naked SCR, Wednesday SCR, Smashed SCR, Who-Cares SCR, etc. These relate more to membership in non-RW groups (military, female, college) than to RW skill (with the exception of the Night SCR which does give you credit for conditions—dark 'n **scary.**)

SCR and SCS are international in scope. You must be SCR to enter a Scrambles meet or tell lies at a new DZ. You must also be SCR or SCS to join the RW Council since they certify that you *participate* in RW with some success.

o Having a USPA license (A, B, C, D,) shows you jump out of airplanes.

o Having an SCR shows that you are a participant in the brotherhood of RW.

o Having an SCS shows that you are a participant in the brotherhood of RW with perhaps a degree of skill (or luck).

o Having an NSCR, 16-Man, 20-Man means you like to participate in group therapy in the air.

o Having an ACE, All-Girl SCR, International SCR, etc. means you gathered enough weird people like yourself and that your group *can* do good RW despite what everybody's been sayin'.

RWu, January, 1973

A History of the RW Underground Newsletter. January 1972. Relative Work had been growing in popularity for some time as ever-increasing numbers of jumpers discovered that freefall together in the same air space was great fun. Largely ignored by the sport parachuting establishment, it had covered the United States and large parts of the world with freefalling friends.

Although relative work had evolved into a competitive sport — there had been 10-man star meets in California and in Zephyrhills, Fla. — it was unrecognized, unorganized and unheard of in national or international competition.

At a party we heard that the U.S.P.A. Board of Directors would soon meet in nearby Milwaukee. After polling key relative workers across the country by telephone, we and Dick Giarrusso and his wife Betty put together a plan. We would propose that U.S.P.A. recognize large-star relative work as a competitive event by adding it to the events at the 1972 National Parachuting Championships. (Four-man RW had been a rather unpopular team event at the Nationals for a couple of years.)

John Sherman was to plead our case at the B.O.D., many of whom knew very little about this popular form of skydiving called relative work. John was a known style and accuracy competitor as well as a hard-core relative worker. Importantly, he's a smooth talker. He made the proposal to the competition committee on Thursday.

On Saturday and Sunday many of our friends showed up to support us. We lobbied in the hallways, in the bar and in rooms. We did everything we could think of to generate enthusiasm for the idea. After some discussion of logistics and team eligibility, the motion to include speed stars, using the existing California Star Rules, in the 1972 Nationals was passed. The speed with which the Board passed the proposal was unprecedented. Never before had they reacted so quickly to a proposal of such magnitude coming from the membership.

Four a.m. and we had won! Sleep was blocked by the nagging thought: All the "big people in parachuting" had suddenly gained a new-found interest in relative work when the motion passed. Many had already dropped unsubtle hints that they would like to be the first Chief of RW in the U.S.A. A few began to campaign for the slot.

No! Freefall should always be governed by participants; not by some ground hog leader! How could we insure that freefall, and in particular this suddenly popular new form of competition, would remain the property of skydivers?

The answer seemed to be communication. Form an invisible Union of Freefallers who could provide their own leadership. Give the brotherhood a name. Have meetings. The idea was that if we banded together and all talked at once we would at least sound big. Big enough for changes in our sport to be presented to jumpers rather than to a small elitist group for approval.

Hastily a list of the names of 30 key relative workers and team captains from all over the United States was drawn up. This was the mailing list for the first issue of a newsletter which eventually became *RWunderground*. (In those days of underground counter-culture newspapers, the newsletter's name made a lot more sense than it does today.)

The list of 30 key star people was divided among the three of us (Giarrusso, Sherman, Works) and we contacted everyone by telephone to explain that RW would continue to be run by RW people if team captains would be responsible for maintaining communications with the national organization on behalf of members of their teams.

There was some fear among the people we contacted that U.S.P.A.'s involvement in relative work was not good, and indeed, they wondered if what we had done was really such a good thing. Yet, everyone was looking forward to the first "real" national competition under the auspices of the national organization.

Other elements of the "underground communication" battle plan included making sure that team captains fully understood the implications of U.S.P.A.'s action, and the responsibility of relative workers to respond in good faith by not showing up for the meet in illegal equipment or sporting cannabis patches (which was sure to incense the image-conscious heads of state, particularly since U.S.P.A. was hosting the World Championships at Tahlequah that year.)

Copies of the newsletter were also sent to U.S.P.A. and to members of the Competition Committee.

Our basic message in those first issues of *RWunderground* was: "you are a member of the loose-knit brotherhood of freefall relative workers known as The RW Council...an informal league of star people who do their thing (not just mine or yours) for RW. Anyone who wants a say in RW should start (or get on) a team. There are no dues but you must remain active in RW. By virtue of being an RW Council member you are also an advisor on relative work to the U.S.P.A. Competition Committee. You should voice your opinion on RW matters. This newsletter will print anything you have to say concerning the betterment of RW."

And in our fourth issue (Fall 1972) we printed The Purpose of the RW Council:

"The Relative Work Council is a loosely knit group of active relative workers who are banding together to see that better things happen for RW more quickly. Some 42 relative workers at the Nationals, representing both 4-man and 10-man RW, agreed there was a need. The RW Council will act to supplement rather than supplant USPA. The Competition Committee recognizes the Council as an advisor to the Committee. All RW Council members must be active in RW and should be a member of a 4-man or a 10-man team. In addition, Council members must be SCR.

"This newsletter serves as the communications media for the Council and interested parties. Duties of all RW Council members are: 1) to voice their opinions concerning the improvement of RW competition to USPA, fellow jumpers and this newsletter, 2) actively promote RW, and 3) make lots of RW jumps. There will be no "Mr.

Big" or nonjumping paperpushers. All RW people will have an equal say in controlling their sport. There are no numbers or merit badges except for the SCR and SCS.

"Good RW promotes itself. Large-star RW is where it is today now. It was noncreated. RW just happened and grew. Being noncreated, RW is transcendent over acceptance or rejection. Unfettered, it does not ossify into ritual mechanistics and so continues to grow. Since it is represented and led by *participants* rather than a groundhog "leader," it grows. If directed by a brotherhood of freefallers this growth can strengthen us through unity in numbers. Look how many of us there are today. We are all just beginning. Let's begin together. Do some RW on the ground so we can do lots of RW in the air. Sincere, active RW'ers should be encouraged to improve and maintain the good vibes of RW. Send us news; make lots of RW jumps."

RW Council meetings were held at the Nationals, at the Z-Hills meets, and at other major meets. Soon we had paying subscribers to help cover the cost of printing and mailing the newsletter which was published "irregularly." We even had subscribers in other countries.

"We're blown away at the number of us," we told our readers in the sixth issue, March 1973. "The good vibe, positive response to *RWunderground* has been overwhelming. We get a fantastic amount of input from our readers — articles, ideas, comments — we hardly have room to print it all. Actually, the 'WE' ain't. It's YOU and US. We simply communicate by having the resulting mess printed. It's work but we get lots of help and have fun doing it. Everyone who gets this newsletter helps in spirit and the printing is just a manifestation of that. We're trying to record what is going down in RW."

Every issue was hand-to-mouth for printing and postage costs. We did have advertising to help pay the bills, including some of the most unorthodox advertisements seen in any parachuting publication. Our art department was right out of Zap Comix — the newsletter's look was definitely "radical funk." Our friends were drafted to help assemble, staple, fold, stamp, address and sort for mailing every issue.

The rewards were terrific — it was great fun to get the mail every day to see what fantastic story or letter it brought from a jumper in another state or county.

We reported on team activities, competition rumors, large-star and speed-star records, meet results, equipment evolutions, competition rule changes and controversies of all sorts. We were right there in the middle of every heated discussion — "speed vs. sequential" for the future direction of RW competition, "soft vs. hard" for head-gear, TSO requirements for gear, even politics...promoting a relative work slate for the 1974 U.S.P.A. elections.

We also initiated the Certificates of Merit to recognize the contributions of individuals to promotion of our sport, and the Combined RW Awards for national competition to encourage participation in more than one form of competitive relative work. The Combined Award has since been taken on by U.S.P.A. as an annual presentation at the National Championships.

The last issue of *RWunderground* was published in June 1976. As we explained to our readers in that issue, our 15th, we felt that we'd "paid our dues" and had accomplished what we had set out to do. "We started *RWu* to spread relative work ideas and news at a time when no other parachuting magazine was printing much RW material," we said. "In 1972 'serious' jumpers considered relative work to be only 'fun-jumping.' When 10-man speed stars were accepted as an event at the National Parachuting Championships, we felt there was a need to bring relative workers across the country together, to let everybody know what was happening.

"Today, RW is still fun-jumping...but it has captured the imagination of the world. We're proud to have been a part of this early growth. We get such a tremendous amount of fun out of jumping, we felt that the work we put into *RWu* for the last four years was just a token return for the fun the sport has given us."
Pat and Jan Works, 1978.

On Becoming A Skygod. Once you've mastered all of the basic relative work maneuvers and have applied this mastery to 30 or 40 stars, you generally sprout a 7-foot wing span to match your inflated ego, will give autographs on request, and are very fast and never miss. When you reach this stage you should take on the name "Skygod" or something similar that goes well with your shiny, cast-iron ego.

Then, jump only with your friends, the other Skygods. Never let turkeys or toads on your loads — they may slow down your star or get in the way. If you do honor anyone with a star, pick a good-looking girl or a close personal friend (if you still have one), and let them go base. They'll then have the entire jump to watch YOUR entry and mastery of flying.

213

If somehow a novice relative worker finds himself on your load, be sure to make him feel at ease with soothing words like: "If you bomb the star, I'll zap your reserve." Or, "See if you can get close but DON'T TOUCH." Or, "If you make a mistake, don't bother to pull."

Obviously words like these don't do much to lessen a novice's anxiety or to teach him anything about what relative work is all about. So, be friendly and helpful to novices, not because you are basically a nice guy, but because you can help build a positive attitude in the sport that will help us grow...and build bigger and better stars. Or diamonds and wedges...

RWu, December 1974

RW Council's Certificate of Merit Awards. "In recognition of Outstanding Services rendered to Freefall Relative Work, this Certificate of Merit is awarded with the Gratitude and Appreciation of all Relative Workers to..."

In 1972, *RWunderground* issued the first Certificates of Merit. This special award was conceived of to recognize and express appreciation to individuals who actively promoted relative work so that it would grow internationally.

By *RWunderground's* last issue in 1976, 33 individuals had been singled out for the award. Nominations were submitted by relative workers themselves.

These people are recipients of the RW Council's Certificate of Merit:

1972

Lowell Bachman (Para-Gear, Chicago); *Chuck Embury* (Parachutes, Inc., Orange Mass.); *Joe Garcia* (A-1 Unlimited, Calif.); *John Higgins* (The Chute Shop, Flemington, N.J.), all for their contributions of equipment and cash which permitted the national championship team that year, Jerry Bird's All-Stars, to attend the World Meet and turn the rest of the world on to large-star and sequential relative work.

Skratch Garrison, chief judge of the first national championships for 10-man competition and author of the first national rules governing 10-man; *Bill Newell,* founder of the Bob Buquor Memorial StarCrest, *Ted Webster,* organizer of some of the first major relative work competitions and an RW philanthropist, and *Dan Poynter,* then Northeast conference director and editor of *The Spotter.*

In addition, a special award was made to Jonathan Livingston Seagull and sent to author Richard Bach with a letter describing how Jonathan's thoughts on flying and excelling have inspired freefall relative workers.

1973

Members of the Jerry Bird's "All-Stars" 10-man team which enthusiastically promoted relative work to competitors at the 1972 World Meet, with wide acclaim. For many, the All-Stars demo jumps, including 10-man star to line to two 5-mans, or a star to snowflake with the outer five tracking away, was their first glimpse at the new phenomenon called "large-star relative work." Team members included:

Jerry Bird	*Chuck Wickliffe*	*Ron Haun*
Bill Stage	*Rich Piccirilli*	*Bob Westover*
Tom Phillips	*Jim Fogelman*	*Sam Alexander*

J.R. (Rod) Murphy, of South Africa, and *Eilif Ness,* of Norway, both members of the CIP relative work subcommittee of the FAI, and instrumental in developing and organizing 4-man and 10-man competition on the international level.

Bob McDermott, U.S. Army Parachute Team, chief judge of the 1973 U.S.A. National Championships, and one of the host officials at the World Cup of Relative Work in Fort Bragg, N.C.

James F. (Curt) Curtis, active competitor and long-time member of U.S.P.A.'s Board of Directors, who helped push relative work competition to prominence at the national and international level.

1974-75

Jerry Bird, roving ambassador for relative work, the only individual to receive the award twice. As captain of three national champion teams ("All-Stars" — 1972, "Columbine Turkey Farm" — 1973, "Wings of Orange" — 1974) he has done much to influence the popularity of relative work wherever he goes. He has organized large-star loads, SCR loads, and training sessions for groups of relative workers in other countries, including drop zones visited after his participation in international meets. In addition, he has helped other teams at international meets with tips on organization, ground practice, exits and other suggestions for improving the quality of RW competition.

Six outstanding and world-recognized freefall photographers:

Andy Keech, from Australia. His beautiful book "Skies Call" attests to his unique talent for capturing the unusual and the beautiful in relative work parachuting. Andy lives in Washington, D.C.

Ray Cottingham, from Long Beach, California. His breathtaking aerial photography of sequential relative work, as performed by jumpers in Seattle and Casa Grande, turned a lot of people on to a new way of looking at relative work. Ray has been shooting freefall film for a number of years.

Carl Boenish, from Los Angeles. He is perhaps the best-known of all freefall photographers — his beautiful shots are seen in all parachuting magazines, posters, postcards, etc. He shot the 26-man World Record Star in 1972. He produced the popular film, "Masters of the Sky." He has shot thousands of feet of film of relative work, and has also turned his camera on hang-gliding.

Jerry Irwin, from Delaware. He is not only a well-known RW photographer on the East Coast, but a very promotion-minded one as well. His shots have found their way into the general media (newspapers, magazines) where they help create a favorable impression for parachuting among the general public.

M. Anderson Jenkins, from Whittier, California. He shot the World's First 20-Man Night Star — a remarkable photograph. He has been shooting relative work for a number of years. His photographs have also found their way into the general media.

Peter Bottgenbach, from Germany. He is probably the most well-known European freefall photographer. He filmed the first World RW Cup at Fort Bragg; his photographs grace the pages of many European parachuting magazines.

1976

Al Krueger, "Captain Hook," who captained his 10-man team of Sky Pirates skillfully for more than three years, culminating in their winning the National Championships in 1975 and then, the First World Championships of Relative Work at Warendorf, Germany, in an unforgettably hard-fought victory. Al, a fair-minded and thorough individual, is a supporter of international competition and a spreader of good will. He has always been willing to contribute his knowledge to others.

B.J. Worth, captain of the U.S. Freefall Exhibition Team which turned-on the world's imagination with sequential relative work at Warendorf in 1975, has been a steady contributor of level-headed thinking to the growth of sequential relative work.

Matt Farmer, an avid progressive-thinking relative worker, is honored for his willingness to help others learn as much about progressive relative work as he knows. Matt, author of numerous "how-to" articles on sequential, ranging from 4-man to 20-man, can always be found wherever the good sequential RW is happening.

Hank Ascuitto, a creative rigger and enthusiastic supporter of competition relative work, was the first to turn out really lightweight gear that was reliable. He has contributed a lot of the innovative thinking that characterizes RW gear today. Others have made lightweight canopies and container systems, but Hank's Piglett II was the first to make lightweight gear popular and practical.

Sam Brown, captain of the "Rainbow Flyers" 4-man Team which has been the winner of two consecutive world 4-man events, is an enthusiastic competitor and promoter of the 4-man relative work event. The "Rainbow Flyers" began as a fun team and grew into a tough competitive team, proving that hard work and consistent effort pay off.

Bill Ottley, an avid supporter of sport parachuting in general, has devoted untiring effort to the improvement and growth of relative work on an international scale. Bill, former vice president of USPA and a member of the current Board of Directors, is a level-headed supporter of both competitive and fun-jumping relative work.

* * *

There are many who continue to support and contribute to the healthy growth of relative work. If Certificates of Merit were still being awarded, there would be several deserving recipients.

"Thank you" is a sweet sound to anyone. Recipients of these Certificates are special people... people who have given of themselves so that all of us who participate in the sport may benefit. We are all served by their positive efforts on our behalf.

Combined Relative Work Awards. In 1976, U.S.P.A.'s Board of Directors officially assumed the administration and presentation of the Combined Relative Work Championship trophies at the Nationals each year, stating that they will be considered as "equal in importance and significance" to the Individual Overall Championship awards for men and women.

The concept of a combined relative work award was originally the brainchild of Dan Poynter. *RWunderground* thought it was an excellent way to recognize all-around ability in relative work, and announced the new award in the June 1973 issue:

"We are proud to announce that there will be an award to the RW competitor(s) who places highest in both 4-man and 10-man competition at the Nationals.

"These awards will recognize competitors who show themselves to have superior ability in both 4-man and 10-man RW. *RWunderground* will present handsome trophies, suitably inscribed.

"The National Champion(s) of Combined RW will be selected as follows: RW'ers on both 4-man and 10-man teams will receive points based on their overall standings in each respective event. (First place = 1 point; Second place = 2 points, etc.) At the conclusion of both events points will be totaled—the lowest score is National Champion of Combined RW. It is likely that there will be more than one winner since many 4-man teams are part of a 10-man team."

The combined RW trophy quickly became accepted as the "decathlon of relative work." Like the Olympics event, the winners of the trophy have proven their competence at a variety of athletic events—both 10-man speed stars and 4-man sequential, in this case. As in the Olympics, there can be no individual overall RW champion because relative work is a team event.

Since the award was initiated, it has become a coveted prize, with teams vying for the combined trophies. Alternates were not eligible unless they actually made the jumps in both 10-man and 4-man events.

Following is an official list of the National Champions of Combined Relative Work, recognized by *RWunderground* from 1972 to 1976, including second and third place runners-up:

OFFICIAL LIST
NATIONAL CHAMPIONS OF COMBINED RW
1972-1976

Year	Name	Stdg.	Team's place in events 10-man	4-man	Total Pts.	Total Time (if tie)
1972	Rich Piccirilli	1st	1	7	8	—
72	Bob Federman	2nd	4	5	9	—
72	Pat Works	2nd	4	5	9	—

Year	Name	Stdng	Team's place in events 10-man	4-man	Total Pts.	Total Time (if tie)
72	Dick Giarrusso	2nd	4	5	9	—
72	Patty Wickliffe	3rd	5	7	12	—
72	Father Farkle (Steve McClure)	3rd	5	7	12	—
72	Ted Webster	3rd	5	7	12	—
1973	Craig Fronk	1st	5	2	7	—
73	Ron Herman	1st	5	2	7	—
73	Bunky Larson	1st	5	2	7	—
73	Rocky Kenoyer	1st	5	2	7	—
73	Curt Curtis	2nd	3	5	8	—
73	Pete Gruber	2nd	3	5	8	—
73	Jan Prewitt	2nd	3	5	8	—
73	Ed Smith	2nd	3	5	8	—
73	Eddie Mosher	3rd	12	3	15	—
73	Greg Reisinger	3rd	12	3	15	—
73	Dennis Downing	3rd	12	3	15	—
1974	Carl Winther	1st	4	2	6	176.2
74	Porter Turpin	1st	4	2	6	176.2
74	Mike Gennis	1st	4	2	6	176.2
74	Sam Brown	2nd	5	1	6	191.3
74	Don Carpenter	2nd	5	1	6	191.3
74	Rocky Evans	2nd	5	1	6	191.3
74	Ken Coleman	2nd	5	1	6	191.3
1975	Mike Gennis (2nd award)	1st	3	4	7	—
75	Sandy Sandoval	1st	3	4	7	—
75	Mike Steele	1st	3	4	7	—
75	Carl Winther (2nd award)	1st	3	4	7	—
75	Bob Feuling	2nd	4	4	8	165.8
75	*Brand X	3rd	6	2	8	194.9
1976	Jay Hilden	1st	2	6	8	—
76	William Murray	1st	2	6	8	—
76	Andrew Reyling	1st	2	6	8	—
76	Mike Cerasoli	1st	2	6	8	—
76	Craig Fronk (2nd award)	2nd	6	3	9	—
76	Thomas Classon	2nd	6	3	9	—
76	Rocky Kenoyer (2nd award)	2nd	6	3	9	—
76	Carl Winther (3rd award)	3rd	10	2	12	—
76	Sandy Sandoval (2nd award)	3rd	10	2	12	—
76	Donald Towner	3rd	10	2	12	—
76	Dennis Murphy	3rd	10	2	12	—

*NOTE: September, 1975 *Parachutist* lists these members of Brand X team: (Alternate not indicated; eligibility unknown because award recipient must have been an active competitor in both events of the meet.)
Brand X: Dennis Dean, Dennis Downing, Gary Henry, Greg Reisinger, Jim West

The Symbolism of the National Champion of Combined RW Trophy(s).

Dear RWu:

...I'm writing on behalf of me and the other 3 guys who won the '75 Combined RW Championship trophies—Carl Winther, Sandy Sandoval and Mike Gennis! What the hell is the silver bowl and spoon supposed to be symbolic of? We've tried everything from Raisin Bran to Pea Gravel and still aren't sure! If there is any particular reasoning we are sure curious! Is it true that next year's overall trophy will be a silver *tea pot?*

—Mike Steele, Sacramento, California

Dear Mike:

Once in the great dim past of featherless birds and other strange pre-stuff, the tradition of presenting a Sterling Silver Revere Bowl to honor people types for great and unsurpassed achievements of human (and non-human) endeavor was instituted.

As a hoedover of this moldy past, we have the America's Cup, the Rose Bowl, the Orange Bowl and the boll weevil. All of these here saying "far-out" about SOMETHING to SOMEBODY so other clods would meby shut up and listen to the music.

At about the same time—in celebration of the decline of the post office, the telephone, the 5 cent beer and free love—a gentleperson, Quaker Oat named Nixon, invented the silver spoon. His motto: "If you're not born with a silver spoon in your mouth, lie a lot. And that way somebody will eventually give you one to stir the shit with when it gets too heavy." (Source: Nixon Papers.)

As you mayhap have noticed, the Revere bowl is of the correct and proper shape for a serving bowl for assorted nuts. The silver spoon is carefully contoured to catch all the dribbles that might otherwise miss the crapper. I mean...need I say more...Raisin Bran! Pea Gravel! Hrrumph!!

RWunderground, June 1976.

Continuous Babble by Pat Works—SCS No. 1. Since the beginning of time (when relative work first began), years have put new heroes and hopes into our collective freefall-frenzied minds. To wit:

1. The common denominator has always been a secret ecstacy that the brothers of freefall relative work engage in and can only call joy. It's

Jonathan Livingstoned Farking Seagull. It's knowing that the constant reward of good swooping is joy.

2. In RW-type swooping we make contact somewhere in the field of our existence, amidst all the sound and fury of the rushing sky. It's our thing, a kind of being, if you will, that happens during an inspired jump.

3. Often, it's a weird feeling after a jump...adjusting back to ordinary reality. Our freefall reality just doesn't mesh with the black-and-white-with-no-gray lines that many people use to delineate life.

4. I like to share what I've learned about swoopin' and relative work with others. After all, good things are to be shared. I've jumped and I've listened to other jumpers. And so, I wrote it all into a book *(The Art of Freefall Relative Work)*. It's all the feelings and the techniques many have related to me, because people who want to fly deserve to know all about flying that has gone before.

5. Right now, my three favorite kinds of jumping are:
Sequential Maneuvers
International 4-Man RW
Big-door Speed Stars (with a 2nd maneuver)

6. A group of us have formed a 5-man sequential-maneuver team. Our goal is to learn how to do stable donuts, fast bipoles, and better flying backwards and sideways. We are having fun.

7. People shouldn't get so uptight about current changes in our sport. I see no reason why we should fix the sport of relative work or parachuting where it is, especially after all the changes it has gone through already. Why shouldn't our sport be a place where we can develop the joy we've been talking about?

Glad to see the Star Crest is doing a magazine. Communications is a very good way to relate to others. The printed word spreads thought thoroughly and reasonably fast. RW intercommunications spreads the germs of ideas that blossom into expanded horizons.

Friction...there'll always be big-mouth stupidoes who will tell you how screwed up you are if you're not into THEIR favorite thing. Since the split between style and accuracy is dying down, some people are cooking up a new schism between speed-stars and sequential RW. Very feeble thinking, to my way of thinking.

It's like an echo. Sounds hardly heard...bouncing around and getting garbled into misunderstandings, with pigheaded cheerleaders egging it all on.

RW is a very personal thing. You should do the kind of relative work YOU like to do. The critical thing to remember is that *no* type of relative work (4-man, speed-star, sequential, static maneuvers, 35-man, night, naked, all-girl, all-collegiate, all-beards, etc. etc.) is either "good" or "bad" or "better." It's all RW.

To do any kind of RW you must relate to others in the air. This relatedness has created a special kinship between us all. We're all "family." We all owe a debt to the RW family. Every RW'er should do his or her best to spread knowledge and joy. Let's let time settle the petty hassles, and let's all do lots of RW!

More boogie! More RW!

Pat Works, Starcrest Magazine, October, 1975

How it's Done: Floating. (Pete Picciolo originally wrote this idea he had for using floaters to improve star times in 1970.) If the first person out can stand outside a twin beech, with only his right foot on the door sill and his right hand holding him upright facing forward, he won't have to worry about getting blown away. There is no wind coming over the top of the wing after the cut.

The first person out the door should bend his right knee and push up and out as he lets go with his right hand, keeping his body in the same line of flight as the aircraft. Don't let the air blast take you away from the base any farther than you can help it. The least resistance to the forward speed of the aircraft will put you closer to where you want to be. While you are doing this, reverse your arch and put your arms out in front of you ovsr your head and bent slightly at the elbows, with your hands down almost 45° to the ground. It's just a good old hand track. This will give you forward speed, while the reverse arch brings you up to the base. If done correctly you will be on the same levee reaching for a set of wrists about the same time the base is hooking up.

Minor adjustments are necessary to keep your heading and to know when to let up on your arch and hand track. The first few tries are a gas. It's easy to find yourself 100 ft. above the base, or with so much forward speed that you have to stand up vertically to stop. Believe me, tracking up is a trip. The second and third floaters out the door should execute approximately a 90° turn to the right, then go into the reverse arch and hand track.

RWu, September 1974

3, 2, 1—GO! Ten-Man Star Relative Work (1973)

Competition exits make a real difference. Exit, leave the plane, bombout...none of these words convey the energy and coordinated scrambling of the sprinting pell-mell rush thru the door. You know what I mean if you've ever felt the power and emotion of a competition exit. It's an awesome attempt to have the shortest possible distance between the front man and the last man in the lineup with the most miniscule amount of time elapsing between the first and the last man leaving the door.

The exit is beyond question the most important part of a speed star. The exit has more effect on your recorded star time than any other element of the jump. All championship 10-man teams agree that fully 70-80 per cent of your recorded time on a jump is directly related to your exit time.

In speed stars, forget notions about good airwork being key. Remember that all good speed-star teams do their airwork well. The only place there's room to reduce speed-star times when everyone is flying good is to speed up the exit. I repeat, the exit is the most important part of your jump for time.

Even a fraction of a second reduction in your exit time will give you stars that are several seconds faster. The overwhelming importance of the exit means you must concentrate four times as hard on exits. Several practice exits should be made before every load until the exit and lineup "feel" right to everyone. When it's too windy to jump many teams practice exits with their gear on. If you have a team member who won't or can't get enthusiastic about fast exits and the practice of them, either help him to improve or remove him from the team. It is *that* important if the team is serious about competition.

Champion teams take *full* advantage of the existing rules on exiting. Team members position themselves like parts of a jig-saw puzzle...contorting, bending, stooping, squatting, perching or whatever to make the distance between the first and last man *as short as possible.* If you're comfortable, you are probably slow. Your position may be so bizarre that the only thing that gets you out the door is the push of those behind you.

The countdown leader must have perfect, constant cadence. The rhythm musn't vary. He starts the count and conducts it like a choirmaster. Everyone counts *loud!* Everyone sways together with each beat. On "GO!" everybody moves. You don't wait for the guy in front of you to move, you move, NOW!

With a small door aircraft, when you dash for the door, stay low all the time so you won't have to bend when you reach the door. Take short, quick, shuffling duck-walk steps. Keep your hands and body on the man in front of you. Dive before you get to the door.

If you do it right, you'll find your face touching the backs of the legs of the man in front of you. If you're any further away than that, then you're just not exiting properly.

Pat Works, RWu, October 1973

Fast Exits. Pete Picciolo, SCR-23, was captain of the Arvin Good Guys, one of the first 10-man teams in California. He sent us a copy of a letter he wrote to the team as they were preparing for spring practice in March of 1970. What he said then about the importance of a fast exit is also true today, and may be useful to some teams. He gave some figures taken from the *Complete Book of Sky Diving:*

Seconds	Distance Fallen In Feet	Total Distance Fallen Each Second
1	16	16
2	46	62
3	72	138
4	104	242
5	124	366
6	138	504
7	148	652
8	156	808

"Take a look at the distance we could save by cutting just two seconds off our exit time. This savings is actually more than it appears on the chart, due to the fact that the first man is still gaining distance on the last man because the last man is still trying to get to terminal."

Fast exits continue to be a vital part of any relative work jump, competition or sequential, but 10-man star times have certainly come a long way. Pete closed his letter to his team with this challenge: "How about a sub-terminal 5-man? Or a 30-second 10-man?"

RWu, September 1974

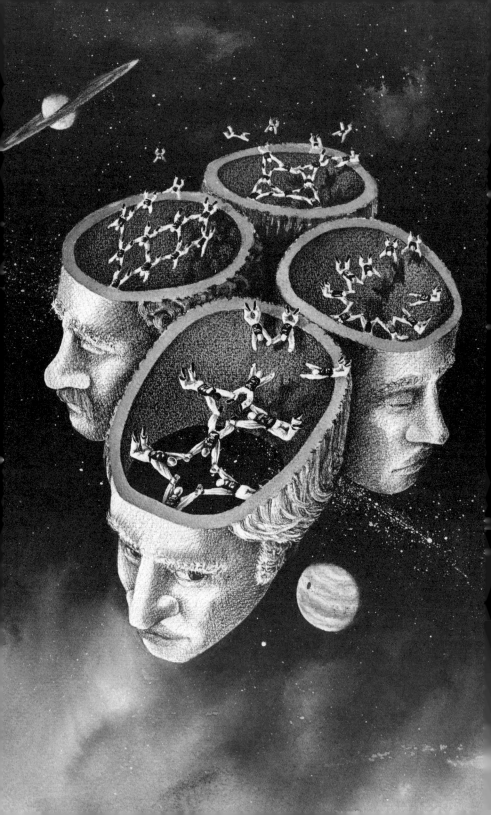

7

Head Trips

Head trips—philosophy and psychology

The skydive experience transcends normal existence. Freefall presents us with the opportunity to enter a joyful condition of flow. We skydive intricate dances on wings made of earth-pushed wind. The music of our sky dance is the rhythm of its flow.

The sky dance philosophy is love of wisdom or knowledge of the art of freefall relative work. The sky dance psychology is the mental process indicated to achieve and retain the sky dance philosophy.

The following articles are some head trips relating to the understanding of the above. Here are different approaches to relating to our thing of doing what we love to do: skydive.

Freefall RW requires other people to relate to.
Smile at the next toad who goofs.

On-The-Ground Relative Work

The Art of "Serious" Fun Jumping, or Avoiding DZ Politics. Fun exciting skydives, hot high-energy relative work, challenging flying assignments, learning more...these are a few of the things that are important to the serious relative worker.

To get more of these desirable high-joy jumps in your logbook, you'll want to jump with others who recognize the relationship of good "ground" relative work to fun, high-energy skydives.

Relative work is still a new sport. We are only now discovering that good-vibe relative work on the ground is the *only* thing that ensures a continuing string of high caliber good-vibe jumps.

Time is a good teacher when we heed her lessons. Lately more and more people have realized that to let old ways of building RW loads prevail, to continue to fall into the habit of forming cliques and exclusive groups so that we always jump with the same people, to allow pressures, politics and hassles to enter into the planning and flow of a relative work jump is no good.

If you continue to follow the old way of thinking, it is certain that you will quickly burn out on unsatisfying skydives and situations. Or if you do keep jumping, you'll probably contribute to attitudes that cause others to leave the sport for happier times.

What Is On-The-Ground Relative Work? Ground relative work is the structuring of good relative work jumps *now* with an eye on maintaining an atmosphere which will enable you to have good relative work jumps *later,* and everafter.

As the term implies, ground relative work is what happens on the ground before and after the jump. The goal is simple: to prepare yourself and others to get maximum joy from your skydives. That means you'll not only participate in making the very next jump a complete success, but (importantly) you'll consider other upcoming jumps for later in the day, later in the week, or later in the year so as to ensure that everyone (new and old) will share the ecstatic wonder of being part of that energy flow we call relative work.

The Organizer. Since RW involves more than one person, the jump must be organized so that everyone knows what to do when and where. If not, a "garbage load" will result. Here are some things an organizer should consider:

• Pre-plan the type of jump, remembering that *quality* RW is generally superior to *quantity* RW.

• After deciding what size load is reasonable for the circumstances, diagram it and manifest it.

• Manifest it using people good enough to fly the slots. That doesn't mean you always get the very best flyers, but rather that you get a mix of expert and novice who you think can accomplish enough of the dive to have a good time, and learn from it.

• Avoid always putting exactly the same people on your loads. Forming closed-load cliques by jumping only with a set group all the time does great long-term damage to the quality of relative work at your drop zone. Instead, organizing relatively open loads fosters learning, fun and friendship, and ensures your drop zone will have plenty of experienced relative workers to choose from next year. Since no one can do RW alone, you GOTTA maintain friendships.

- Recognize that there will likely be more qualified people than you have slots for. Nevertheless, don't turn your planned 4-man, 8-man or whatever-size load into a larger load just to be accommodating. Do the load you planned. As organizer, you are repaid for the hassles of organizing by being able to direct the jump the way you want it.
- Organize loads for learning purposes as well as tricky fantastic wow-ers.
- Make sure the base formation has the more skilled flyers in it.
- Show everyone the diagram of the load. Ground practice, from line up/exit to wave-off and pull at least twice and preferably as many times as is needed for *everyone* to feel comfortable with the dive and their role in it.
- Learn to be tactful.
- You must be able to say "No" to preserve the size and objective of a particular jump, as well as your credibility as a thoughtful manifestor.
- You must be able to say "yes" to new people and new ideas.

The Organized. Like it sounds, the folks "organized" by the organizer should be chosen individually to maximize the dive, and they should be willing to participate to the best of their abilities. When you pay for your slot on an organized load, you are not buying a jump as much as you are agreeing to make a specific jump as well as you can.

That means you'll not only want to do your best as an individual, but help others to do their best, too.

Helping others can be as simple as letting your positive good-vibe attitude externalize so that others can add your confidence and joy to their own. Or, on those days when you're feeling down, to just keep quiet and do your best not to spread your bad feelings.

- Find out when the load is going up.
- Pay your money promptly.
- Don't leave the area after the load is manifested unless you tell the organizer where you are going.
- Be suited up and on time for ground practice.
- Until the organizer has walked you through the dive at least once, keep quiet. You can blither and make your suggestions later.
- If you don't like the dive, you have an option to not get on it in the first place and to organize your own dive.
- To give the organizer a hard time, simply because that person *is* the organizer, is shortsighted.

- Participate fully in ground practice.
- Always be willing to do more ground practice.
- Help the organizer by helping to keep things going smoothly. That may include finding people, asking people to be less actively destructive, etc.

All over the world there are good-vibe drop zones that foster fine, high-energy RW. Those are where all the hot new ideas come from. Likewise, there are bad-vibe, bridge-club drop zones that foster adequate RW and shorten jumping careers.

Think about it. It is your choice.

Pat and Jan Works

"As an unlimited idea of freedom, your whole body, from wingtip to wingtip, is nothing more than your thought itself."

R. Bach

Jumping "Prime Time" — More Skydiving for the Freefall Dollar!
There is for each of us a period of time after the exit during which we are performing sub-optimally: getting squared away on heading, relaxing, evaluating the exit situation (where is everybody?) and accelerating awareness. Then the solid quality skydiving starts.

Similarly, on the far end of a dive we phase into another period of time in which peak performance RW becomes less important than altitude awareness, leaving the area and dumping.

The time in the middle is where the best RW gets done. The end times may vary in length among jumpers, but for each person they are probably fairly consistent. They are translatable into distances and, more importantly, are independent of exit altitude. If that altitude is low enough, there is nothing left in the middle. Peak functioning is never realized.

A community average is probably around ten seconds on top and five on the bottom. With increased experience, confidence and skill, the end times become shorter and better defined. We learn to perform better sooner out the door, and the shift of attention on the lower end is delayed to an "acceptable minimum." These things also tend to lessen the variablility — we can make more accurate subjective predictions of how much "dead time" will bracket the good RW.

To get to the point... if it takes five seconds after exit to get stable and comfortable, find everybody and figure out where to go and how fast, with five seconds later on devoted to "saving yourself," you will have 20 seconds of "prime time" from 7200 ft. It takes a transition to do sequential and one formation can eat up most of fifteen seconds.

If you had jumped from 4500 ft., there would be virtually no prime time at all. However, from 9500 ft. you get 50 seconds or more of freefall which leaves 40 seconds of prime time — twice that from 7200 ft. at *much* less than twice the price. More good RW for your jumping dollar! (And fewer pack jobs per freefall hour, or completed formation, or adrenalin rush...or whatever.)

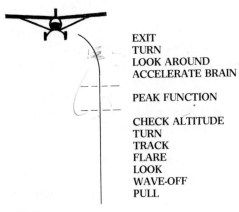

EXIT
TURN
LOOK AROUND
ACCELERATE BRAIN

PEAK FUNCTION

CHECK ALTITUDE
TURN
TRACK
FLARE
LOOK
WAVE-OFF
PULL

Roger Hull

Song of the Godfrogs

Oh come with me and we'll go up there
Where the wind blows cold and there ain't much air,
Where the clouds are ice and your blood runs thin...
But don't worry, toad, we're comin' down ag'in.
Like a frog, a screamin' Godfrog!

When the airplane gets so high she won't go no more
With a laugh and a holler it's out the door!
Down amongst them clouds to play
Like that ol' eagle who does nothin' else all day.

Then back on the ground when the Whuffo's ask "how come?"
And you really don't know,
And you are feelin' sorta dumb...

Well, you may wonder but I know why —
You're a screamin' Godfrog and you love the sky.
C.G. Godfrog (Pat Works)

Expanding Awareness. Walk and chew gum...aviate, navigate and communicate...do more than one thing at a time and you are developing and using increased awareness to get more accomplished for the time invested. You do that now in relative work; you have to time-share your attention with other flyers, your body position and the ground.

But there can be much more. For the same investment of time and money and with your usual number of jumpers, your skydives can be planned to place greater demands on your attention and awareness...to produce greater rewards. Doing two or more sets of formations at the same time is a good way to start.

Most of us started doing relative work as if we were looking through a tunnel, staring at whatever was straight ahead with little or no peripheral awareness. For instance, it is fairly easy to "sneak up" on a student relative worker from the side, tap him on the shoulder and watch him react with surprise. Later on, our awareness expanded to the sides. We saw left and right and generally did acceptable RW as long as no one flew over or under us — they were usually unseen until after the collision.

Vertical transitions and three-dimensional maneuvering are interesting and often appropriate or efficient — and they also condition us to look up and down. If we have learned to scan the space around us vertically as well as horizontally, then awareness has been expanded into another entire dimension. Result: better skydiving.

There are a lot of skydives that can be done not only because they are interesting or fun, but because they gently force us to do more, to see more and to become more aware. Sequential RW was a quantum leap in that direction. Instead of bigger or more complex statics (which still have their place), a whole new open-ended form of free-falling expression was upon us. It extended our extra-sensory perceptors.

During the exploration and development of sequential RW we are finding that along with the complexity, even more time has to be spent on the basics. Long sequences turn out to be short if the initial formation consumes half the free-fall. Complex moves and transitions are nice, but funnels and bad entries can still happen if poor basic techniques are used. Techniques have to be almost second nature if our attention must be directed to remembering a long or complex sequence.

Timing and flow awareness must also be an integral part of the planning and the execution of a good skydive. We have to think about, plan and practice awareness from the first dirt dive just like we have to think about, plan and practice the exit, the moves and the communications.

Although we may see or be aware of much of what is going on around us on a dive, our attention is typically directed to only one spot: the leader (base) for a formation or a reference point around which the formation is being made er the person we are to dock on or fly no-contact with. Having to pay attention to or concentrate on two or more points or activities at the same time (by making it *necessary* to accomplish the dive) is a means of promoting expanded awareness and can result in a much more challenging dive. And with the challenge comes reward.

The dives that follow are based on these ideas and have no doubt made better, more aware skydivers out of those of us who have done them. They are some of the ones that have been done at Pope Valley and are included to illustrate the ideas and to serve as examples of what can be done.

As a start, take an even number of people, split them in half and design a sequence for the number in each half. Alternate the people in the exit, build the formations side-by-side and execute the sequences at the same time...simultaneously, if you will. Each transition should be initiated just as the slower of the two groups completes the previous formation, with the formations being mirror images of each other.

The objective is *not* speed; it is not a race between the two groups. Try to keep the two formations level with each other and only about ten to fifteen feet apart. Avoid letting them collide, overlap, drift apart, develop vertical separation or get off heading. To do that successfully, you will need to concentrate on the transitions within your own formation *and* the position and progress of the other. It may require looking over your shoulder or across other people who are closer to you. While making transitions it will take good "situation flying" to correct for a position error between the formations while keeping your own formation level and intact.

FOUR-PERSON

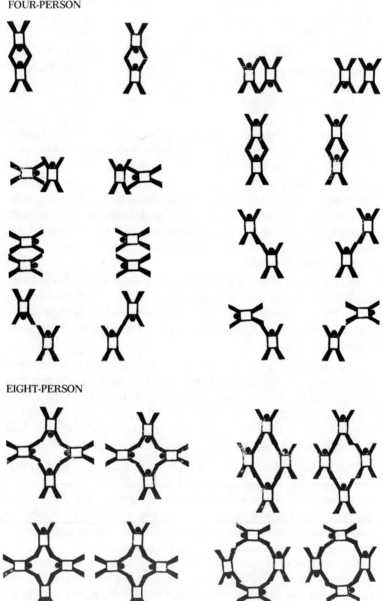

EIGHT-PERSON

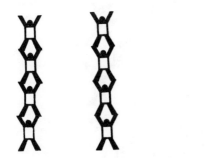 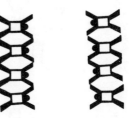

Now to add to the complexity and the enjoyment. Do a similar dive, but as each transition is made have one person from each formation swap places with his partner in the other formation. A different pair swaps at each transition so that if the number of transitions equals the number of people in each formation, the original groups are together again at the end, but on the opposite "side."

We call the dive "Transmutation." It is designed for eight people but something similar to it could be designed for any even number. To do it, set up the two leads facing the direction of flight and have the two floaters dock on the outsides of both formations (facing each other). The first pair of flyers dock on the insides; then the last pair flies straight into the open slots to close off the stars.

Plan to make all the transitions without overt signals. If everyone looks around, they'll know when it is time to move and signals will be unnecessary. Shaking usually does more harm than good anyway. Once completed, the formations need be held no longer than a heartbeat.

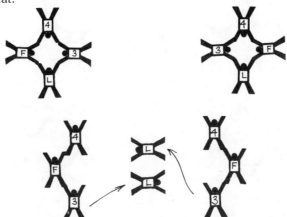

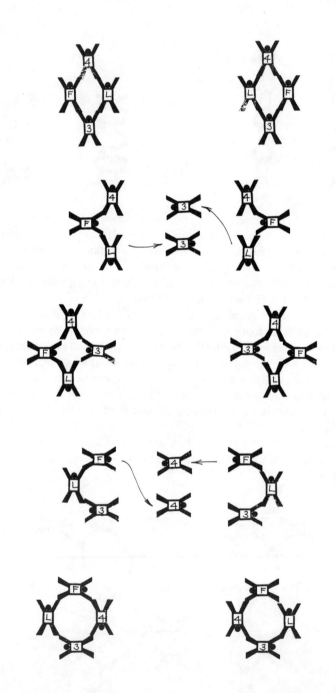

Expanding on what can be learned from the dives described so far, we get into more simultaneous sequential, but with formations that vary in size while transitioning.

"Metamorphosis" starts with eight people in the feeder formation. At each transition one person flies to the receiver formation so that one diminishes while the other expands. A transition should not be made until the preceeding flyer has docked on the receiver formation, so that only one person is moving at a time. Here it is even more critical that the formations be kept level, close together and on heading.

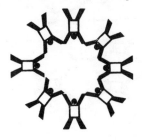

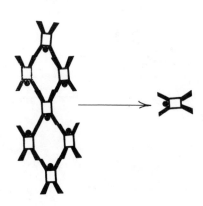

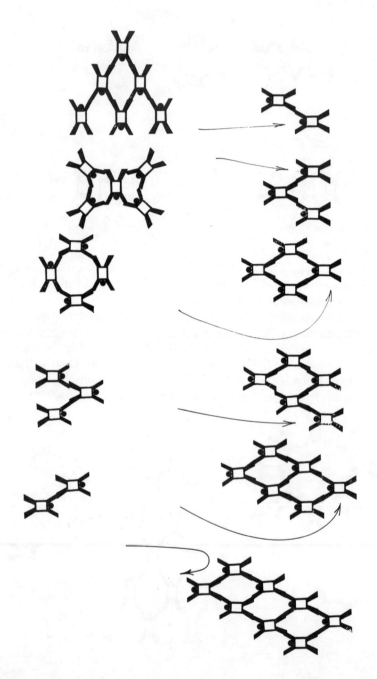

Speed will help get more done but the real objectives are smoother, more precise flying and timing and increased awareness, not merely larger numbers of completed formations. As a variation for six people, move all the receiver formations down two spaces and start with a six-wedge or six-star.

To make things even more interesting, up the ante to three formations and have them all change to a different shape at each transition. More to look at...more to be aware of.

TEN-PERSON

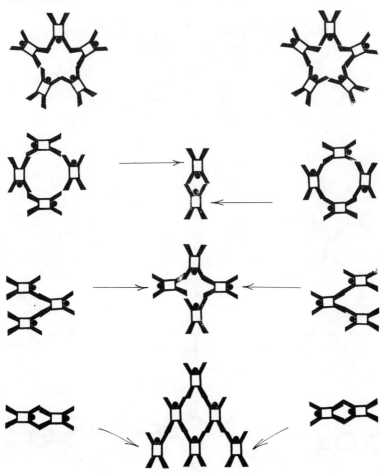

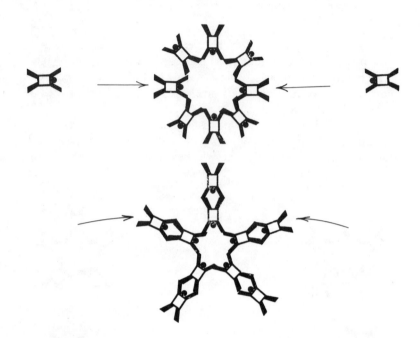

EIGHT-PERSON

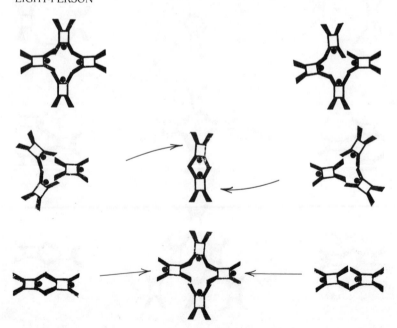

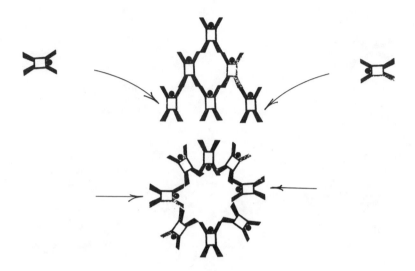

On all these dives, and any sequential dives for that matter, try to conceive of the transitions as taking place within a transparent cylinder, then fly to make the diameter of the cylinder as small as possible. Backing away from a formation — outside the cylinder — then flying back in from several meters away after your slot is ready *has* to take time...time that could be used to get more accomplished later in the skydive.

Your relative position during a transition, while you are waiting, should be treated, practiced and flown as precisely as your position when you are occupying a slot in a completed formation. Allow only enough room for the planned movements of the other people near you, keep your head on a swivel, and never let your slot wait empty when it is ready for you. Be there.

Here is a skydive that can help you practice that concept. You may be surprised to find that the sequence will go faster with the five people than it would if there were only four, *if* the person on the perch at each transition is close and ready to take the slot. It's called "Isotosis."

A different person sits out each time so that everyone "misses" one formation. Unless you are a completion freak, repeat the cycle by backing one person out of the five-star, leaving the original set-up, and keep moving. Besides being intense and enjoyable, it is a great way to use a team alternate, if you are into that.

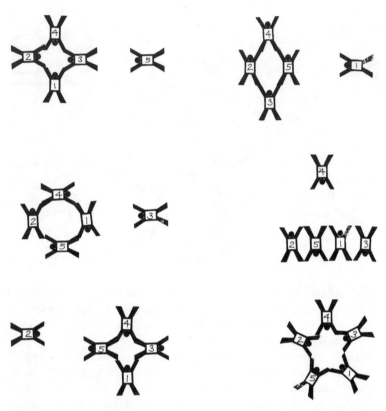

When you have practiced these dives, understand the objectives of their design and have begun to plan a few of your own, avoid treating them as isolated techniques. Integrate the multiple-formation concept with other sequential styles to develop more appealing skydives. Mix in some piece flying or vertical transitions so that your dives are well-rounded. Don't bog down on any one technique or style at the expense of others you find enjoyable, unless you want to.

Try this mixed-technique dive: The two four-stars open to lines, one flies over the other, then they both turn 180°, level and dock into a single star. The eight-star breaks on the opposite axis, each line transitions to a bi-pole and the bi-poles dock on each other. With only two grip switches, that opens out into an eight in-out. Put some canopy relative work on the bottom end and you will be out of breath when you get to the ground. More intensity...for not a penny more.

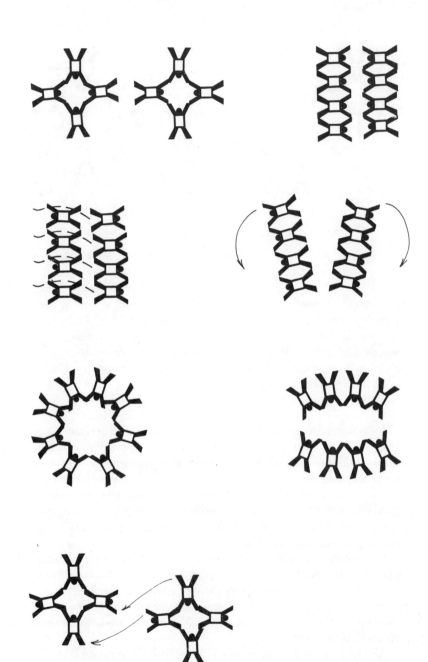

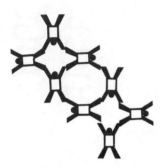 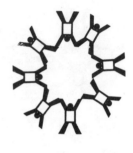

Awareness...it's part of what this skydiving trip is all about. From the first jump right up through the most recent one we are able to sense a little more of ourselves, others around us, what our bodies are doing, the ground, relative positions and speeds and the relative wind. If your jumping stagnates — if you find yourself doing the same skydives or making the same mistakes — it may be because your awareness has stopped expanding. It is often hard to tell which comes first.

If you are more aware, you can do more. And *trying* to do more helps with the awareness.

–Roger Hull, Parachutist, January 1978

Metamorphosis Into Icarus. I jump out of airplanes because I like freefall. It's an ultimate experience that satisfies some deep existing need within me. Freefall is a release, a state of clarity, a metamorphosis into Icarus. I fly with wings I have won for myself.

For me, the most fully satisfying skydive is sequential maneuvers. A good sequential maneuver fulfills the need to do good relative work. It fills the freefall with the intense beauty of doing that which I love — it's full-on 500,000 watt ecstasy.

Flying is motion, and motion is poetry. There is a special purity and unrestricted beauty about freefall flying. And in a way that is uniquely personal, this purity and beauty directly reflect your ability. Your body, mind and imagination all work together to synergize into the most perfect flying machine you can be. You become a symphony unto yourself, if you will.

Although perfection itself doesn't have limits, the expression of perfection through flying must be limited by time and space. Thus for each body, every freefall maneuver has a theoretical limit. If you fly too fast or if you fly too slow, you get further from your goal of perfection. But when you fly at perfection, you are unlimited. When you fly at perfection, you are There.

New SCR holder Richard Bach said the same thing in one of his famous books. The Elder advises Jonathan Livingston Seagull: "Heaven is being perfect...you will begin to touch heaven, Jonathan, in the moment that you touch perfect speed. And that isn't flying a thousand miles an hour, or a million, or flying at the speed of light. Because any number is a limit, and perfection doesn't have limits. Perfect speed, my son, is being there."

In sequential maneuvers the most important thing is to be where you are supposed to be at the right moment with a clean, fingertip docking. Being good at it comes from everyone in the group doing RW together. You learn these things by practice.

Ground practice and sketches of each maneuver are absolute musts for RW maneuver flying. If you are unfamiliar with grip switching, flying backwards and nonmomentum relative work, then practice in four-man RW is where to start.

Four-man practice teaches you how to fly from one maneuver to the next without going low or being sloppy. GOING LOW IS THE MOST COMMON MISTAKE IN SEQUENTIAL MANEUVERS. Four-man RW also teaches you control and precision. Precision is critical because you must dock at your assigned position so as to have no effect on the building formation's stability. Good nonmomentum RW requires full control of your entire body.

Learn how to gain a bit of altitude while you hand-track. You will very likely need it as the next maneuver builds.

Never expect a maneuver to absorb any excess speed you have. Be precise. Be perfect. Put your body where it is supposed to be. Make a no-wrinkle docking and get a firm grip on your contact man's jumpsuit.

For building a maneuver, and in sequencing from one maneuver to another, your flying is mostly of the nonmomentum type. You fly instead of coasting. You feel a lot like an eagle whether you're closing the tail of a diamond, or lining up backward as the point-man.

As you approach a maneuver in freefall, the electricity starts when you spot your contact man and swing toward your position. Use every part of your body to fly toward that invisible, intuitive spot. You may be flying sideways, even backward.

If you're entering after the "base" in the second maneuver, grab extra altitude and be headed for your docking point before it happens. On contact, be absolutely sure your entry will assist the entry of another flyer in the maneuver.

If you and your friends decide to get together with a serious maneuver team, you'll need a few ground rules, just as you would with a competition 10-man or 4-man team:

1. Always be there for practice at the appointed time.
2. During designated practice periods, team jumps come first.
3. Always do practice sessions on the ground before each jump.
4. Participate in a debriefing immediately after each jump. This is where you figure out what happened, and what you'll do next time to make that maneuver faster or better.
5. Apply enthusiasm and stick-to-it-ness along with imagination.

Your first several jumps together may be disheartening. It will seem impossible. But keep at it; try to think of new ways to make things work better. Soon it will begin to click.

On-the-ground planning sessions are vital to maneuver RW. Every team member should be provided with sketches of the maneuvers and each man's position. Everyone should think about them and contribute their ideas on the best way to do them. These ideas all add up to a game plan. The game plan need not be written, but it should show each man's position and how he should get there. A master team logbook would be a definite advantage as well.

After the plan for each jump is developed, talk it over. Discuss each detail. Try to think in terms of the best team and the best maneuver instead of the best "you."

Ground practice is absolutely essential to making the maneuvers happen in the air. Use it to learn to work together and coordinate your movements on the ground so that every maneuver becomes practically second nature. It may be compared to football or any other team sport practice where coordinated interaction with one's teammates is required.

Slowly walk through the entire maneuver(s) on the ground at least four times before every jump. Build each maneuver just as you will in the air, starting from exit. Imagine that you *are* in freefall. Don't build a maneuver in 10 seconds if it usually takes 35 seconds in freefall. Walk into the next maneuver in sequence and in proper timing. Then imagine break-off time and pull sequence.

Spend a *lot* of ground practice time learning the mechanical steps of building each maneuver so you won't have to waste a lot of time in the air learning them. With good ground practice, you'll learn the cadence of each jump so that you'll all feel every maneuver together, and they'll fall together beautifully in the air.

Good sequential relative work is, in part, a matter of mental approach. It's your attitude, or in other words, the programming of your mind's eye to achieve the best flying results.

To learn to fly RW maneuvers well and with perfection, you must do a lot of relative work, learn to relax, and be able to fly with your imagination. Then truly you will be riding on wings of wind.

> "We dance
> to a whispered voice,
> overheard by the soul,
> undertook by the heart,
> and you may know it
> if you may know it."
> — Neil Diamond

–Pat Works, Spotter, May-June 1975

Grafitti. *RWu* spotted the following words on the wall of the hangar at Columbine Parachute Center at Casa Grande, Arizona, and would like to share them with you. They are attributed to Terry Cooper, SCR-486.

"When we know for sure that we all fall through the same air, then big stars will fill the skies...Psych *yourself* — or someone else will and they may be thinking negative. Refusing to let a person on a load is like burning his canopy...you might as well torch it, he has no use for it on the ground. If you think someone is not worthy of being on your load, throw him off — but remember this: nine people make a lousy 10-man star."

RWu, June 1974

Hear! Hear! In case you missed it, we think the following excerpt from Norman Heaton's March *Parachutist* editorial bears repeating:

"...It makes no difference what is one's 'bag' in this game; we all do

exactly the same thing: *jump out of airplanes.* This is the root, the very basis of any amount of camaraderie inherent in this sport of parachuting. Any attempt to belie this is an attempt to destroy the common good of all. No one can justifiably degrade or isolate someone else because their thing in parachuting doesn't happen to be your thing. And vice versa. We all put our rigs on one strap at a time."
RWu, June, 1974

The Skydiver: (Male Variety).

Between the insecurity of childhood and the insecurity
of second childhood, we find the *Skydiver.*
Skydivers are found everywhere: in bars, under bars,
behind bars, looking through bars, in trouble, in debt,
in love and in the air.

Skydivers come in assorted sizes, shapes, and weights
in states of sobriety, misery and confusion.
Girls love them, mothers worry about them,
Unemployment Checks support them,
and, by some coincidence, they manage to get along
with each other. The skydiver is laziness with a deck
of cards, a millionaire without a cent, bravery with a smile.

The Skydiver is a composit, sly as a fox, has the brains of an
idiot, the energy of a turtle, the sincerity of a liar, the
appetite of an elephant, the aspirations of a Cassanova,
the stories of a hero. When he wants something, it is usually
free jumps, more money, a good piece of tail. He dislikes
ASO's, getting up early, small planes, hot-shot pilots (who
never hit the DZ), the week before his payday, his girls'
father's curfew, and legs (that is a landlover). He likes
girls, women, females and all members of the opposite sex.

No one can think of you so often and write so seldom.
No one can get so much fun out of your letters, old jumpsuits and sex
movies.

The skydiver is a magical creature; you can lock
him out of your house, but not out of your heart.

You can take him off your mailing list, but not out of
your mind.
–Author Unknown

How to Lose at Tennis (Or Anything) Without Really Trying — And What to do About it.

Introduction: *The nation's pioneer expert in the field of sports psychology and author of the new book, Sports Psyching: How to Play Your Best Game All of the Time (published by J.P. Tarcher, Los Angeles) explains why sports has us talking to ourselves and tells what those inner voices mean.*

IF YOU started carrying on a conversation with yourself on an airplane, in a restaurant, or standing on a sidewalk, people would probably give you wide berth.

Not so, however, if you do same on a tennis court or golf course or other sporting arena. No one seems to think there's anything particularly strange about a tennis player saying to himself, "Not that way dummy!"; or a golfer blurting out, "Come on, now, follow through, keep that head down," as he steps up to the tee; or a pitcher saying to himself, "Steady, steady;" or a grown man having a tantrum at the 10 yard line after missing a long pass. We often see famous athletes talking to themselves and, when we play, find ourselves doing it too.

What would otherwise be classified as irrational behavior seems to be socially acceptable in sports. This does score a few points for the R.D. Laing set who see sanity-insanity as social definitions anyway. But, mainly, it says something about athletic games themselves. In them, we not only talk to ourselves, we hear voices. Not that we hallucinate actual spoken words; it usually takes the form of those little ideas whispered into our consciousness as we play. You are lining up a particularly tricky and dangerous downhill putt and the voice says "go for it." You lose caution, putt too hard, and roll the ball six feet past the cup. The opposite happens just as often. You've got an 18-inch putt and suddenly the idea pops into your head that this is *The Big One*. You then feel like the abominable snowman has embraced you. A condition known to golfers immemorial sets in. Bobby Jones used to call it the "yips." You freeze and the ball rolls to a sickening stop six inches short of its destination.

Carryovers From Childhood Often Defeat Us As Adults. Although these are all common experiences, most of the time we overlook them when trying to figure out why we did well or poorly in a game. The context for describing sports action is largely in terms of the physical.

We tend to talk as if sports were little more than an elaborate set of calesthenics. The serve was out because you tossed the ball too high; you guttered the bowling ball because you rolled your wrist; you missed the putt because you didn't follow through. You want to improve your game and keep from repeating those mistakes and, following this conventional logic, you look to physical solutions for what you think of as purely physical problems. You read the instruction book, study the diagrams, watch your favorite pro on TV. Then you go back and make the same mistakes again.

This is because most of the time the root cause of the fluffed shot is an *emotional* reaction. The immediate cause may be something physical. But it was an emotion that set it off. You wanted to make the play or felt you had to make the play and as a result, in your anxiety, you either muscled it — exaggerating some motion — or you froze up. We've all had this happen to us. But few wish to explain or deal with it on psychological grounds. This is because, again, the conventional explanation paints you into a corner. If someone reacts to pressure, the verdict usually is that he "choked," or is "a flake." So a lot of people ignore their reactions to pressures in a game. They say they don't feel any pressure; that they are only playing for fun. Or they use a superstitious explanation. They were "jinxed" on this play, or they should have worn their lucky green socks.

All of this sidesteps a very real component in the nature of all sports. All athletic games are emotional experiences. The feelings are the very reason we all play. All sports involve challenge — you try to sink the basket, get the strike, can the putt, and so on — and that leads to some amount of anxiety in anticipating whether or not you'll make the play, win the game. Pressure is part of every game and every player — no matter how cool he may pretend to be — feels it.

We attach great importance to the outcome of sporting contests. We are encouraged to do this all the time by pervasive social influences. You can't help but be tempted to measure yourself when you go out — for a game of tennis or golf, *(or to do RW),* no matter how friendly. And to some extent, this is part of the fun, a little game you play against yourself to make things interesting. Part of you becomes a spectator in each game you play, rooting from the bleachers.

The trouble starts when the spectator comes down out of the stands and onto the field — throwing beer cans; when the "spectator" in any way begins to distract the player. We talk about how tough it must be for professional players to perform in front of huge crowds. But lots of recreational athletes create their own imaginary crowd of jeering, hooting, cheering fans — this being made up of their own inner expectations and anxieties.

In sports, as in life, what you want isn't always what you need. You are playing Jack, your old buddy, and this is match point and you want to win it. But what you need to accomplish this has nothing to do with whether or not it is match point or how many games you've won or Jack has won. What you need is to be relaxed enough to be limber, fluid and flexible on the court and to be concentrating on the ball and not on your thoughts about the score or anything else — not on the goal you want. The ball, the net, your racquet, the court are all the same whether it's match point or just for practice. You have to make the same moves to complete a successful shot whether it is only a warm-up or a hot rally for the big prize.

In other words, the things you need to do as player have to be smooth, cool, *focused* on the action, while as a "spectator" you are putting on all the pressure for the things that you want.

One of the trickiest things to learn in sports is separating those two modes of behavior. All the traditional rah-rah, "up for the game" stuff we hear is misleading. Certainly, players need to be motivated to put in the kind of time and effort needed to perform at high levels. But usually it is the exaggeration of the importance of the desire to win that caused the problems. The pressure becomes so predominant that it takes a player's attention away from the game. Performance suffers rather than improves.

Great athletes are those who can stand the pressure, as we all know, but they don't do this by necessarily piling it on themselves. Instead, they have found ways to shut out those pressures when it comes time to play and to channel the energy into their performance. Veteran pro players commonly talk about concentrating so much that they are not even aware of the thousands of people in the stands. Likewise, their own inner thoughts are less of the spectator variety ("Come on, now, do it!") and more of the calculating "player" variety ("I notice a weakness on the right side: next play I'll go in that direction").

A good first step in getting a handle on pressure is to start listening to yourself. Become aware of the kinds of things you say to yourself in a game *(or on a jump)*.

Do this non-judgmentally, by the way, or you will be defeating the whole purpose of doing it in the first place. Monitor yourself during your next few games, casually, without trying to ochange anything just yet. Separate the "spectator" type things you say — or think to yourself — from the "player" type strategy thoughts. The frequency and the force of the "spectator" type things you say or think to yourself almost certainly will correlate with how nervous you become in a game and how much your performance suffers from exaggerated, self-induced pressures. The more you yell at yourself — like some desperate coach — the worse it is. But just realizing what is happening — that this isn't something real, but a habit we internalize from outside influence — will help to get it under control. For example you could be saying to yourself, "Damn it, get the hell in there. Why can't you get it right?" over and over while your performance gets worse and worse without realizing that it is precisely your own "spectator" exhortations that are getting in your way. To understand how this mental habit is operating is to help put it back into perspective, so that you can concentrate on the game.

In addition, the kinds of things you *say* to yourself are an important indication of the way you feel about yourself in relation to sports. Emotions can become a problem in sports in a variety of ways, depending on individual reaction. Some people, for example, tend to be too aggressive, so much so that they become ruled by anger in a game, often becoming vulnerable to being provoked into unwise moves by cooler opponents. On the other hand, some suppress the normal amount of aggressiveness needed in most games and tend to be too easily intimidated. You might lack confidence, or have too much of it. You might be too easily discouraged into an "I don't care" attitude, or be so driven that you are a perfectionist who is constantly tied in knots because you never seem able to reach some impossible goal.

Some of the typical things players say to themselves tie in with long standing attitudes and characteristic ways a person has learned to react in *any* game. If these reactions are continually a problem, the best way to start getting at them is to listen as they manifest themselves in terms of those inner voices. In this way they will soon become understood and predictable and lose some of their hypnotic potency.

The More You Yell At Yourself — Like Some Desperate Coach — The Worse It Is. Some of the typical "spectator" statements are: "You'll never get it right... That was a good shot, but it could have been better..." and the like, which indicate that chances are the speaker is overly driven.

"I'll show them . . . I'm going to ram this shot down his throat . . . Now I'm *really* mad . . ." and the like usually are connected with over-aggressiveness.

"I'm uncoordinated . . . I'm just a klutz, I guess . . . I'll never do it . . . Wow, that was a great play, you're terrific . . . What's the use . . . Looks like I'm sunk . . ." and such are tied in with lack of confidence, tendencies to be too easily intimidated, feelings of inadequacy which discourage players from practicing or taking lessons to improve performance.

"You dummy . . . You can't do anything . . . You're no good." . . . and so on, which are often tied into the compulsion to feel guilty every time one misses a play or loses a point *(or zaps a formation.)*

If you mull over some of the things you say to yourself in a game, you'll find they will lead you back to the ways in which you were conditioned to feel about sports as you grew up. You probably fell into certain patterns as you played in the school yard and now you carry them with you onto the tennis courts and golf courses *(or your playground in the sky)* even though now they no longer make sense. This doesn't mean you have to psychoanalyze yourself in order to play better. We can safely say that, for the most part, the way all of us are conditioned to react in athletic games during our school years is a disaster wherefrom the superior players are survivors who have gone on *in spite* of the system rather than because of it. The rest are left with some degree or another of negativ attitudes which interfere with our playing to our best potential, whatever that may be. The school gym and athletic programs are little more than a continual calling out process for the more talented kids who, step-by-step, participate in higher and higher levels of competition, from Pony Leagues to high schools to college and finally to pros, as all along more of us are being relegated to the status of spectators. At one level or another someone always loses and, what's worse, is made to feel that there is something shameful in this. Kids are thrown into complicated, competitive games usually before they have learned the simpler kinds of exercises that let them develop subtle motor skills needed for sports, and, just as importantly, confidence in their abilities. We are set up for Walter Mitty daydreams about sports superstardom without the wherewithall to even attain fundamental skills with any consistency. The results are disappointment, frustration, anger, guilt. It's the reason Charlie Brown is such a compelling character. There's a little of him in all of us.

What was learned, however, can be unlearned. You don't need to drain sports of their emotions. On the contrary, you can clear away lots of societally-inspired emotional baggage that gets in the way of being able to feel the real joys of sports, the exuberance that comes when you make a play that is your best, that is better than you thought you could do. If you keep that spectator part of you in the stands and behaving himself as an encouraging, supportive fan rather than an *agent provocatuer,* you'll have made the initial big move toward that happier situation. It isn't always easy. Old habits are hard to change. But if you keep practicing the new ones of being more aware of *yourself,* they gradually will replace the old ones with more and more regularity.

Being aware of the psychological dimensions of what is happening on the playing field also can make all games much more interesting and rewarding. It is essential to what is colloquially known as "playing your own game." You can't play your own game until you start to know it up close.

–Thomas A. Tutko, Ph.D. and Umberto Tosi, Golden West Airlines Magazine, July 1976

High Flight
Oh, I have slipped the surly bonds of Earth,
And danced the skies on laughter-silvered wings:
Sunward I've climbed and joined the tumbling mirth
Of sun-split clouds — and done a hundred things
You have not dreamed of — wheeled and soared and swung
High in the sunlit silence. Hov'ring there,
I've chased the shouting wind along and flung
My eager craft through footless halls of air.
Up, up the long delirious, burning blue
I've topped the wind-swept heights with easy grace,
Where never lark, or even eagle flew;
And while with silent lifting mind I've trod
The high untrespassed sanctity of Space,
Put out my hand, and touched the face of God.
John Gillespie Magee

The Joy in Joy. Have you ever noticed that during an inspired jump, time expands so greatly that the recounting of the jump takes longer than the jump itself? Instants become moments sung by the heart and remembered with ecstasy.

When we become totally immersed in a sport of creative action like relative work, we lose sense of time and the external world. Instead, we experience joy, the ecstatic feeling that everything is going just right. For me, this is the highest form of enjoyment, and I call it "the joy to be had in joy."

This feeling is expressed as "flow" by other individuals who experience it. Flow, as psychologist Mihaly Csikszentmihalyi of the University of Chicago describes it, develops when we are completely immersed in what we are doing. In this state, a person loses a self-conscious sense of self and time. He gains a heightened awareness of his physical involvement with the activity. The person in flow finds his concentration vastly increased and his feedback from the activity enormously enhanced. Ultimately, he enters an ecstatic state to such a point that self-awareness doesn't exist.

"How are we to know that the mind has become concentrated? Because the idea of time will vanish. The more time passes unnoticed the more concentrated we are...All time will have the tendency to come and stand in the one present. So the definition is given, when the past and present come and stand in one, the mind is said to be concentrated." Vivekananda

Dr. C.'s studies of flow, described by individuals participating in activities that are rewarding in and of themselves, are the subject of an article by W.B. Furlong in *Psychology Today,* June 1976. What is said about others' involvement in their sports can be directly applied to relative work. Good relative workers radiate energy. They can fly sideways...and backward. They become one with the air, effortlessly. The article suggests that the high joy of relative work offers its participants pleasure by its very nature.

In Furlong's article, a rock climber describes it: "You are so involved in what you are doing you aren't thinking of yourself as separate from the immediate activity." Said another rock climber, "It is not moving up but a continuous flowing; you move up only to keep the flow going. There is no possible reason for the climbing except the climbing itself. It is a self-communication."

The article goes on to relate how others define flow: People in flow undergo an intense centering of attention on the activity. They do not try to concentrate harder; the concentration comes automatically. "The game is a struggle but the concentration is like breathing — you never think of it," said an expert chess player. A dancer described it, "Your concentration is very complete. Your mind isn't wandering, you are not thinking of something else, you are totally involved in what you are doing. Your body feels good. Your body is awake all over. Your energy is flowing very smoothly. You feel relaxed, comfortable and energetic."

In flow there is a sense of being lost in the action. The individual experiences an altered sense of time. "Time passes a hundred times faster. In this sense it resembles the dream state," said a chess player. Sometimes the centering of attention produces a spatial alteration akin to the changed sense of time. Baseball players in a hitting streak often say they see and hit the ball so much better because it seems much larger than normal as it comes up to the plate. Ted Williams said he could sometimes see the seams turning on a ball that was approaching him at 90 miles per hour. In his prime, Arnold Palmer could look down at a putt and see a line on the green that led from the ball to the cup.

Thought Destroys Flow. There is no sense of the self in the period of flow, says Dr. C., but there is what he calls a "merging of action and awareness." Take a reader absorbed in a book. He is turning the pages and he knows he is turning the pages, because that is the only way his reading can go on. But he does not notice that he is turning the pages.

Flow is a floating action in which the individual is aware of his actions but not aware of his awareness. A tennis player who is intensely aware of the ball, and of hitting it, does not reflect on the act of awareness itself. He is not bothered by such thoughts as "Am I doing well?" or "Did everyone see that shot?" These thoughts destroy flow. If the moment is split so that the player perceives his action from the outside, then flow halts.

Another factor in flow is the clarity of response that the individual gets from the activity. The feedback in sports is a good example; the tennis player knows instantly whether his shot is a good one, as does the basketball player, the marksman, the billiards player. It is a trifle more subtle in the creative arts. The performer may get immediate responses from his audience, but the non-performing artist — the composer, sculptor, painter, writer — must get it from an internal sense of rightness.

The feedback is not an end in itself, but rather a signal that things are going well. The person in flow does not stop to evaluate the feedback. "The action and reaction have become so well-practiced as to be automatic," says Dr. C. "The person is too concerned with the experience to reflect upon it." A teenage basketball player put it, "I go out on the court and I can tell if I'm shooting OK or not. But if I'm having a super game, I can't tell until after the game."

Flow can make a person feel an almost Godlike sense of control. All the dichotomies, polarities and conflicts of life are resolved. A basketball player explains, "I feel in control. Sure, I've practiced and have a good feeling for the shots I can make. I don't feel in control of the other player, even if he's bad and I know where to beat him. It's me and not him that I'm working on." Said another, "Although I am not aware of specific things, I have a general feeling of well-being, and that I am in complete control of my world."

To induce flow, an activity must allow each individual to meet a challenge at the outer limits of his capability without testing him beyond those limits. Once he goes well beyond his limits, he begins worrying about the severity of the test and about himself — his safety, or his success. These worries break flow.

To flow, an activity must offer fast and direct feedback. For this reason it should be very simple and have clear, noncontradictory rules. It should lack the ambiguities of real life. The participant sees clearly what is "good" and what is "bad" and how to seek the good. One stamp of flow activities is that they do not demand incompatible things. Games and sports are good examples. The ball is in the air; we can catch it or not. So we focus on the ball and on catching it.

While a surprisingly diverse number of activities have the potential of producing flow, not all activities will yield a deep flow experience. And not everybody can get the sense of ecstasy associated with the most intense moments of flow. Whether flow happens at all, and if so, how deep the experience is, depends not only on the activity but on the individual's attitude toward it. Some people cannot surrender completely enough to the moment to allow flow.

A person who feels severely over-matched in a competitive activity will be blocked from flow. For example, if a weekend tennis player is matched against Jimmy Connors, he is likely to be overly concerned about how he's doing, and so become too tense for flow.

"Thought is time and Time creates fear."

***

Time and Space Exercise

Ask yourself: What time is it?

Answer: Now.

Answer the question until you can hear it.

And, on jump run, or wherever, focus your thoughts in the present.

Don't Think About the Future.

Just Be *Here Now*.

Don't Think About the Past.

Just Be *Here Now*.

Then, reflect on the thought that if you are truly Here and Now —

a) It is *enough,* and

b) You will have optimum power and understanding to
   do the best thing at the given moment. Thus,
   when "then" (the coming jump) becomes Now — if
   you have learned this discipline — you will be
   in an ideal position to do the best thing, and
   need not spend your time now worrying about "then."

Adapted from *Be Here Now, Baba Ram Dass, P. 90.*

By Pat Works
Partially reproduced from Psychology Today, June 1976,
"The Fun in Fun" by W.B. Furlong

To Whom It May Concern. There was a time when the time did not matter, but now there has come a time when time matters, and it is time to think about time. And it's about time that we think about time because up until this time we have really not taken the time seriously. So, seriously, the question is, what is the matter with the time this time? I got seven hours sleep, and still stumble but that has nothing to do with time but merely body chemistry. Which has something to do with subjective reasons (I guess) objective time, but I don't think that's really what we're talking about. I think what we are talking about is time, and time passes by and we all get older and a little wiser (very little), but most certainly old, and does anybody really know what time it is?

Weird Al (Warsh), RWu, June 1976

A Formula for Flow

1. Fit Difficulty to Skill. One prerequisite for flow is an even match between the difficulty of a challenge and a person's ability to meet it. If the demands are too slight, the person feels bored; if too great, he feels anxious.

But a match of skills and challenge does not guarantee flow. The other prerequisites are internal.

2. Focus Attention. Some people can flow simply by focusing their attention to allow the merging of awareness and activity. This pathway to flow does not require a controlled environment such as a game; any activity can spark flow if a person focuses well enough.

3. Forget Time. We can flow in any activity if we are in the right frame of mind, even while changing a flat or taking out the garbage. Among the attributes which should make things flow is the ability to focus on the moment, so that we can respond to feedback from the immediate situation. To do this, lay aside thoughts of the past or plans for the future. Too much of the time we race from one thing to another, preoccupied with the next or worried about the last. This frame of mind takes us out of the moment so we lose flow. Flow exists only in the present.

4. Relax and Wake Up. To flow, let go of worrisome concerns. Relax. But stay alert. Become fully aware of what is happening in the immediate situation. Notice what your body is doing.

The domain of flow is the band between anxiety and boredom. An alert mind resists boredom by keeping us involved in events around us. A relaxed body is the physiological opposite of tension. The two together — alert mind, relaxed body — combine to make us ripe for flow.

5. Training for Flow. There are specific kinds of training that make us more open to flow by teaching habits counter to speediness, tension and distraction. Any discipline that focuses us on the here and now brings us closer to flow. Dance and some Eastern martial arts, for example, combine awareness and movement to center attention. Certain meditation techniques instill mindfulness, the ability to focus on whatever is happening at the moment, no matter what it may be. The meditator also gradually becomes more relaxed and alert.

Psychology Today, June 1976.

Ask the Wind
What could I write about relativework
What could I?
What could I write about the way of the wind

and working it with you
to go
and flow.
You can ride the wind
always
but it always wins
always
always sings its own song.
Ride upon wings of wind?
sure
but first sing its song
go along
ride where it takes you
and smiling
direct its flow
to ebb and coincide with your brothers and sisters
as they dance and flow with their own wind song.
come 'listen
come sing
come ride with us the wind
and let it tell you its story
in voices of sunset
in valleys of light
in chasms of clouds towering
to lend foundation to the words
that the winds sing
Joy! sing joy!
in voices deeper than all our understanding.
what could I write about relativework when you need only ask the
wind?
Pat Works

Freefall Physics and the Relative Worker

Total energy…maneuvering potential…energy maneuverability…words borrowed from those who design and fly airplanes.
Terms which have direct applicability to jumpers and relative
work…concepts which are probably more widely understood and
used than expressed. Without fear of trying to over-simplify or to
quantify at all what we are doing, we can explore the realm of potential

by looking at subjectively definable boundaries expressed as velocities.

How fast and in what directions can we go and how can we use those velocities to our advantage?

All of the physical energy we use (or have available) in relative work is Newtonian — it comes from the act of descending under the force of gravity. **"Gravity is a geometrical phenomenon" — pause for reflection — "and we are doing geometrical things with potentially definable velocities."**

Our total energy control on one dive, on one day, is the n-dimensional sum of the jumpsuit, the gear and the mass of the jumper. The amount of energy that is, or can be, used constructively in relative work depends on several things. The most important one is the "thing" we are trying to do relative work with. Be it a person, a grapefruit or a frisbee figbar flake minus one (you!), it is falling at *a* speed at any one moment. Allow me to refer to that speed as the reference rate of fall.

Then there is judgment. Judgment, developed and tempered by experience and forethought, allows us to exercise the limits of our potential without exceeding them or the restrictions imposed by the nature of the dive.

Another and perhaps more directly influential factor is state of mind — our willingness to fly at or near the edge of our "known" potential capabilities.

We do not develop energy as an airplane does with its engine, but we can and do convert it, redirect it, channel it and use it to accomplish our purpose: being in one place in the sky with respect to a *moving* reference and staying there. It is that moving reference that prevents our easily defining such things as potential energy which, in the usual sense, depends only upon vertical separation from a fixed reference.

The one phenomenon which keeps us from accelerating constantly to some hypersonic velocity in a mere two mile fall is *lift.* At a rate of descent we refer to as "terminal velocity", that lift is sufficient to counteract the force due to gravity and we no longer accelerate, all other things being equal. It is by changing those things which were assumed to remain equal that we can do relative work. We can block the air (projected frontal area), redirect it (deflection and friction) or compress it and expand it (aerodynamic lift). Drag and friction allow us to change our rate of descent from some loosely defined "normal" by changing body size or projected frontal area (the number of fractional acres your shadow covers on the ground). Deflection is the means by which we sideslide and delta and backslide. Aerodynamic lift is the essence of the maximum track — forming ourselves into a wing with airfoil shape.

In freefall, there is for each of us a maneuvering envelope that is *independent* of anyone else in the air. Each of us has an absolute (for now) fastest and slowest descent rate. There are other boundaries to this conceptual space but allow me to harp on the vertical ones for a moment.

Reverse arch...maximum recovery...de-arch...whatever you call what you do when all your friends are looking down on you is a position most of us are all too familiar with. It is a fact that if you are moving in any direction other than straight down with respect to the air, you can not be falling as slow as possible. You may be falling as slow as you know how, but not as slow as possible. To explain: acceleration results only from a force.

In order to move laterally, something has to push you. That something is the result of air that has been deflected laterally to some extent. Only so much drag and friction can be generated by one person at one time when it is "all hung out". Consider it a quantity of force. Any fraction whatsoever of that quantity that is used to move laterally in any direction *must*, by the Law of the Apple, be subtracted from what is making us fall slower, or would have made us fall slower. If you are moving forward slowly in a reverse arch, you ain't optimizing. (Try putting you toes together with your knees spread).

But I digress...try to accept the fact that there is an upper limit today. In the opposite direction, there is similarly a maximum return to the firmament speed. And, here again, if you are moving forward at any speed at all, you aren't going down as fast as you could (maybe just as fast as you know how). If you could go forward *and* maintain maximum vertical speed, then a sailboat could run directly into the wind without tacking.

We were talking about an envelope, and now we have the upper and lower boundaries. On the front end (forward speed) is your max track; and then there is the back track (track backwards?) and the sideslide left and right and the do-see-do, swing your partn...

All of these parameters are more or less proportional to the maximum and minimum surface areas we can expose and maintain into the appropriate component of the relative wind. Whether or not we can actually achieve these maximum velocities on a particular dive depends on the time available and the precision with which we can shape ourselves into our best "known" body positions.

Virtually all the positions used to operate on or near the edge of the maneuvering envelope are inherently unstable and require a high degree of concentration. Witness those who flip over trying a reverse arch or Z into front loops learning to track. The reward for operating at the edge without exceeding it can be called maximum performance. The price paid for exceeding a "limit" is loss of control and gross inefficiency. Flying in the interior, short of the edge, when maximum performance would have been appropriate results in a cost which is ordinarily manifested in terms of time — delay in reaching a point in space.

Each of us has a unique envelope. The "reference point" in any envelope is determined by an *external* source, like another jumper's neutral frog rate of descent. The envelope for a single jumper falling alone has no reference other than zero *horizontal* airspeed. The vertical zero reference would be whatever speed the jumper happened to be falling. The external source may be one jumper (the leader) or several (a formation). Each jumper's maneuvering potential is given in rough measure by the amount of envelope that lies between the reference point "in use" at the time and the edge of one's *personal* envelope. The time required to correct a displacement error is a function of maneuvering potential available and the willingness to operate at or near the edge of one's own ability.

In determining what sort of maneuvering is appropriate to correct a displacement error, there are rates of change in velocity — accelerations — to consider. Quite often this is where the greatest judgment is required. How long will it take to accelerate to the planned closure rate and, more importantly, how long will it take to dissipate it to zero one microsecond before "arriving"? How much slack is there in case the *reference point* changes its velocity in some random direction — say, toward a jumper who is attempting to correct an error in position as rapidly as possible?

The maneuvering envelope so far drawn is purely imaginative. There are no numbers to support it (yet!). But we are not as much interested in numbers as we are in subjective comparisons and evaluations of jumpers. We know that some people simply do not know how to track as fast as others. Some do not know how to backtrack at all (at least intentionally and under control), probably because they have never tried. By comparing maneuvering envelopes, we can plainly see...

That reminds me of the bullshit phraseology used in a lot of math books: "Clearly, the triple integral...", or "It is obvious that the solution..." while you sit there mystified and insulted. But I digress...

Let me put it this way. *If* the envelopes had numbers on them, we could draw them on something transparent, stack them up and look for that area that was common to all of them. That range of velocities is where we have to be to have any hope of completing something with that group of people on that dive. By comparing envelopes this way, even mentally, it may be apparent that if the reference rate of descent is established above the upper limit of a particular jumper, he will go low and stay there unless he is holding on to someone with more "room at the top". The converse may also be true for a featherweight in photographer's bells with a Protector for a main who can just get down in a dive but bobs up out of sight, even in a stable fetal position. The reference point is at the lower limit of his envelope.

We do little more now with numbers than to assign exit order and entry positions and this is no attempt to increase their use or influence. Numbers are finite and finiteness is a temporary condition. Most of us have not even begun to explore the maximum of our potential for controlling ourselves in the air. Besides, at the very best these limits are "fuzzy". Like, today for some inexplicable reason we can track faster than we could yesterday but slower than we will tomorrow. True, for some people the variance is small — the limits are almost subjectively predictable. For others they may vary widely with mood or how interesting the dive is.

Reasonable familiarity with your own maneuvering potential can allow you to make value judgments on other than a purely intuitive basis about what your "best" moves might be *even prior to exit* for various directions and distances from where you want to be.

For instance, your maximum track may actually result in a rate of descent equal to or less than the reference, in which case it could be used for a *level* lateral correction even for a moderately short distance. Knowledge that your smallest stable frog or "RW stable" is not fast enough to catch a heavy student with a T-10 and coveralls should induce you to *plan* to dive below him and pin him on the way "up". In that case, virtually all your maneuvering potential is above the reference established by the student and you could stay above him in a backslide, sideslip or a max track. Using a dive or exiting first are your only alternatives.

Once you develop a feel for your own neutral rate of descent, you should be able to determine early in the dive where the reference rate of descent is in *your* envelope and to start making contingency plans, especially if the dive plan calls for multiple formations or no-contact flying or vertical transitions.

See. There is nothing new about this envelope thing. You knew about it all the time.

In the interior of the envelope lies the entire gamut of minor correction moves, hand tracking and position-maintaining maneuvers. It is the area where we spend most of our time and expend most of our effort. We have all seen the jumper who seems to have flip-flop controls. He is either flat out to get someplace or hanging it all out to stop. Perhaps "thrashing" is a better term. The smooth, reliable and consistent jumper is the one who blends one move into another, constantly aware of and responsive to the changing situation, tempering his speed and direction of movement with time and distance to go, thinking ahead about qualitative and quantitative measures of his potential. He probably has an intuitive feel for what this curve says without consciously realizing it.

The little arrows on the perimeter of the curve are like "degrees of freedom". There are none on the max track or the max back because there would be a conflict of definition. However, you can fall faster in a reverse arch just by closing your mouth. The hand track is up near the top of the envelope because I felt like putting it there. The arrows say that you can move forward faster or slower, and you can fall faster with the same forward speed. The same applies to a backslide. Sometimes floaters have to backslide and fall slow; if you are directly over your slot and the formation is moving toward you, you might need to backslide and fall faster (or just beat feet and set up again). In the first case you are on the upper limit of your envelope and to the left of the vertical reference; in the latter you are down inside the envelope but on the same vertical line, left of "center".

And on and on. This is just a way, a different way, of trying to express more concisely an overall concept that has allowed this aspect of the sport and the people who participate in it to develop to the present state-of-the-art. Maybe just one small bit of the ultimate awareness.

Roger Hull

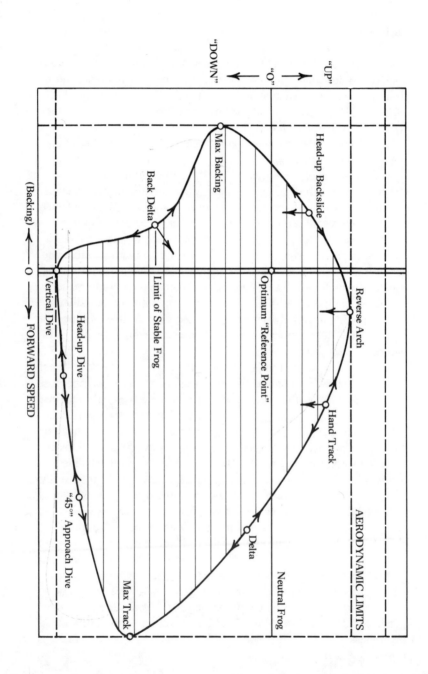

8

Jump Stories
With a little help from fairy dust

It's Got Soul Today
It's a beautiful day—
Look at those clouds!
Clouds, as they form and change,
Are like stars as they cruise around the sky.
That is a beautiful sky up there...
I see a sky like that and I want to get up there
And touch clouds
And hug clouds
They make my heart big.
It's got soul today.
Donna Wardean

Cloud Jump
 The ride up is always a pain in the ass.
 If you fly at the back of the bus, the windows in the Beech are too high to see out of. Conversation and the guys clowning at the door pass the time.
 On jump run, you sit as long as you can so you don't have to stand crouched in the thin air.
 When you do stand, ready for the sprint, you put your head in that state of aggressive, relaxed, total concentration that you've found really lets you get it on.
 Cut. Ready? 54321! Go! go go go go
 Head low, down the hall, sharp right and out, you arch to dive and your left side stalls briefly in the subterminal air.
 Into the dive. Far out! A valley of clouds!

The base disappears into the puffy side of a cumulus mountain and the swarm follows.

You dive, swoop, brake and set up your approach in sinewy movements,

While grey-white masses roar up around your ears.

Reflexive paranoia: Cloud-Rush freight-trains you and the star.

Wet air. Your vision flashes in and out like a strobe light. The adrenalin rush bobbles your approach and slows your entry.

Drop your ass for a wrist entry — and you're in.

Shake and break. Check out the star as the white world waterfalls up around you with an eerie, silent roar. Awed and exhilarated, you split as the star explodes like a Fourth of July rocket.

Sit up, pull, and the world starts.

Pat Works, RWu, Fall 1972

"Bonus Days." Safety is survival. You should practice safety nearly as reflexively as you automatically blink when a raindrop nears the eye.

As a jumper, and interested observer of and participant in a few "Bonus Days", my more than 17 years of jumping suggests that you will likely become more safety conscious the longer you jump. In other words, you'll come to recognize the subtle distinction between a "might survive" and "comfortably survivable" situation.

Safety consciousness in parachuting can be described thus: The easiest thing to "do" is nothing. Unfortunately, in parachuting doing nothing is deadly. Occasionally a parachutist, or pilot, or motorcyclist, or mountain climber or hang glider will do nothing —

or the wrong thing —

for too long...

There are some adventures that are hard to squeak past. There are some adventures that are fairly certainly terminal ones. So whenever anyone slips past a "real close one," a new calendar is started and *ALL* the days survived thereafter can be termed "BONUS DAYS."

These are those extra days you get after the near-crash. As Freak Brother No. 2 Roger Nelson tells it:

"I reconfirmed my membership in the Bonus Days Club watching the ground 'stop coming' at about 100-150 ft. SPORT DEATH!

"What had happened was a typical brain malfunction, yep, I packed a total! So I really shouldn't have been doing a 3-man after-star. 'Cause when I threw out my pilot chute, it went 8 feet and stopped fully inflated!!! So, immediately I pictured Waldo Jecker, FB No. 22, and Tony "Frit" Patterson, FB No. 181, (both deceased), as I looked at the ground.

"Time was vital. I had a choice of two things, dump your reserve and chance an entanglement and streamer in, *knowing* I'm gonna bounce (the way Frit went in at Deland), *or* reel in my small 29" pilot chute and take it lower for a clean reserve opening. See, when I looked at the ground right after realizing my problem, I said "3 seconds" in which I had to play. So I decided to reel as I counted to 3. I hit 3 just as I grabbed the bottom. I dropped my head to get some air on my back as I dumped my reserve.

"Well, at this point, seeing where I was, I kind of thought dropping my head might not of been too smart 'cause I was about to bounce head first on the side of the runway. When all of a sudden, "YEA, BONUS DAY CLUB!!!" (To become an *active* member in the Bonus Days Club you must very narrowly escape eternal freefall...one exciting time.)

"I looked down, saw my shadow, screamed excitement and saw a jumper clapping my Z-Hills act."

That was a Bonus Day.

Pat Works

Blue Sky...Black Death

1. Thunderous energy of flight!
   Flashing sequences roar into
   geometrical perfection
   ...for instants
   among the blinding blue.
   Artistry...
   precise physical and mental movements translated
   into the reality of perfect flight.
   Flight, perfect flight, in harmony
   and close formation, we relate to the
   actual
   moment of
   Now.

2. Ho, push!
   You and the Formation
   ebb and flow from the rhythmical entry sequences

into an 8-donut...to 8-caterpillar.
Energy
Flight
Perfection
Problems...one out...
He enters, donuts, and we
pause for the camera.

3. As predetermined, the front man on the cat pulls
   (for the photo, of course.)
   On pulling, he glances to the ground and
   high speed dirt ground-rushing up.
   And mouths, "Oh my god!"
   as you, too, pull
   and
   perversely perhaps ('cause it *is* low)
   you look up to see the entire formation in the puppet-like dance
   called line stretch.
   "Separation is nice to have
   but
   an open canopy is better...
   much better."
   You look to
   see...
   to experience
   ground rush.
   "Okay, I'll give the main three seconds..."
   One!
   2!
   3!
   ...Not bad. Thirteen-five.
   Stupid!
   Funny, 'tho. Everyone had 1,000+ jumps!

Pat Works

Sport Death "Going low is a rush...But it's not practical..."
Everybody understands about that. It has to do with reaction time on
those days when everything seems to be going wrong at once. Recently
I have noticed a lot of people with stratostars pulling high...

That is sport death too...

"Sport Death" is a phrase that seems to bother a lot of people. But the concept came from a drop zone that understands the reality of watching people die. Friends and strangers... students and experienced... for every reason in the world... none of which make the slightest difference. It doesn't matter who is moving and who is holding still... the impact is the same.
Skratch Garrison

12.5
"For two miles up in the heavens
Is a cold and lonely spot
That's where you find out what you are
And indeed what you are not.

"Some men roam the heavens
And some men sail the seas
But most men sit by the fireside
And wish that they were free.

Some men try, and some men die,
And other men just fail,
Some fly the sky like the eagle
And others like the quail.

For two miles up in the heavens
Is a cold and lonely place
And if you can't keep up — Get Out
It may not be your race.

Some men should never fly at all
It wasn't God's intent,
They should stay and walk the earth
As mortal man was meant.

But for the breed who are lonely
The sky is the only place,
They'll rot on the face of mother earth
Looking heaven right in the face.

Then some men die with a mournful cry
Some with a smile on their face,
Some men call it an act of God
But most say an act of Fate.

For two miles up in the heavens
Is a cold and lonely place
You bet on skill and Lady Luck
To lose is no disgrace.

If you last, you'll give the whole thing up
But then you'll crawl on your knees,
For another chance to race the wind
To be a man again and free."

Charlie Straightarrow

Introduction. *R Wunderground does not ordinarily print stories or poems about death. But we're printing this piece by Matt Farmer because we think it is more about life than it is about death, and we want to share it with you.*

A Friend Goes In. The Story of a Jump. This is going to be a good one. I can feel everyone psyching up for it, as we turn jump run. Quinn is up front, keeping everybody loose and the vibes up.

"Alright, let's do it!"

"Air dive, Air dive, feels great."

"Air dive, Air dive, can't wait."

The twin Beech vibrates at a new pitch, as the driver throttles back. Floaters swing through the door and hang waiting. We move quickly to stack ourselves in the door. Heydorn is in the door. I slide in behind him and Luginbill leans tightly over the two of us. Melroy, Captain, Wooten, Herman and Gruber take their places.

Between Heydorn's back pack and the top of the door, I can see Chuck and Quinn watching me intently for the start of the count. Their jumpsuits are already flapping in the wind we will all feel in a second.

"Ready!"

Gruber starts the count.

"Ready," comes back the response.

Stacked in the door and counting, I can feel the adrenalin flow, mind and body winding up—

"Go!"

We explode from the tight confines of the Beech into a bright blue sky two miles deep and stretching from horizon to horizon.

I catch a good exit and look for Heydorn. He's right in position and the floaters are close behind him, tracking up on the still slow air. Quinn is up and on first with a beautiful fingertip dock. I close facing him on Heydorn's left hand. Chuck's up from the other float slot as Luginbill docks beside me on Heydorn's right arm. A five-spider fast, clean and stable.

Looking out for Melroy's side-in approach, I catch in my periphery above us Gruber's flare to the back door. He is perhaps fifteen feet above us, head down to the point of being nearly vertical, fully flared against the momentum of his approach speed. He looks for all the world like a flying squirrel in a desperate full spread flight to a small tree branch. Melroy slides into his side-in slot and Quinn and I catch him with no trouble. It's going great.

I glance over my shoulder to see where Wooten is. He's on a smooth final to the tip slot on Melroy's leg. Gruber's already in on the point and Captain has finished his side-in when I look back across the now nearly complete ten-wedge. Only the two tips are out and they close a heartbeat later, right on the pace. Little more than 25 seconds have passed since exit, the base formation is complete.

Everyone's attention is on Heydorn. He will key the break with a simple nod of his head. Ready—*Now,* he nods, hands release grips, the ten-wedge breaks into three pieces. Two three-man wedges separate from a four-man diamond. The two wedges are side by side, facing the diamond.

As the pieces begin to separate, the wedge that I am a wingman of turns a quick 180. The other wedge turns with us, between us and the diamond. Melroy, Wooten and I are the base wedge. We take up a heading, trying hard to hold it and fall straight down. I take a quick look over my inside shoulder and see the other wedge move into position behind us, ten feet up and ten feet out. The diamond is right behind them, on their level or maybe a little lower.

My gauge reads five grand. We've got the time. Three pieces are in position and we can dock them to triple diamonds, if we hurry. I take a glance at the ground, then back at the gauge. Coming up on four grand—still no dock. I look back over my shoulder again.

The other wedge is almost on us. They are shooting a very vertical approach, carrying a lot of speed. Captain on the point of their wedge has his arms back and up; Luginbill and Herman, his wingmen, are tucked up tight. The diamond is in close, already on our level, moving for the slot that will be there when the wedge docks.

Crash, the wedge, unable to brake all their vertical approach speed, comes on hard. Captain catches the grips and we struggle to regain stability. Before we can dampen the effects of the hard dock, the diamond, already committed, piles into the back of the two struggling wedges. Heydorn, on the point of the diamond, comes up with a grip on Luginbill. We fight for stability. The oscillation begins to dampen but the formation distorts where the grip is missing between Heydorn and Herman. Tension pulls at the formation; we struggle to stabilize and connect the open grip. It's no good — *Snap,* we lose a grip. The formation starts to break up.

I let go, turn to my left and lay it back into a track. Right at three grand, safe and sane, I track hard, then sit up and look over my shoulder. Above and far off to my right, I see Heydorn unload his P.C. Nothing over the shoulder, I wave and punch. My rag comes off clean and I feel the steady pull of opening. Just as I'm getting the opening shock, I see Heydorn again, not a hundred feet away, still at terminal velocity. His P.C. is streamering.

Words flash in my mind. Streamer... Streamer... cut-it-away... cut it... Long before the words can be verbalized I see — seemingly in the very instant I perceive his situation — a flash of white, his reserve.

The scene screams away toward the earth. I watch. Stark white against the dark red and black of his tangled main, the reserve streams out. It doesn't bloom. It's tangled; tangled in the mess of line and canopy over his head.

Fear! Fear for this man, my friend. Fear borne of knowledge. Knowledge of time and speed and the ground.

The words pour out.

"Come on... Come on... pull it out, pull it out."

Seconds tear by. I watch, far below, the ground, the still hurtling figure, the flapping tangle of red, black and white. I watch, small now against the enormous earth, the man and the flapping un-opening chutes.

Fear and helplessness — my thoughts race — the time — Christ the time — come on — come on. I can see it's too late only an instant before he collides with the planet. A ring of dust and sand explodes outward from the violence of the impact. The flapping tangle of nylon lies still against the hard brown desert.

Dead. Oh, God. He's dead. Not ten seconds have passed. Ten seconds, a life time. I hang spent, drifting slowly toward the desert under my breathing canopy. A deep sadness washes over me. I feel empty.

On the ground I can see cars stopping on the highway. People are running from the hangars to form a small circle around the smashed, lifeless figure. I am momentarily angry at these vultures. What do they want here? Do they think they will understand something of their own impending deaths by staring blankly at this man's?

I land and walk toward the hangar. The spectators drifting past me look curiously at the parachute rolled in my arms. Their eyes are bright as they hurry to see violent death. They don't understand the loss. What can they know of Heydorn — of fast hands and a quick mind, of an easy laugh and his intense personal sanity. To them it is only an opportunity to see a newspaper headline in real life. — Chutist Falls — Something to tell at work Monday.

Those of us who were on the dive drift slowly into the packing area. Eyes sad, movements strangely slow and deliberate. No one quite knows what to do with themselves — I am here, but my friend is dead. We stand in a small circle around Ron's van. There are short snatches of conversation.

"It doesn't seem real — not somebody like Heydorn."

"A streamer."

"No cut-away."

"Entanglement."

"Fought it all the way in."

"God, did you see him hit."

The conversation dies out; each of us lost in his own thoughts.

Thoughts about dying — about this odd chain of events we call life that leads us to it. He made a mistake. You can throw a reserve past a streamer sometimes. — A chance. He rolled and lost. Now he's lying in a broken heap out by the highway and I'm sitting here feeling the hot sun on my back and wondering. Wondering what it is we seek in freefall. Why are we here?

"Hey, that was a good dive."

Someone breaks the silence.

"Yea, that spider was right there."

Someone else picks it up.

"Quick wedge."

"Really."

"That was a nice swoop, Grube."

"The break to pieces looked good to me."

"Yea, but, when the lead wedge turned, it dropped down and away."

"Right, and vertical separation makes it hard."

The conversation rambles on slowly. I'm half listening and thinking—Well, what are we doing? Our friend is dead and we are standing here talking over the dive. But we're skydivers and so was Heydorn. Our lives and perhaps our deaths are tied up in this thing we call skydiving. Who's to say? We are only human, so we all live to die—and there are many ways to die—many ways. You can be so afraid of dying that you can't live.

Life is what skydiving is all about. In free-fall you know you're alive. You're right there on the edge where the world is moving. Where time is right now. Jimmy Hendrix said it right—

"I'm the one who has to die when it's my time to go, so let me live my life the way I want to."

The talk is slowing down. I glance up, squinting against the setting sun to see who's talking. It's Luginbill, big hands thrust deep in his blue jean pockets, kicking aimlessly at the gravel with his toe and summing it up in one easy sentence—

"Yea, well, no sweat, we'll get it. All we need is a few more dives."

Matt Farmer

"Skydiving is an invitation, a privilege audaciously
and impolitely granted, perfumed with danger and surprise, offering greater freedom of movement, inviting one to live life at some other level. If one dares."

Adapted from Tom Robbins, Even Cowgirls Get the Blues

How Far is Up? (A True Story) There I was, at 12,000 feet. We're flying close formation with a Twin Beech. We're in a 182. The crazy pilot is flying us in *real* close. The spotter in the Beech is just giving the "Cut" as I step out...and fall off the wheel.

Goddam! I fell outa the stupid airplane! And oh, woe! I'm supposed to be part of a 15-man formation. A 15-person triangle that will grip change into a three-man star *inside* of a 12-man star, which, if there's time, will become a 15-man star with three people entering from the inside. Horrors, what if everyone gets in but *me?* Finally they exit...slow-motion out the doors far up and far away. Now what in the hell am I gonna do on a solo 60-second delay?????

In a split second I decide I'm gonna be in that formation. I look straight down and reverse arch til I ache, pulling every trick my skinny body knows about going up. I do this forever, it seems. I've even got my mouth open catching all the air I can. Looking up, *nothing* is in sight. My heart sinks further. More arch! And oh god, I'd just been talking like a plastic Skygod, too…"I never miss…blah, blah, blah…"

There, I can see them!…but they're a *long* way up and far away. I concentrate on horizontal movement and recovery. Then I'm getting close enough to see colors. I gotta pick out my spot. I'm closing way too fast…I've built up an amazing amount of horizontal speed. I actually have to flare and slow down (slow *up?*). Spencer, who'd seen me fall, sees me enter and laughs like a madman. We sequence to part of the second maneuver and run out of time.

On the ground, many who had observed the jump wanted to know how I did it. A perfect shot for a heroic rejoinder like, "Oh, that…well, I never miss." But I'd learned too much; I was still stupefied, over-wrought with adrenalin. I walked in circles for 30 minutes, sorting it out. "I haven't got the foggiest idea how I did it," I said. But my muscles ached from the strain for two days afterward.

I'd fallen out 3-4 seconds before exit. Think about it. *It means you can put out eight floaters with base-pin going out 9 and 10!* My physics teacher would be amazed, too.

Pat Works, R Wu, December 1974

Jumping Into A Volcano. It all started at the Z-Hills Turkey Meet. I was eavesdropping on a conversation between Jerry Keker and Dave Williams and heard some key phrases like "rock concert" and "demo." I eased my way into the conversation and found out that they were talking about the January 1st demo jump for the Sunshine Festival—which is held smack dab in the *center* of Diamond Head Crater in Honolulu, Hawaii. When I found out that much they had to stop talking for a while and fill me in on who to get in touch with if I should just happen to be in the neighborhood.

When I arrived in Honolulu at two in the morning, December 30th, I called up Randy Cordes and introduced myself as a visiting jumper who wanted to make the demo into the Volcano. I was warmly invited to their house, called "Toad Manor," one of the highest houses perched on the cliffs that overlook the city.

They informed me the next day that there wasn't a jump planned for this year due to lack of interest. With the interest that I showed and the interest that was generated when I mentioned that it might make for an interesting article in the *RWunderground,* the demo was planned New Year's Eve.

Randy, Flip Hollstein and myself were going to make the jump the next day, or later on that night (it depends on how you look at it). Just an hour before we were ready to go to the airport, veteran crater jumper Randy came up with a cold sweat and chills (really!). So "Rag Man" Frazier took his place on the load.

On the ride up the plane flew over Pearl Harbor. I saw a ship with the smoke blowing straight up which suckered me into thinking that there were no winds. But there were and they blow over the crater and create the same effect as blowing into an empty coke bottle. Veteran crater jumpers know this and do two things: 1) jump round canopies, and 2) stay in the middle of the crater. I did neither and felt the "crater effect" at about 100 ft. when the swirling gust hit me sideways and turned my Strato-Star the same direction with a few cells closed. The landing turned into one of those "keep the toggles up and try to hit a clear spot 'cause your ass still has to pass over stuff" landings.

Flip and Rag Man landed where they were supposed to and I didn't break any bones or take out a bunch of junk by the stage — so we called the demo a success.

P.S. — Randy asked me to add that he would like past crater jumpers to get in contact with him at Toad Manor, 821-A Puunani Pl., Honolulu, Hawaii 69817.

Whitey, RWu, June 1976

Unconscious and Falling! In Texas on December 22, 1966, 16 expert parachutists met at a small pasture five miles from the Gulf of Mexico between Galveston and Houston. After two weeks of planning, they were ready to attempt free fall jumps from the edge of space.

At 12:15 that afternoon the first five loaded their jump aircraft: a 206 Super Cessna Skywagon. It roared down the narrow grass runway and climbed upward into the 21° below zero temperature at 25,000 feet, into air so thin it robs a man of useful consciousness in minutes by oxygen starvation, or hypoxia as the doctors call it. They were climbing into trouble.

We were manifested for the second lift to 25,000 feet. So, as the plane took off, we watched with more than casual interest. Tim, an ex-jet fighter pilot who had lost his left eye flying for the Marines, turned to me with a grin and a shrug, "Well, they made it off the ground, but I'll lay you odds that one of those clowns screws up before they even leave the airplane."

Some 37 minutes later, when the Cessna reached jump altitude, the thin air and cold had done their deadly work. Only two of the five skydivers aboard were able to jump. One of the others had been so affected by the cold, or his nerves, that he froze in the door and did not jump; another had accidently unhooked his oxygen line so that when it came time to jump he was only able to turn blue and babble. During the ascent he had been sucking on an oxygen line that wasn't connected to the oxygen tank and as a result, the necessary state of mental alertness was replaced by confusion and euphoria.

The third jumper had suffered the consequences of gas expansion which occurs at high altitudes. When he was carried from the aircraft on the ground, I solicitously removed his lined jump suit and carefully scraped the frozen vomit from it. Warmer than mine, I wanted to use it for my upcoming jump. Little did I realize that before the day ended, I, too, would be lying unconscious at 25,000 feet far out over the chilly waters of the Gulf of Mexico in a plane piloted by a man whose oxygen-starved brain convinced him that north was best reached by flying south.

The two that did jump grossly misjudged their exit point so that they landed some five miles away. Although we blamed it on stupidity at the time, later events indicated that their misjudgment was caused by the insidious dullness which accompanies hypoxia. Just what is hypoxia?

Hypoxia means not enough oxygen in the bloodstream. It is a silent killer, as the symptoms are seldom unpleasant and there is no pain. The accompanying impairment of muscle coordination and judgment is not noticed by the pilot or jumper. In effect, you can suffocate without ever being aware of it.

In the thin air of 18,000 ft. you can breathe less than half as many molecules of oxygen into your lungs as you can with each breath at sea level. As a result, your body undergoes rapid and severe psychological and physical changes. You experience headaches, light-headedness, marked fatique, labored respiration and mental impairment: you just can't react or perform in a normal manner. Collapse is imminent. At

23,000 ft., 8 to 15 minutes of exposure leads to convulsions, cessation of respiration and circulation, and death.

The onset of hypoxia could cause a pilot suffering from its effects to fly straight into a mountain without blinking. He feels exhilarated and weak at the same time; he may see the mountain and know it is there without being able to do a thing to miss it, or care.

Some people maintain that they can hold their breath for two or three minutes. This, they feel, should give them a longer time of useful consciousness in the event of oxygen failure. What they fail to understand is that your whole body needs oxygen to survive, not just your lungs. The human body is porous so that even a saturated system of oxygen will rapidly diminish and induce cellular damage in the brain, leaving you a babbling idiot.

To avoid the devastating effects of oxygen starvation, all aircraft which operate at altitudes over 12,000 ft. must supply supplementary oxygen to the pilot and passengers. Big commercial airliners pressurize their cabins to an oxygen content of 4,000 ft. to avoid having an oxygen mask for each passenger. On light aircraft, however, such as our Cessna 206, 100 per-cent pure aviation oxygen is carried in a tank. When the plane reaches 12,000 ft., passengers and pilots simply plug their individual oxygen masks into this central tank and hypoxia is avoided.

To we jumpers on the ground the possibility of hypoxia seemed remote. We were more worried about the cold.

The sun shone through broken clouds and above their scattered whiteness the sky was clear all the way up to 12,000 ft. where a light layer of broken cirrus clouds seemed to divide the sky. Below these clouds is most of the air we breathe: 90 per-cent of the earth's oxygen. Above is nothing except dark blue sky and cold.

The temperature drops ten degrees for every thousand feet you climb. Above the clouds the air is too thin to retain any of the sun's heat. On the day we made our ill-fated jump the temperature was 21 degrees below zero at 25,000 ft. At the wind-chill effect at that altitude makes the cold even more deadly.

Like most jump craft, the twin waist cargo doors of our Cessna had been removed, creating a large opening 2½ ft. wide by 39 inches high, for easy in-flight exits. This leaves a gaping hole in the side of the airplane which acts as a funnel for cold air. Air so cold it will freeze a gloved hand in minutes.

But we were confident that we would be in complete control of any situation which might arise. We didn't expect to be at that altitude long enough to encounter any danger. We were grossly overconfident.

Our aircraft was a good one. The 1966 Turbocharged 206 Cessna Super Skywagon has plenty of horsepower even in the thin air at 20,000 feet, where the rate of climb is 500 to 700 fpm.

Average round trip to and from 25,000 ft. is 45 minutes. Our trip was to take over two hours.

To take care of the oxygen requirements of the pilot and passengers, this Cessna has a tank behind the baggage space. A pressure gauge is located on the bulkhead and is easily visible for in-flight reference. Overhead, above the windows, each passenger has a female receptacle to accommodate the plug on his oxygen mask hose. Masks are simple rebreather types held to the head with an elastic band. Unfortunately, all of the masks in our aircraft were either broken off or removed from the oxygen line, leaving the jumper with a bare hose to stick in his mouth and suck on. Each individual system has a small spring-loaded check valve in the clear plastic oxygen hose. When oxygen is flowing, the valve is held open.

Thirty minutes after the Cessna returned to the ground, we were rigged up, loaded and ready to go. As the wheels lifted off, I tried unsuccessfully to adjust my position so that the coming cold would not blow directly across my body. In the back of the plane Tim sat and fiddled with his oxygen line. Beside him sat Don, inscrutable in a cold weather mask and dark glasses. Ed, a 23-year-old dental student from Houston, was sitting in the door. He was to act as jumpmaster and pick the spot over which we would exit. His choice of an exit point would determine where we would land.

In the front, next to the pilot, sat Skippy, a field engineer for a construction firm in Houston. Skippy, a short and muscular fellow, had been a pro boxer in his youth. I was sitting on one side of the open door, facing Ed.

As the plane climbed we tried to assure ourselves that our jump would go better than the jump which had preceded. We decided to keep up a rapid cross-talk so that anyone suffering from the altitude would be quickly noticed by his friends even if he himself was oblivious to his condition. In addition, we assigned partners. Each man would have someone to look after. We weren't going to make the mistakes that the first load had made. My partner was Ed and I was to look after Skippy.

Some 20 minutes after takeoff, at about 12,000 ft., it began to get cold. Plans were forgotten as we attempted to assure that we would not be too cold to move when the time came to exit. My face went completely numb.

At 16,000 ft. we hooked up to the oxygen supply. With the tubes stuck in our mouths, conversation was difficult; later it would be impossible.

It took me several minutes to get accustomed to breathing through a thin tube. I let the oxygen trickle into my mouth until my cheeks were puffed out with the pure oxygen, and then I'd breathe in. As I looked around, everyone seemed to be having the same difficulty. Except for the pilot. Having been up to 25,000 ft. once that day, he apparently felt that he was an old pro and didn't hook up till the plane reached 18,000 ft.

From 18,000 ft. the ground looks strange and unreal. Most of the color which you would expect to see is replaced by a cold gray. Thin clouds that looked like wisps of ice made things seem even more unreal.

At 20,000 ft. the wind rushing into the cabin has a different sound — a higher pitched whistle instead of the usual roar. The lower pressure and thinness of the atmosphere gave me an airy bloated feeling. Climbing at over 1,000 ft. per minute, the Cessna reached altitude in just under 40 minutes. However, we remained at that altitude for over one hour.

The temperature was well below zero. The cold whipped in the open door, driven by the 175 mph speed of the aircraft. My legs grew numb. The five of us sat and sucked on the oxygen lines as if they contained pure ambrosia.

My altimeter still showed 20,000 ft., but it hadn't been working properly lately. Anyway, as long as I could see the ground in freefall, the trees rushing up would paint a graphic picture of my altitude and tell me when to pull my ripcord. If you have to depend entirely on your altimeter to tell you how high you are above the ground and when to pull, you are likely to dig yourself a hole on impact if something goes wrong.

The plane turned onto jumprun. Ed threw off his blanket, nodded to us and began to sight along the edge of the door to the dropzone far below. Still sucking on his tube of oxygen, he made thumb motions to Skippy up front who relayed the direction of turn to the pilot. Looking over Ed's shoulder I could see the target area: four miles down, a bit ahead and to the right.

One small ten degree turn and two minutes more and we would be directly over our exit point. Excitement began to build. Just two more minutes.

I got on my knees to unhook my oxygen, then passed it up front for Skippy to stow out of the windblast. As I awaited Ed's command to exit, dizzyness came over me like a cold fever. My head throbbed and my stomach turned. Ed made circular motions with his hand to the left; my head moved with his hand. The two minutes had passed and despite his repeated requests for a ten degree left turn, we had continued straight ahead and up; missing the exit point by over a mile. Ed wanted another pass; I wanted some oxygen. Still, instead of a hard bank and a quick pass we began a slow sweep to the right, out over the Gulf of Mexico. I suddenly lost all of my energy. I knew I needed some oxygen, and quick.

Others had their problems, too. When Ed shifted in the door to spot, Tim slid over to watch and double check. He braced his hand on the open door sill where it froze almost immediately. Meanwhile, thinking that we would soon be around for another jumprun I borrowed "drags" of oxygen from Don and Ed and waited for the plane to turn.

But for some reason the pilot refused to turn the aircraft. He sat hunched over the controls, dark glasses, his parka, and oxygen mask shielding his face. He hadn't hooked up his oxygen until 18,000 ft. and was now floating in the mental confusion of hypoxia. He probably understood what the signals meant, but couldn't relate them to turning the aircraft. We were at 25,000 ft.

Unable to figure out why Ed was wasting time, Skippy pushed back to the door. "What the goddamn hell is going on? Let's go!"

Wordlessly Ed pointed down to the gray waters of the Gulf of Mexico; then out to the receding coastline of Texas. Skippy took one look and returned up front to convince the pilot to turn.

I had a strange floaty kind of feeling: somehow I felt more like a spectator than a participant in this crazy game of getting the aircraft back over land.

I watched nature unfold a panorama of conditions at 25,000 ft. The most noticeable thing was the ice. With the onset of hypoxia the cold had ceased to bother me. But ice was everywhere. My chest and lap were covered with a light frost of moisture frozen out of my breath. All of the metal fittings on my chute and boots had grown snowy beards of frost. Ed had icicles frozen on his chin from his running nose. It was like the winter scenes in "Dr. Zhivago".

Around us the thin air seemed to turn darker. Below, the waters of the Gulf were an unpleasant black, spotted by soft cotton puffs of clouds.

Inside appeared even more unreal. Don sat blue-lipped and silent, sucking on an oxygen tube with the intense concentration of a hash smoker seeking release. He held the frozen hand of Tim who was now curled on the floor crying words I couldn't understand. The inside of the cabin was done in a soft yellow fabric, fuzzy like a blanket. The instrument panel was the only thing alive, it seemed. Its gauges registered four hundred feet of climb per minute and a slow motion bank to the left. The cold surrounded me.

Oxygen — who ever misses it? Here I was dying without it. Man, what a gas...had to get some air, and soon. But Skippy was arguing with the pilot and I couldn't break in to convince them to give me my mask. Besides, I didn't have enough wind to whistle, much less shout. Tim was still curled up in a tight ball. His shaking was causing the wing tips to quiver in harmony. Ed was still trying to get the plane turned and Skippy had quit talking and was pounding the pilot on the back and shoulder. It was like an oldtime movie.

Don gave me a drag from his tube and I laid down and shut my eyes. I was unable to think sitting up. Slapping me, Don peered closely into my face. He stuck his oxygen in my mouth while he tried to get someone up front to pass my mask back to me.

Shaking so hard he could hardly talk, Tim addressed the world in general: "I'm freezing, really I'm freezing...I can't take much more...I'm goddamn freezing to death. We have got to go out or down...I don't care which...I'm freezing."

We turned, but in a circle.

By then I couldn't care less. Don handed me my oxygen equipment. As I fumbled with the tubing which had become stiff with the cold, the plane began to return to course. Unable to hook up the oxygen with my numb hands, it seemed like a good idea in my addled brain to remove my gloves. Working in slow motion, I finally got the line plugged in and secured.

Then came the problem of putting my gloves back on. It just couldn't be done. I didn't have enough coordination to clap my hands together. I knew that I wanted to put them on, but couldn't figure out how to make my hands obey the commands of my brain. The effort was making me dizzy. My fingernails were blue, which struck me as funny. Attempting a stern frame of mind I tried to will my hands to work. I got my gloves on only to discover that I couldn't feel them. Further, the exercise had worn me out so I laid back down, thinking that perhaps if I didn't move I could resupply my blood with the needed oxygen.

Meanwhile, Ed and Skippy somehow got us pointed toward the drop zone. I don't remember much of what went on. I do remember my altimeter swinging wildly from 22,000 to 25,000 ft., with the intermittent buzzing of the plane's stall indicator warning device for punctuation.

Suddenly Ed unplugged his oxygen and said, "Jump run." Tim seemed to come out of shock. Don unplugged and turned to me, "Are you OK?"

"Yeah. Be glad to get some air..."

"You sure you're OK now?"

"Yes...Hell yes, if you think I'm going to stay in this plane you're crazy."

We unhooked and waited. The nightmare repeated itself. The pilot refused or couldn't make the final corrections necessary for us to reach the drop zone. We needed still another turn.

When we realized we couldn't jump yet, we spent the next several moments hooking up life-giving oxygen lines with clumsy hands. By now we were all suffering from the cold and lack of oxygen. But for some unfathomable reason, no one considered going back down.

Except Tim. His frozen hand had thawed enough to really hurt. In addition, he was getting the full force of the freezing wind across his body. There was an expression of hurt on his face that was total and complete. He leaned toward Don and spoke a voice that wavered for control. "I'm hurting bad. I think my hand is frozen. You've got to convince them that I'm hurt." His voice broke. "Make them understand...I'm hurt...We've got to get out or go down..."

Don didn't reply. He held Tim's frozen hand between his own and kept nodding his head, like a mechanical Santa in a store window.

Finally hooked up, we all sat immobile, content just to be still and breathe. Then, in a rushing panic, the implications of our inaction hit me. Pulling off my mask I began to pound on the pilot's back and scream, "Turn this sonofabitching airplane around! Turn around...!"

Don grabbed my fist and said crisply, "Shut up." The pilot didn't even glance around.

Dizzy from exertion and somewhat ashamed, I tried to explain, "Tim's right; we've got to go out or get down to some air."

Punctuating his speech with sips of oxygen, Don replied, "Next pass — we either go out — or take the plane down."

His eyeglass frames covered with frost, Ed spoke for the first time. He had removed his oxygen mask and stuck the tubing down his throat so that, with the bone whiteness of his frozen face, he resembled a hospital patient who wasn't going to make it. "What the hell — we've made it this far — let's go one more pass — then jump."

No reply was made or expected, so we each turned back to our own problems. Skippy and Ed worked in a team to get the airplane back around over the field. Skippy would relay Ed's hand instructions to the pilot and prod him into carrying them out. Completely absorbed with pain, Tim sat and shivered convulsively while Don sat like a mother hen over the two of us. I had returned to my prone eyes-shut position to wait. The time had to come when we would exit — get out in freefall where there was plenty of air.

My mind began to wander crazily: Don't trust airplanes. All you need is some air and a parachute and zingo, *you're* an airplane. Boy, from this high — just like a jet airplane — whoosh, with clouds hitting you in the face. Clouds? Now is the time for all good men to come to the aid of their country and fellow man. With a silly smile, I opened my eyes and stared at Skippy who was slapping me in the face. He had stuffed the mouthpiece of his oxygen bag into his mouth. The bag expanded and contracted with his breathing like an extra lung. There was ice in the bottom of the bag. He said to Don, "Should we let him jump?" Don shrugged; I smiled. Come hell or high water I am going to jump.

"Jump run," but nobody moved to disconnect their oxygen. I taxied to the door and prepared to take off, still happily sucking at my oxygen. Ed yelled "Cut!" the engine slowed, and the roar of the wind abated.

Ed hopped out into the blinding sky. I spit out my oxygen and took off after him — only to be caught by an iron fist of cold and flung tumbling. A slow roll on my back silhouetted the airplane which perversely seemed to be falling up, white oxygen masks streaming in the wind. Grabbing air I arched and stabled out, excitement rushing through my veins like ice water. Outstretched on the air, the other jumpers floated. Hands at sides, I dipped my head and air roared by as I dove down to them. They loomed up like overstuffed man-birds, all wearing intense grins. Skippy sailed past, his boots covered with frost. I turned and followed him. He turned to face me and we slid together for a perfect two-man hookup. My altimeter read 18,000 ft. 16,000 ft. to go till pull time.

A wave of uncomfortable lassitude came over me. With mild curiosity I watched the rim of the world below go dark and narrow around me. The dark slowly closed in, leaving a large-ish spot of vision that rapidly grew smaller. It was as if I were falling into a black funnel toward the small end which was snapping shut in front of me.

Just before I went totally unconscious my mind unvoiced the realization of the "tunnel vision" phenomenon. There was nothing I could do. I passed out exactly when the tunnel snapped shut, at about 7,000 feet.

How much time goes by while you are unconscious? I aroused slowly, knowing I was skydiving, unconcerned about having just awakened from oblivion. I knew that something was wrong. Unable to focus on the particulars, I began a systems check.

I couldn't see my altimeter. In fact, nothing was visible except a diffuse bright glow. It was like looking at the sun through clouds. Was I falling on my back looking up at the clouds? If so, then I was falling upward because the light was getting brighter! What could cause this to happen?

Hmmmm, I can't relate to what is happening. I pull my ripcord chanting "When in doubt, whip it out." Opening shock saddles me into the parachute harness and a sharp pain, unnoticed before this, washes over me so that I cry out.

My head...no, my eardrums are exploding. I still can't see. I tear off my goggles and the suddenly visible ground is right below me. I am open over a Texas pasture. The grass is yellow and dry under the warm sun. It was the feeble reflection of the sun off this grass that I'd seen through my frozen goggles. It got brighter as I rushed toward it in freefall. Now my overwhelming feeling is pain in my eardrums. I let my arms drop to let observers on the ground know I am hurt, steering only enough to soften my landing.

Touchdown brought a blinding flash of pain to each part of my body that touched the ground...feet, then knees and hands. My hands burned. And my legs tingled. Too stiff to rise. Too pained to think. My hands were too cold to remove my helmet. My eardrums and eustachian tubes hurt badly. I stayed on my hands and knees, moaning and shifting my weight from hand to hand as the ground crew rushed up.

My hands eventually thawed out and I finally got warm. The tremendous change in air pressure from twenty-five thousand feet down to under one thousand feet in just over two minutes of freefall had put painful pressure on my eardrums. The hooded parka I wore under my helmet had sealed off my ears so that the pressures couldn't equalize. When it finally did, days later, the return of full hearing startled me with its volume. I spit up small amounts of blood from whatever had ruptured for several days.

Tim developed painful frostbite in his right hand. Skin peeled off his hand in sheets. His glass eye had frozen, frostbiting his eyelid. Don developed stomach cramps. While Ed didn't feel well for days, he and the other two had no serious problems.

The hazards of high-altitude jumps are serious enough that the United States Parachute Association has promulgated regulations to help ensure greater safety for participants. Experience in a high-altitude simulator pressure chamber is a must.

We thought we could handle it. We couldn't.

Pat Works, 1966

> "To follow the sun
>   And romp the clouds
>   And race the Wind"
>   *Charlie Straightarrow*

Mexican Madness with the ParaMatadors in Juchitlan, Jalisco. It seems invariably that when one first hears stories about Mexico, he usually stands there taking in the last gruesome detail and then says something like, "Oh well, that's almost as good as what happened to me in T.J. back in '67." But this one is different — *honest!*

Mexican Intrigue, that's what it was, Mexican Intrigue. See, there's this guy standing there, grinning, and casually telling me I'm going in there and fight the next bull. "But after all Senor, didn't we just jump into this bullring, now why do we have to fight the Toro?" Must be because he thinks that if we're skydivers, then we'll make good bullfighters. He hands us another beer. The crowd's cheering of the real matadors is diminishing as we swallow the last foamy dregs. I just toss my bottle into a corner and the gates in front of me open, we walk into the ring, amid the renewed cheers and shouts of the crowd. As we walk we are handed the capes. Thank God the alcohol seeps quickly into the blood in the late afternoon heat. We turn and face the opening where The Bull will appear and fan out into a Vee. I shake the cape, more like canvas than the soft flowing material I had expected. The door swings open. The crowd seems to quiet, perhaps it's only focusing my attention.

The Bull stomps into the ring. First, he looks towards us, then around the ring and immediately right back to us. A quick thought flashes through my mind — *Estamos en Mexico.* I move in on the Bull, shake the cape and shout, "Toro, Aha, Toro!" I've got his attention now. I steady myself for the first pass...

Hey, Hey, let's wait just a second, I'm getting way ahead of myself relating this thing back to you. Let me start by explaining who we are, and just what the hell a bunch of jumpers are doing in a bull ring in Mexico.

We are Rick Hinchman, Efren Perez, "Chepe" Perez, Adan Perez, Alfonso, Dan O'Leary and a cast of a few more, whose names I can't pronounce much less spell or I never knew formally, but without whose help it might never have gone down the way it did. The place was a town called Juchitlan, an hour's flying time from Guadalajara, in the state of Juchitlan, down in Mexico.

I first heard the tales of Juchitlan through an old jump buddy, Rick Hinchman, currently a medical student at Guadalajara. Rick was up in the States on one of his periodic trips North. He was bubbling over with this wild story about a demo into this bull ring where the jumpers actually fought a bull after they landed. This sounded like a bit too much to believe, I thought, but I went along as I listened. But as Rick continued, it began to sound better, *much better.* In fact, I could even almost see Hemingway himself sitting there in the stands, a Tequila Sunrise in one hand and his free arm wrapped around a Margarita. Rick went on painting word pictures of the town, the people and the jump. Almost before I realized it, I said, "When do we go?" I had locked myself in.

Rick picked it up, "Sometime around Mardi Gras I'll count on seeing you. I'll send the particulars." During the few months between September and February I met with Efren and his brother Adan several times at Elsinore and we began firming up the trip's many particulars, tying the thousand and one loose ends. Finally January drew to an end. Efren and Adan set off on the two thousand mile trip by truck. I made it down to Tijuana and boarded an Aero Mexico flight to Guadalajara.

Rick and Dan O'Leary, another medical student, met me at the airport, armed only with a bottle of Suaza Commeritive, Mexico's finest liquor or best grade of antifreeze, depending whether you are man or machine. This was January 31st. The demo was scheduled for the fourth of February, so we had some spare time on our hands. Rick and Dan took it upon themselves to get me acclimatized. We spent the next few hectic days and nights in hard preparation — daily doses of street corner cuisine, rural fiestas, long nights of tequila, dark-eyed muchachas and not too few Mexican songs sung in Irish brogue.

The evening of the third we met with Efren and Adan, and for the first time, met the rest of our "team." There would be six of us jumping into the ring. Rick, Efren, Adan, "Chepe" Perez, a Major in the Mexican Army, and Alfonso, another Mexican Army officer and, oh yeah, me. We'd fly in from Guadalajara in a Cessna 206, buzz the town to announce ourselves, then climb to altitude and make two or three passes. Chepe and Alfonso on the first and the rest of us on the second or third, whatever. Organization and good planning are the key to a good demo.

We spent the rest of the evening packing, bullshitting, telling jump stories and talking cape technique; good idea if you would rather get the bull than get the horn.

We ended the evening by producing a bottle of moonshine tequila Rick and I had found back up in the hills the day before. The booze proved to be safe; at least, I wasn't blind when morning came.

The morning of the fourth seemed to be one of the longest mornings I had spent since waiting for my Army discharge, afternoon reminded me of waiting to graduate from college, but finally everyone showed up around three o'clock and we headed off for the airport. The adventure had really and finally gotten underway. We expected to hit Juchitlan about an hour or so before sunset. Since there is really no one to notify in Mexico about when or where you are going to jump, our main concerns at the airport revolved around readying the plane, briefing the pilot (incidently, he had never flown jumpers before, and probably had never seen any before either) and wondering if we should stash some beer in our jumpsuits for when we landed.

Standing around in an International Airport with a jumpsuit and rig on is really kind of a laugh, especially when you aren't quite sure what the natives and tourists are saying but you've got a good idea about what they are thinking — Sorry ma'am, they only give parachutes to passengers in First Class, bye now.

We took off behind a 727, and sat back for the flight, another fifty-minute eternity. We came in low over the hills and headed up a long valley. Chepe saw it first. "There's Juchitlan!" We made several low passes and I got a glimpse of the target.

"Christ, you couldn't even get a tennis court in that sucker," I thought, "and no alternates either."

Rick looked and grinned then he said, "Told you it was tight, didn't I?"

"No Brown Material," I said.

We climbed and came in on jump run; suddenly, there were three people spotting. I was next to the pilot and couldn't see anything, so I kept giving him rights. Chepe turned around and gave a cut. He and Alfonso disappeared out the door. We circled and watched. Both of them went right 'in,' perfectly. We were losing daylight and time, so we decided all four of us, Rick, Efren, Adan, and myself would go on the next pass. Rick and I would do a two-man. We hit four grand and headed in.

Rick spotted. Cut. Efren and Adan tumbled out. Rick looked at me like "Well?" and I yelled "Go!" We rolled out and I looked for Rick to start for the pin. Then I remembered, the *smoke!* I reached around and pulled the thing, then looked for Rick, then the ground, again for Rick, then the ground, at the horizon, at the ground, at the bull ring, which was the ground, saw the whites of their little brown eyes, gave a quick wave and dumped it out. Rick opened to one side and just a bit lower. The smoke was a dud, wouldn't you know it, but I could see Efren and Adan make it two more "in" perfectamente.

Rick and I weaved in for the target. Rick on a PC, me on my Piglet. Both of us looked like we were in a good position to make it. Rick hooked in beautifully. I started in — No brakes, No wind, No low turns — I ended up just outside the ring. Oh well, five out of six in, but why me?

People were coming from everywhere, helping me back into the ring. Then the six of us joined up in the ring. The crowd went wild. After a few minutes of the limelight we exited to the stands for some liquid refreshment and were met by O'Leary, who had patiently acted as ground control and guardian of the moonshine.

I guess that sort of explains what and how and who had gotten into this thing so...

I tensed for the first pass, dangling the cape off to my left. The cape is the key, I remembered; you move the cape, not yourself. "Ah ha Toro, Ah ha!" I moved in closer, his head dropped, then suddenly he rushed me, I shook the cape and he headed right for it. At the last instant I pulled it aside and he brushed on by me to the next 'Para-matador.'

The contest between men and beast continued and we all became bolder. Chepe was first to grab the Bull's tail and soon Adan, Efren and Hinchman were astride El Toro, the fight was becoming a circus. Then it happened. O'Leary was moving in on the bull, when he suddenly charged, goring Dan with his horn in the chest and throwing him back out of the way. We all froze. Dan stood clutching himself. Slowly he pulled his hand away and for a moment seemed afraid to look, then his eyes slowly dropped to his chest...Nothing; no hole, anyway.

He stiffened, drew himself up and charged the Bull, his own head lowered now. He caught the Bull near the shoulder, simultaneously grabbing his forefeet. The Bull was down, successfully gored by an Irishman, undoubtedly a first in bullfight history. We all jumped on the Bull and held him down as the crowd yelled, "El Gordo, El Gordo, El Gordo, Ole El Gordo!" Dan O'Leary had been renamed.

That night we were the honored guests of the town of Juchitlan. We wined, dined, danced and sang around the town square with the entire populace until the last reveler went home and the long purple creepers of dawn streaked across the sky. Then we fell into our pickup and headed back for Guadalajara.

Pound, Pound, Pound, Pound, "Hey 'Dirty Billy,' are you awake?"

"No, I'm having a nightmare, I must be!"

"Dirty Billy, it's me, Joe."

"Well," I said, "I guess I'm awake, what day is it?"

"Tomorrow." says Joe.

"That's what I was afraid of," says I, "What time is it?"

"Almost noon," from Joe.

"Oh yeah, well look, I know I said I'd teach you guys to jump at eight in the morning, so I guess it's too late to jump, Good night," says I.

"Too late to jump," says Joe, "But not too late to teach, right Teach?"

"I was afraid you'd think of that, why, just tell me, if you medical students have to be so smart, why can't you be dumb? OK, let's go, is everyone here?" I ask, as I try to hide a monster green hangover in the closet.

"Yeah, since eight, how'd the jump and bullfight go?" inquired Joe.

"I think we won, but I'm guessing, some little rascal named Tequila has been putting funny notions in my head lately."

Our jump stories and rap sessions of the last three days had generated enough interest with Rick's classmates that five of them had decided to make their first jumps. So we began First Jump Course, Mexican Style: Five students, a T-10 with a Stevens Cutaway System, reserve, black board, tree limb for malfunction procedures and a pickup truck for PLF's.

By five that afternoon I was amazed. After training hundreds of students, I found that this was the best group I had ever been associated with. Here they were doing their own critiques, pin checks and packing. After an oral exam, we broke class for the day and prepared for the morning.

We got an early start for Magdellena Airport near the town of Tequila (God, that's a popular place) with hopes of renting an air taxi to put our students out of. We were in luck and in a short time we had the door off a battered 206, marked a target in a nearby cow pasture with a cheapo canopy, and put O'Leary to work holding the windsock on the DZ. Luckily we managed to borrow another canopy and reserve from the Mexican Army bunch, rig up another Stevens System and voila! We began jumping our students two at a time, Rick and I both jump-mastering. Each pass brings more and more spectators until the field is nearly full of kids, farmhands and interested bystanders — Whuffos, Latin-style. The last Show of the Gringo Barnstormers draws to an end as late afternoon descends with the last student and a two-man over Tequila. We pack ourselves, our students, cervesa, and tequila into the pickup and head off into the sunset, five new brothers initiated into the sky.

Adios till next year,
Billy Bishop

Note: Billy Bishop, (Dirty Billy, as his friends knew him), was killed in an automobile accident near Guadalajara, Mexico, on September 15, 1976.

–Dirty Billy Bishop, Starcrest, July-August 1976

The Fable of the Godfrogs. Once and then there was, of all things, a frog. Not your usual bumpy or horney frogs, but a nice slick-type frog by the name of Clyde.

Now Clyde achieved his standing as the Godfrog while I was still a tadpole. So the first days of the Godfrogs, as the entire group of slick frogs came to be called, are somewhat muddled in my mind.

Anyway, near as I can tell, Clyde was brought up in the waters along the runway of old Beeline DZ, just 40 feet from the rock-hard target. The terrible tadpole fear he had of the roar of the airplanes would always turn to ecstasy and hopping wonder at the pop and glide of the pretty, oh-so-beautiful, waltzing of the colorful canopies as they passed overhead to crash on the ground.

More than anything else in the world, Clyde wanted to be a parachute. He dreamed and he schemed. And he figured that he could do it. After all, he had made it from a fish to a frog, so why not from a frog to a parachute? Frog logic at its finest, pure and simple.

So he set at it. He figured and pondered. He compared the waltzing glide of the parachutes to their unfortunate demise into a limp nothing. They reminded him of the windsock which always died with he wind. But careful study showed him that it wasn't the wind that killed canopies, but rather their contact with the ground. This was proven beyond doubt when on several occasions Clyde distinctly heard terrible screams, curses and moans of pain when the canopies crashed into the ground. The fact that the wind sock was snapping with life added further proof to this theory.

On his way one day to do a postmortem on a recently killed canopy, Clyde discovered the People-Totems. Up to this point, he had naturally assumed that the limp objects which dangled beneath the beautiful parachutes were ballast — deadweight and nothing more. (This theory is still adhered to in some government circles.)

At this point, things become rather fuzzy insofar as frog lore goes. it is a pity that so many frog facts have been lost in the mind-smashing quivers of frog fear. For when grasped by one of the People-Totems, Clyde went into the active stage of frog fear, which is to say he was so scared that he wet his pants. He also wet copiously on the People-Totem at the same time.

And thus it was that frog fear led to the discovery of the 7200-foot Swoop and the foundation and propagation of the Godfrogs. Because shortly after Clyde did his frog fear bit, the wrath of the People-Totem caused him to be thrown with vigor out the open door of a jump aircraft at 7200 ft.

Once in freefall, Clyde really began to work on becoming a parachute. while he enjoyed the fun of freefall, he nevertheless felt it his duty as a frog to avoid becoming a flat frog as a result of sudden contact with the ground.

So as he fell, he thought. And as he thought he got the frog fear which looked so beautiful from the ground that people began to copy the effect using smoke as a substitute. In order to think better, he stabled out. He was seen to do so by an old Frenchman who stole the idea and named it the French Frog.

Then in the midst of near disaster (89 feet) came the glimmer of the idea which was later to make Clyde the Godfrog. Putting his hands to his sides, he started into the Froggian Swoop. Now since the initial stages of the Froggian Swoop cause a surprising amount of horizontal displacement, people types on the ground were heard to remark, "Man, wouldya watch that crazy frog! He's flat trackin'!"

And thus, the "track" position was born. Unfortunately the newspapers got Clyde's name wrong so today the "track" is miscalled the Max-Track, when it should be called the Clyde-Track.

Anyway, performing a perfect sequence of swoop-arch-upswing-touchdown, Clyde landed right in front of a group of young frogs who were protesting the increasing use of frog legs as a food item, and the term "demonstration jump" was born.

More importantly, however, the Godfrogs were born.

The young demonstrating frogs hailed Clyde as their leader and gave him the title "Skrow" which roughly translates into English as "God, did you see that guy? This we gotta try!" which is usually shortened to "god" with a small "g" so as not to stir up the religious tribes.

Clyde, feeling that it is better to give than to receive, refused the title by shouting "Skrow You!" which was gladly accepted and followed, creating many tadpoles on the spot.

* * *

Time passed and only the frog who was called J.C. remained of the original group. Clyde died when he tried a low snap roll over the graveyard. He caught a tombstone which turned out to be his own.

Many bad things befell the rest of Clyde's first flock of followers. Iron Tooth, the Hungarian frog, broke his back. Nick Frog blew his cool on a demo and had to be buried as a result. Hawk Frog lost an eye and had to be renamed Hawk-Eye Frog. Another member of the tribe broke his leg and thus became known as Hop.

After Clyde's death, J.C. Godfrog came into power. Under his reign all Godfrogs wore black hats and indulged in the consumption of much beer. Further, the healing rites of the full moon and speed streak were perfected to an unheard-of, but often seen, degree. Because of these developments, a joint body of the Nerds and Feebles dubbed the Godfrog clan "outlaws." Things went from bad to terrible.

The Godfrog clan continued to engage in the practice of things which infuriated the Nerds and Feebles no end — three-frog stars from 3500-ft., low-pull contests, low-swoop contests...

The Falcons Against Anything (F.A.A.) arrived on the scene and ate every freefall frog they could catch, claiming that air space was for the birds and God had never planned for frogs to fly in any case. The Godfrogs hotly denied having ever flown in a case, much less *any* case. Being democratic, the Godfrogs delegated Doc Frog to head up the newly organized Protective Cover-All (P.C.A.) for freefall frogs.

Then light (not to mention Joy) was spread over the scene with the arrival of Happy Harry, the Hippy Frog, and his chick Joy. Their presence generated a mood of peace and contentment, what with their motto being: "Make Love, Not War." Unfortunately, however, Joy was buried in accordance with local health laws. Happy Harry burned his draft card in protest, claiming that she had *always* smelled bad.

* * *

Then, as it has a way of doing, considerably more time passed. The mountains didn't get any older, but things changed as if they had.

Newcomers came. They looked and listened and learned. We taught them because, somehow, we have always known that teaching spreads the joy faster.

And the Godfrogs watched too. They grew and changed with the times. Fast-learning new arrivals tested new skills. Happy Harry made over a thousand jumps, developed the chronic 1,000 jump surlies, burned out on skydiving, and hung it up. J.C. Godfrog had less and less influence until at last he, too, disappeared.

Meanwhile, a newcomer was following in the footsteps of Clyde and Harry. A callow, green upstart by the name of Carlos Gene jumped into the scene. Looking back at the glories and mistakes of past Godfrogs, C.G. stumbled blindly into the present. With him he brought lightweight gear, tennis shoes, soft helmets and ram air parachutes.

In order to get ahead, he graduated from a relative work seminar, then headed south, following the yellow brick road to California where, he has heard, is where it's at...

So one day our hero, C.G. Godfrog, is hippy-te-hoppin' along the yellow brick road, wearing a suave new frogskin pair of jeans. His worn webbed Addidas mark him as a frog of considerable depth and experience.

Though life had been good to C.G., problems of his psyche marred his overall self-image of suave, cool, collected Bon Vivant Skygod skydiver. He felt there was something missing in his life — and he knew just what it was. He was having trouble getting laid. Tears welled up in his eyes as he contemplated the inequity of it all. Blinded by grief he moved forward, heedless of a large rock in his path. Danger lurked. He stubbed his toe.

With a croak of outrage and pain C.G. hopped madly in circles on one foot, clutching his stone-bruised foot in one hand while shaking the other heavenward in contemptuous defiance to the unjust gods who not only had meted out serious uglies to him, but had now punctured his left Addidas as well.

It was more than C.G. could stand. He wailed in rage, shouting to the wind: "My Addidas...my foot! You've gone and done it now! I'm gonna burn a church...I'll put a rubber check in the collection plate. I'll..."

Cut off in mid-blasphemy, C.G. was deafened by the thundering roar of an 18-wheel Kenworth semi which ran him down, squishing him flatter than a pancake across several cracks in the yellow brick road. Nine massive sets of tires gave him a close intimacy with the roadway that C.G. would have thought to be impossible.

The hot sun glared down at the aftermath. The Kenworth kept on truckin', and C.G. was laying on the roadway, pressed real close to the warm concrete, tire tracks across his back, soaking up the sun's rays and meditating on skydiving and swooping.

After an undetermined amount of time had passed, C.G. Godfrog was startled from his deep and holy sleep of meditation by the sacred mantra screamed in his ear by a mischievous imp of a first-jump student. She screamed those powerful words which have snatched the quivering attention of skydivers over time: "Pull! Pull! Pull your reserve, for God's sake!"

C.G. jumped up and gave her a froggy stare. "Don't scare me like that," he croaked. Then he glanced speculatively at her. "Want to get your SCR, pretty lady? I'll be happy to put the load together myself. You just lay there and remember the most important rule: Beer! Are you interested?"

Sizing C.G. up as a flaky, horney Skygod, she calculated that she could gain some much desired swooping experience by playing his silly game. "Sure!" she purred, staring boldly into his eyes. "I always like to get ahead..."

Suddenly six voices raised in unison from the shadows: "Head? Who said head? I'll take some of that!"

So it was that they had enough for the load, and prepared for the SCR attempt. The sacred ritual was followed:

The student was first instructed by the Ego Priests of New SCR's and told to fear not, that their skill would earn her the coveted merit badge, plus a kiss pass and a chance to get together later, plus help opening the beer. Her instructions were simple and direct:

1. Don't make any mistakes.
2. We're thirsty. Don't forget the beer.

And it went well. And they were happy. And they multiplied. As they all learned together, their happiness grew until giggles could be heard even in freefall.

The excitement of the challenging skydives they made was increased by their plans for more skydives to be made. Several imaginative frog-thinkers thunk up ever new ways to fly. Three-dimensional formations...even four-dimensional formations!

The average intelligence of jumping frogs soared to new heights as a result of the demands placed upon their minds and memories by sequential formations and multiple maneuver practice dives into the frog pond.

Soon more novice swoopers — tadpoles — joined the fun in the air. The newcomers learned fast from the more experienced Godfrogs. The happiness and good vibes quotient increased along with the fun factor of the dives.

The reintroduction of magic allowed the Godfrogs to build formations that looked like flowers. Practice in the art of freefall flower-building enabled individual frog flyers to transform themselves into individual flower petals while flying into a formation. They won every flower show they entered with their specialty, the 75-frog carnation.

Everyone prospered because the TV networks bought the Godfrogs' jumping story for much gold. Several frogs even won key parts on the famous frog show, The Muppets. The wealth was used to pay for jumps and new frog suits for swooping.

New, colorful jumpsuits helped the beauty of their flight by allowing frogs to fly like butterflies. With a really big frog suit, any frog was able to do less more slowly on every jump — and in living color!

Frog-eyed scribes recorded the fun the freefall frogs had. Teachers studied the condition of frog joy and related it to longtailed tadpoles. The pathway to perfect flight and good skydiving was written with bright, sunny words on clear-shot blue-sky paper. Thus, the attitude of joy became available to any frog who would listen to the music of the sky or read the words of the sacred Book of Frog: *The Art of Freefall Relative Work.* Every Godfrog, both old and new, learned to work together to maintain and build up the good vibes required for long-term sky fun.

Life was good to the Godfrogs until, one day, death came swooping from the sky. Great wings blocked out the sun. Terrified froglins looked up to see a great falcon snatching frogs from the sky. His talons held entire formations as more frogs were drawn with horrible certainty into his craw.

The falcon wheeled and circled in the sky. Tadpoles and godfrogs, young and old, perished under beating wings that filled the sky's four corners, from heaven to earth. Mothlike, to meet the flame of their destruction, the frogs plunged headlong into a fiery falcon gullet.

In the midst of this destruction, C.G. Godfrog jumped up. "Tell me who you are, you feathered turkey, and why do you bother us!?"

Opening its horrible mouth, the creature spoke: "I am called Time, destroyer of people and frogs. I wait ever ready for that appointed hour that faces everyone. I am Lord of fire and death, of wind and moon and waters. To you I am double horseshoe malfunctions, main-reserve entanglements, collisions and other nasty, fatal stuff. All who see me and cannot answer my questions must die horribly. Prepare to die, frog!"

C.G. gulped and hopped back, his eyes bugging out of his head. He croaked, "Not so fast there, you obnoxious windbag. First, ask the questions!"

The falcon asked:

"What is the road to heaven?"

And C.G. answered:

"Truthfulness."

"How does Man find happiness?"

"Through right conduct."

"What must he subdue in order to escape grief?"

"His mind."

"When is a man loved?"

"When he is without vanity."

"Of all the world's wonders, which is the most wonderful?"

"That no man, though he sees others dying all around him, believes that he himself will die."

"How does one reach true religion?"

"Not by argument. Not by scriptures and doctrines; they cannot help. The path to religion is trodden by the saints."*

With the last correct answer, the terrible falcon disappeared into a dark cloud, hurling thundering threats of revenge behind him.

C.G., of course, was a hero to the saved Godfrogs. He was rewarded by having his parachute packed for him free for the rest of his life. And he and his froggy friends lived happily ever after in the big frog pond in the sky.

*Adapted from the Mahabharata, 500 B.C.

Pat Works, 1962-1978

Mass Jump. The world's largest parachute meet (Z-Hills Thanksgiving, 1972) also saw the world's largest mass exit. 162 nervous RWers and one 6-ft. frog left six monster airplanes at the scary altitude of 3500 ft. The pilots flew in tight formation and in freefall the sky looked like a beehive. There were several small stars built. The only fatality was C.G. Godfrog, a 6-ft. bright green, stuffed 10-lb. tree frog who opened too high and drifted off into the alligator-infested swamp. C.G. was a beloved member of the Godfrogs 10-man team. His competition experience included the invention of the Swoop.

RWu, January 1973

C.G. Returns. Comes this mysterious letter. "Thought you would like to know that I ran into C.G. Godfrog the other day. Seems somebody gave him a bad spot at Z-Hills and he landed his cheapo in a swamp where he was rescued by some Zephyrhills swamp frogs. I guess they were pretty impressed to have such a celebrity drop in, even though most swamp frogs don't know much about skydiving except what they watch from their quagmires.

"Anyhow, C.G. taught them all about swoops and other neat stuff like that, so now a bunch of swamp frogs are logging swoops in their frog logs. C.G. says they didn't know much about skydiving, but they really turned him on to the Bayou Boogie. He used to sit around on toadstools, but down there they use mushrooms; 'puts a whole new perspective on things,' says C.G.

"C.G. heard about a 30-man attempt at Elsinore and thumbed his way out here. As it turned out the Hueys didn't show so they used two Beeches and two Howards. We thought it was a 27-man, but Ray Cottingham's pix the next week showed that it was only a 25-man with two guys breaking wrists less than half a second after a grip was lost, and another less than a second after that. Well, C.G. was pretty upset about that so he split back to Z-Hills for a Big Swamp Stomp they have planned for Easter."

Love,

Father Farkle

RWu, March 1973

"Sunward I've climbed and joined
the tumbling mirth
Of sun-split clouds..."
   "High Flight"
      John Gillespie Magee, Jr.

The First Relative Work Festival. A beautiful new event happened...a lot of people who love to jump outa airplanes in groups drove a buncha miles to be with their people in Richmond, Indiana on September 9 & 10, 1972. A hundred-twenty RWers jumped at the first RW Festival...there were no prizes or competition, there were no judges or hassles, just RW for the sake of RW. The City of Richmond hosted it, Tag Taggart honchoed it and *everybody* loved it.

The city charged admission to whuffo cars and made several thousands of dollars to support the Boys' Club. The RW people made several big stars out of a Twin Beech and a DC-3. All the self-styled, super-hero RW types made three tries at a 30-man and succeeded in FUBAR-ing all three in front of the lens of Carl Boenish. Everyone else just giggled and went up and made 18-mans and other big round things with no problems on "garbage" loads. Saturday night saw bonfire, boogie and the most beautiful RW films ever seen — Carl Boenish's great flicks of Jerry Bird's All Stars flying at the XI World Meet.

I believe the Richmond RW Festival was wonderful for the sport. The fact that 120 people from all over the Eastern half of the USA (plus California, Australia and Montana) came reflects the tremendous interest in good ol' RW jumping. I doubt that any recent local competition drew as many people. A lot of people had a lot of fun. More people oughta have old-fashioned RW Festivals, trackin' contests and Scrambles.

RWu, Fall 1972

More music-making at Hinckley where an 11-man accordion was built recently — sans jumpsuits. Plain old ordinary accordions built the hard way — start with a 2-man, add to ends only, with jumpsuits and regular "para"-phernalia — were getting dull. Sure was cold on the way up.

RWu, September 1972

Unplanned Twenty-six (26!)-Man Star at XI World Meet. It just happened. It was supposed to be mainly just a free, fun mass jump/star attempt. Three monster helicopters chugged up to about 11-grand and 28 RWers jumped at once from both sides. 25 for the star plus 3 cameramen. It built to 22 and broke. Three people entered on this line to make 25 as they flew it back together (*can you imagine trying to fly a 25-man line??*). One of the cameramen got antsy, couldn't stand it any longer and entered. It broke at about 5-grand and everyone did a severe track. The beautiful thing about it was the fact that it was a true RW-USA star...Army guys, East Coasters, Southerners, Mid-Westerners, Californians, etc. Everyone got together...and got together.

There was also an 11-man "everywhere" star including people from many countries. It was reported that the East German Team made their country's first ten-man after several tries.

RWu, September 1972

Jonathan's Creator Tries it Himself. Author Richard Bach *(Jonathan Livingston Seagull, Nothing By Chance),* who received an RW Certificate of Merit from *RWu* on behalf of Jonathan several years ago, decided to try his own wings in freefall. He took up jumping in Florida this winter, progressed rapidly into relative work (flying an SST with Strato-Star), and wrote in a letter to *RWu* after participating in his first 10-man that "The great thing about RW to me now is the sovereignty and independence of each jumper *choosing* to reach out in the sky and touch and touch and be touched by another. In the air or on the ground, that's exciting!"

RWu, June 1975

"...the most important thing in living is to reach out and touch perfection in that which they most loved to do, and that was to fly..."
  Jonathan Livingston Seagull

***

There is always another destination, and, ultimately, it is the availability of everywhere that make the plane a hero, that makes flying miraculous. When Wendy, John and Michael finally got the hang of air travel, the bed-mantel route wasn't enough. "I say," said

John, "why shouldn't we all go out?"

And they did. And the prospect of the unknown wasn't all that frightening, even though Peter Pan hadn't bothered to show them how to stop, because "if the worst came to the worst, all they had to do was to go straight on, for the world was round, and so in time they must come back to their own window."

J. Barrie, "Peter Pan"

RWu, March 1973

Celebrity News Note. Famed Jonathan Livingston Seagull, who has gained 27 pounds eating royalties from his best-seller book, was reported to have moved to New York where he got his beak shortened and has a part-time job at the United Nations as surrogate Peace Dove.

"As an unlimited idea of fat, son, your whole body, from wing tip to wing tip, is hard to fly and lands harder," said Jonathan heavily.

RWu, March 1973

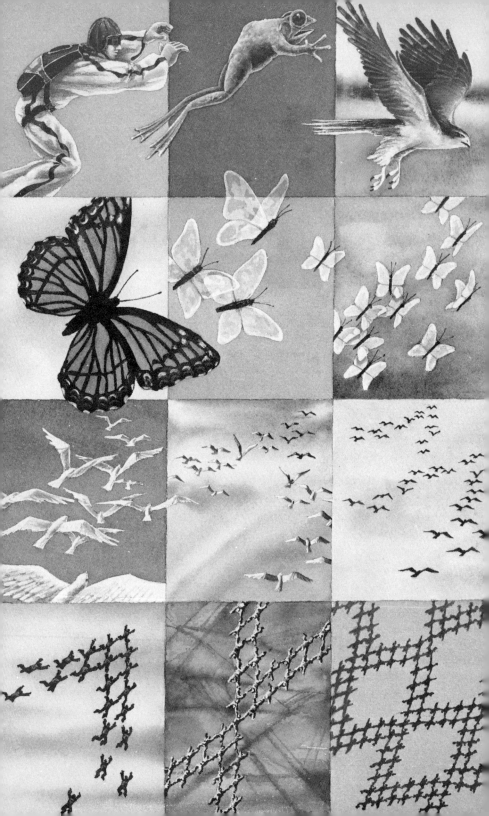

9

Sequential

Part I: Musings on Sequential...The Skydance Philosophy
You're always a one-man star. To build something bigger, you gotta do RW.

Why Sequential? Sequential Relative Work exists only because it is possible within the freefall environment. It is not the preconceived idea of any one group or individual. It is a natural step in the evolution of relative work. Sequential relative work is bounded only by the physical realities of freefall and our own skills and imagination. The sequence is the means. The joy of sequential is the flying necessary to accomplish it. Relative Work is a human possibility. A potential. Sequential is the pattern of the resulting *flow*.
Matt Farmer

Sequential Relative Work: Tempting Our Imaginations
The Concept. During the past few years, the art of relative work has been progressing at an amazing geometrical rate. All around the world on small drop zones, as well as on large ones, relative work has been rapidly expanding, limited only by the imagination of those involved. Everywhere jumpers have discovered that we, personally, have the ultimate control over all of our actions in freefall, even if some of these are not our intended actions.

Since a large majority of skydivers have become involved in this free-style form of relative work, it is inevitable that there has been a growing desire for a refreshing new concept in skydiving competition to test the freefall skills involved.

For November, 1976 the Third World Cup of Relative Work has evolved as a means to encourage international skydiving meetings where exchanges of new ideas will be highly persistent and most of all encourage progression within our sport. Due to the jump aircraft readily available in most countries around the world, the size of teams was established to include 4-Man teams. This will enable most of the teams to have as equal a chance as possible to practice for this competition.

In the past, all forms of parachuting and skydiving competitions have maintained the physical test as a constant, and scoring has been determined by maintaining time or distance as a variable. This has resulted in limiting the maximum performance of this test to a finite 0.00 seconds or centimeters. The events for the Third World Cup, however, have been designed so that time is a constant and scoring is determined by the number of points acquired during that allotted time.

This concept results in there being no limit for the maximum performance, as an infinite number of points are possible.

Exit requirements and restrictions have posed many problems for past relative work competitions. The split second decisions required of judges on speed events to determine exactly when the first jumpsuit has shown in the door when a no-show exit is required, has been a very difficult job at best. It has been harder to determine if that blob that piles out the door has anyone holding on to each other. These, along with the most serious drawback, that of continually battering the bodies of the skydivers, have inspired the World Cup organizers to remove all exit restrictions, as long as no-one's safety is jeopardized.

In determining the skydiving requirements for the World Cup, every effort has been made to establish a combination of events to test a multiple of relative work skills demonstrated by the skydivers. The exit and time to build the first formation is very important on each jump, and the quicker a team is able to perform this exercise, the better chance they have to score well. Once the first formation is finished, it is also of great importance to use the remaining freefall time to its fullest extent. On each jump a team will have a sequence of maneuvers to perform within the maximum working time, during which points will be scored for each correctly completed formation. All formations and intermediate requirements must be completed in the predetermined sequences as explained in the rules or scoring will stop.

The judging of the World Cup has been made as simple as possible. It is up to the judges to determine whether or not each formation has been completed correctly. It is not required that a completed formation be held for any length of time. There are no requirements governing symmetry or heading of the formations. Also, complete mirror images of the illustrated formations throughout the entire jump are acceptable. It is up to the competing team to execute the correct and complete required maneuvers in a manner that the judges will be sure that this has been achieved. A computer will be used to determine the elapsed time between judge's exit announcement and each additional call signifying each successfully completed maneuver. If a maneuver is recorded complete after the maximum working time has elapsed, no points will be scored for that completion.

The Events. The actual events, formations and sequences of maneuvers for the Third World Cup of RW have been carefully constructed in order to insure a great deal of variety from one jump to the next. The 4-Man and 8-Man events are basically identical in concept. The 4-Man has 35 seconds working time and 8-Man has 50 seconds.

The emphasis for the first four rounds is on "flying groups", or doing relative work with two or more jumpers gripped together as they fly from one formation into another. It is through the use of mandatory intermediate requirements between the specified static formations that this is accomplished. If there are no intermediate requirements indicated between formations, the team may choose any method to go from one formation to another. Also, a total break of grips is not necessary if this is the case.

Understanding exactly what is required, allowed, and not allowed during these specific intermediate maneuvers can be quite confusing. Hopefully this explanation will make everything perfectly clear. The mandatory intermediate requirements shown in the rules must be observed by the judges between the previous and following completed static formations. If this intermediate requirement shows two or more divers gripped together, then they must break from the previous formation gripped together. They must maintain this contact through the completion of the following formation. These divers gripped together may have to switch grips to form the necessary intermediate requirement, but they must not loose contact between themselves. If a team does not follow this procedure, such as a total separation occurring between two or more divers who should remain in contact with each other, scoring will stop until they rebuild the last completed formation and continue to work from there.

Once the intermediate requirement has been achieved, the divers must fly these sub-groups as they are until completion of the next formation, unless additional grip switches are necessary to complete the next formation after docking. In no case may contact be totally broken between the divers within each flying group. If this procedure is not followed, scoring will again stop until the intermediate requirement is rebuilt and the team progresses from there.

On the transitions requiring rotations of flying groups, such as turning and docking stairsteps, the turns may be in either direction on the horizontal plane.

The exact sequence of formations for rounds 5-10 will be drawn prior to the practice jumps at the meet site. The first formation for each of these rounds has been established. The random selection for the remainder of each round will be from the pools of formations established in the rules. There will be four additional formations to build after the pre-determined one in the 4-Man event and two additional ones in the 8-Man event. A total of all grips must occur before continuing on to build the next formation. All the additional formations must be performed in the order drawn from the pools, or scoring will stop. Again, it should be stressed here that it is up to the jumpers to make it evident to the judges on the ground that these maneuvers have been completed correctly.

The Dives. In the 8-Man event for rounds 1-4, two points will be scored for each correctly completed formation, and teams that complete the entire sequence correctly will score two bonus points for that jump. In rounds 5-10, three points will be scored for completing the entire sequence. In all the rounds in the 4-Man event, two points will be scored for each correctly completed formation.

In the case of a tie at first, second or third places, the tied teams will go into a Sudden Death jump-off. The competition will continue as in rounds 5-10 for one or more additional rounds. However, one additional formation per round will be added until there is a difference in the teams' scores so that the respective places can be decided. It is at this point that the advantages for the concept of limitless maximum performance can be truly appreciated.

The sequences of maneuvers for World Cup events were designed as fun dives for anyone to do at any time, as well as being a means of international competition. These dives will add a new freshness and challenge to our skydiving, but it should also be stressed that limiting our dives to include only these will quickly pop this new bubble. Mastering these dives will help establish basic skydiving skills which can serve as an important platform for infinite future skydiving possibilities.

Boom Or Bust. Will all this complexity lend itself to a reliable form of relative work competition? Time and a great deal of effort by a wide variety of people will tell. A foundation to work from has been established, and experience will test its worthiness.

As is often the case, the quality of the skydiving at this point is at a far more advanced state than the quality of the judging. It is for this reason that the judging has been simplified as much as possible. And it is for this same reason that the skydivers have been required to make it perfectly clear to the judges that they have completed the required maneuvers, even if it is not the most efficient method to do so.

The widespread use of video tape from a multiple of angles on the drop zone, and even in freefall, will greatly improve the judging. This will, in turn, allow the divers to be judged closer to their possible maximum performance, which will also be continually improving.

If the concept of the rules for the Third World Cup of Relative Work is to be successful in future national and international competitions, it will be necessary to change and improve the sequences of maneuvers to keep up with the progression of our sport, and to continue to challenge our abilities.

B.J. Worth, Canpara, August 1976, and Parachutist, July 1976

Progressive Sequential. The best way to learn sequential relative work is to practice it, of course. And the practicin' is as much fun as the "doin'." Here's an idea that will help you master the mystery of sequential easily — practice "Progressive Relative Work."

Progressive Relative Work is found in all phases of the RW arena. It is that outermost creative edge of a swoop where you test your imagination. We all do it. It evolves from the conscious act of pursuing perfect flight.

Two kinds of Progressive RW give *fast* increases in sequential skill: 1) no-contact sequential, and 2) four-man sequential. No-contact is, simply, sequencing from one formation to another on a dive without taking actual physical hand-grips with each other. It's a fun, challenging type of flying.

The most successful sequential teams have two things in common:

they do Progressive Relative Work, and they have a core which does four-man sequential RW. In many cases, that four-man core was the beginning of a larger team.

Learn four-man sequential first and you'll do better eight-man sequential quicker, cleaner, and in less time. In four-man, you fly every second. Importantly, four-man requires the same multi-dimensional levels of thinking and flow that eight-man (and larger) sequential requires.

You learn to do RW right out the door, subterminally. You learn to carry completed formations out the door. You learn to fly pieces together around the sky. You learn to fly sideways with elan. You learn to fly backwards with crisp aplomb. You learn how to rotate a wedge or a diamond for a clean dock whether you are point, tip or wing.

Additionally, it's easier to organize and there are more available aircraft for it. Try it, it works!

Aircraft. The type of airplane you jump from doesn't matter. However, be sure the pilot flies jump-run moving at least 75 mph. Subterminal relative work is easier with fast exit jump-runs. If you can emulate a DC-3's air speed on exit, your RW will be easier from any type of airplane (with the bonus of having few problems switching to different types of aircraft).

Air Speed. Faster air speed makes smooth relative work more possible by reducing or shortening subterminal time. Think of it...if exit speed is close to terminal velocity for flight-suited sequential relative workers, it means you can start flying better sooner!

If you learn right away to fly the Relative Wind on exit, your swoop is easier to control because the buoyancy of the air cushion from the earth-pushed wind of freefall stays more constantly controllable. One immediate benefit is being able to shoot clean subterminal back-ins.

Equipment. Because jumpsuits are very important to precise sequential RW, always jump a functional flight-suit...one made for sequential RW by an expert.

The rest of your equipment should include a light, reliable reserve and a main canopy weighing under 12 lbs. Piggyback systems are preferred by nearly all sequential relative workers.

Boots/shoes and helmet should be as lightweight as *you* feel are reasonable (unless there's a rule to the contrary).

More Isn't Better; or Quality vs. Quantity. Shortsighted relative workers understandably want to jump in *larger* groups out of *bigger* airplanes as quickly as they can progress from student status to Skygod.

Fine, but recognize that someday you'll have to do some four-man sequential to learn to be as good as you could be and probably already think you are.

Attitude. Give up all your inhibitions and all your beliefs that you can't fly. Touch the wind as though it is a part of your life. Know that it's all right for you to fly well, and let your subconscious self take over your flight plan.

Remember that in Progressive RW there is really no base and pin. There are divers, floaters, and a two to four-or-more base that launches from exit to begin the sequences. Don't give any single exit position too much thought because you must learn them all.

Always plan the dives with the cleanest, fastest, quickest-thinking and most adaptable flyers in the base four-man. Be sure everyone exits smoothly. Practice the exit. Work on making the exit as fast and consistent as speed-star exits are.

Keep in mind that while teams may break up because of a problem of flying, most of the time they disintegrate because of poor interpersonal relationships. Bad vibes, hassles, ground politics and egomania all rend teams apart.

To avoid this, practice on-the-ground team relative work as if it were as important as time in the air. It is! Every serious relative worker is responsible to the sport and to himself to look further ahead than the next jump, the next meet, or the next season. If you want to ensure continuing fun and challenging jumping for yourself, spend ground time wisely. Don't just *have* good vibes. *Spread* good vibes! *Organize* good vibes! Practice more skydiving, less hassles.

It's a simple fact. Many experienced relative workers quit jumping when the ground hassles overpower the joy of skydiving. If you want to keep jumping, don't be such a bitch about *this* jump, or the *last* jump. Just pay attention to doing your part, organizing joy, and helping build good jumps for tomorrow and for next year. If you make a thousand jumps in your jumping career, remember that no jump is worth jeopardizing the rest.

Be patient. Have a relaxed attitude toward ground practice and de-briefings. Do your best flying. Don't ever over-fly or over-boogie the dive, but *flow* with it. Let yourself learn early that in progressive sequential relative work you mustn't force it to happen...you *let* it.

Beware the mindless monster we call "The Team". Recognize that the team must be well-directed or it can seek to destroy itself. The team is part of none of its members, yet its members are all part of it.

Structured fun jumping, progressive relative work, open jumping, hot dives... these are the many names relative workers give to the kind of skydiving that becomes the basis for competitive jumping. For example, 8-man sequential, 10-man speed-stars and 4-man international sequential all evolved from "fun jumping". All of these forms of RW are still both fun jumping and competitive.

Although these traditional designations help to *describe* relative work, they do not limit it. If RW competition were to end today, Progressive Relative Work would certainly continue.

Pat Works

R/W's Imaginative New Direction. "We're here to jump and have fun... we don't need any rules or restrictions — we're restricted enough by our own abilities... Rules or no rules, when we cut on jumprun, we're going to hang as many guys as we can get outside the airplane and build the fastest, cleanest formation we can..."

This was the philosophy of the "Clear-Eyed Homegrown" 10-man team at the 1974 Casa Grande "Chute Out" as expressed by Matt Farmer. It essentially states the outlook of the majority of jumpers at both Seattle and Casa Grande, the two areas most responsible for promoting sequential RW in the country.

Sequential is where skydiving is going. It's dynamic, different, new and it requires finesse if it's to be done right. It's a rush, and anyone can do it. We'd like to turn you on to this high and share what we know — and don't know — with you. The key to it's attraction has best been explained by Pat Works when he wrote "...(In sequential) your imagination is your reality."

Rande Deluca, Spotter, May-June 1975.

Part II: What's what in sequential...Glossary of ideas

Glossary of Sequential Terms

Accordion (Open)—

Accordion (Compressed)—

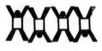

Bi-Pole—A four-man base unit of 2 facing the center of the star and 2 facing out:

Cat(erpillar)—all jumpers hooked-up in series, head-to-tail:

Cluster—A double-star type maneuver wherein the jumpers comprising the outer ring(s) hook up between the legs of 2 differing jumpers:

Connection—A series of connected, like, base units to form a chain:

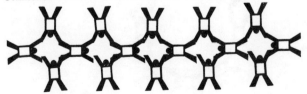

Diamond — A maneuver of 4, 9, 16, 25, 36…jumpers with an overall diamond shape:

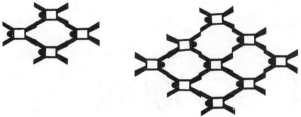

Dock — Flying 2 or more separate formations (each containing 2 or more people) together to form another maneuver:

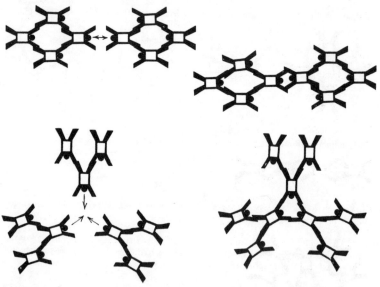

Donut — A formation wherein the jumpers form a 'caterpillar' star — all grips are one hand on the other jumper's same leg (i.e. right on right), and the people are sideways to the center of the formation.

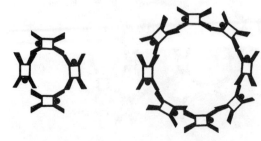

Donutize— To form a donut from another formation or position in a formation:
From a diamond:

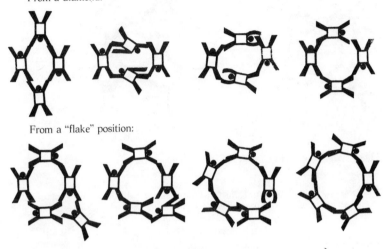

From a "flake" position:

Facing— All jumpers in the maneuver have the same heading:

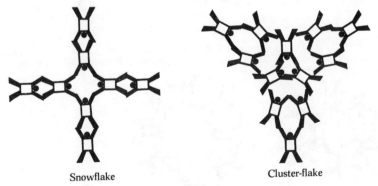

Flake— The outer portion of a maneuver, similar to a cluster. The jumper(s) hook-up to one person's legs, or, in the case of a donut-flake, to the outside leg of one jumper and the outside hand of another, or, in a cluster-flake, between the legs of two jumpers:

Snowflake   Cluster-flake

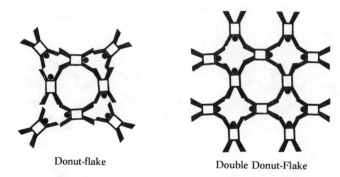

Donut-flake   Double Donut-Flake

Float — What most maneuvers, especially large ones, do.

Floaters — It's a good idea to use floaters on maneuvers loads; those who will exit the aircraft ahead of the base-pin and enter the formation on the back side — try it, you'll like it.

Fold-Out — A member of a maneuver who will hold on with one hand, or be held in by a leg, and rotate around that grip to either open a slot or rotate into another position in the formation.

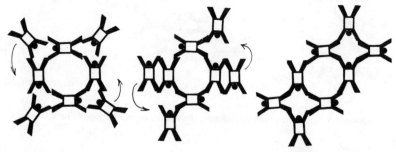

In-Out — A star of even-numbered people, half of whom are facing the center and have the commanding grips; half of whom are facing out and are being held in by their legs:

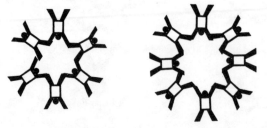

Maneuver — More commonly, a formation, where the jumpers connect in any combination of grips to produce a geometric pattern.

Pod — 2 or 3 jumpers connected to form an additional section on the outside of a maneuver, on the legs of a person in the base formation:

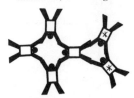

Point — The front man on a wedge or diamond:

 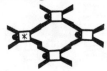

Opposed — Members in the formation may be facing each other directly:

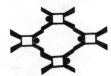

Sequential — A series of maneuvers completed on one jump, effected thru grip changes, grip breaks and flying, or both.

Spider — A 5-man base unit for wedges, diamonds, or anything you like:

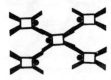

Star — A round formation or maneuver.

Stairsteps — 2 jumpers hooked-up hand to opposing leg to form an offset cat:

Swoop — Time between your exit and entry to the maneuver.

Tail — The back or slot man on a diamond.

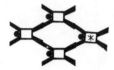

Tip — The corner men on a wedge or hourglass:

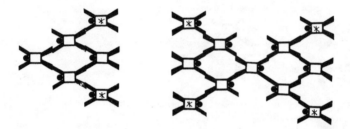

Wedge — 3, 6, 10, 15, 21, 28 . . . jumpers forming a triangle or wedge shape:

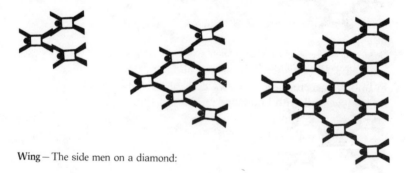

Wing — The side men on a diamond:

Spotter, May-June 1975

**PART III: Words of wit and wisdom on skydancing...shared
sequential dream flakes**

Sequential
pure energy flow
faster than words can go.
pure action and reaction within the framework of

a startling blue sky
that shocks you with its vividness
and redefines life
and cold
and colors flashing by
so crisply
so finally
that all those questions you took up
unanswered into the sky

float down on canopies of softer man-made color.

satisfied and smiling
bursting with energy
wanting to hug the whole of the experience to you
of sky

and wind and brothers and sisters all sinewy flying
in bubbling memories
that answer all with knowing
and those who know can
only answer with a smile.
Pat Works

Practicing "Aware" Sequential Diving. Freefall relative work
requires unique awareness. Relative work also bestows awareness.
No ground sport has the added dimension of a vast and
undifferentiated void as you find in freefall. In racquetball, the floor
and the wall stay put. In basketball, the basket is in a fixed location.
However, in freefall there is no such constant reference. There is
nothing that is firmly set to take your bearings on.

In RW, the formation you fly with and in is also moving in the sky as you move. It would be like driving a racing car on a road or track that is always moving...or playing tennis with a net that raises, lowers and moves around while you play. That's why relative work requires multi-dimensional flying awareness.

Likewise, sequential relative work encourages and fosters even more dimensions of awareness. Keeping several formations flying together to sequence, rotate and dock with each other means that you must be aware of the flight pattern your formation of two to 10 persons must take to synergize with the others at some imaginary spot in the vast blue void.

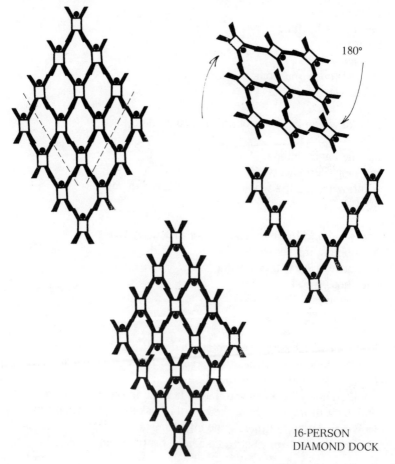

180°

16-PERSON
DIAMOND DOCK

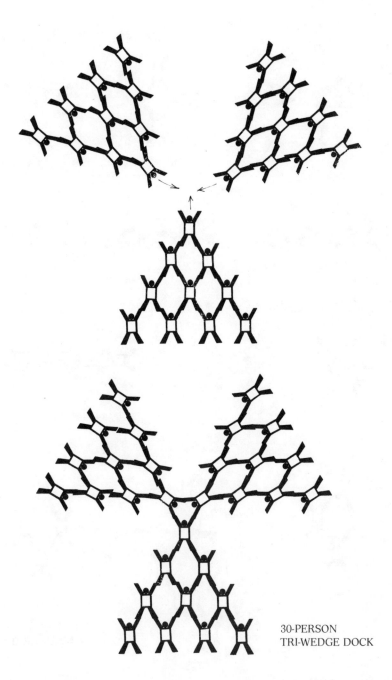

30-PERSON
TRI-WEDGE DOCK

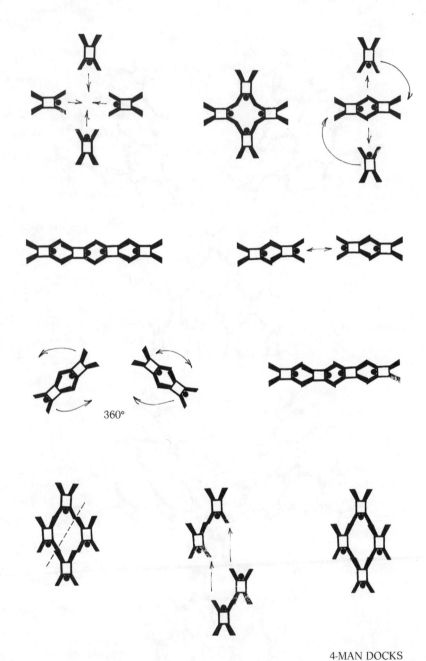

360°

4-MAN DOCKS

Building awareness starts with being good at no-contact relative work. You must be able to fly yourself precisely and with happy imagination — to park just outside a grip and fingertip dock only when the flow of the dive prompts you to pick up the grip, with a smile.

Awareness is generated by doing basic 2-person and 4-person group flying. Practice pre-stars whenever the flow of the dive allows. Always track the "pieces"...diamonds, cat or wedges...away as a last sequence. Practice flying as you track. Don't overfly your portion of the piece. People at the rear of a unit control its speed and share buoyancy control (relative fall). People at the point or front direct its turns and also share buoyancy control.

The unit flies like a unit when each member gets grips that do not hinder anyone else's flying.

Good timing is very helpful in successful sequential. Each relative worker should get to his slot at the optimal time. Not half a second too early, nor half a second too late, is right on.

One gets there at the right time by flowing with the dive. A sequenced skydive goes only so fast, like a river. Rivers flow and carry flotsam on their watery backs to highlight the currents. In freefall the uprushing air creates torrents of wind in which we flow. Do this in sequential relative work and you will have better completions. Flowing with the dive permits you to concentrate better on the changing panorama of sky, ground and sun-flashed colors of those who ride on wind.

Awareness and flow start in the airplane. So does the jump. Building a subterminal donut, carrying a 4-man diamond out the door, exiting with a clean 7-man contact which sequences into a 10-man star still tilted on its side in sub-terminal air, flying a 2-man cat out the door all require a good competition line-up and exit. A good exit allows more time to do RW. That is what you're paying for, so do it right from the beginning.

To achieve a really good exit and first formation, you must ground practice both the exit and the formation. The better the ground practice, the better the skydiving. And the better the skydiving, the easier awareness becomes second nature to you.

Pat Works

A Ten-Man Wedge That Floats and Moves With A Purpose

Much inspired by these fantastic flying feats, RWu has proposed the following maneuver and will give a GRAND PRIZE!!! to the first group to execute and photograph it.

All participants should be unflinching. Also, you need a pilot with a sense of humor. It is very likely that this dive will attract the attention of the local press, so have coffee and donuts ready.

We will assume that the coordinate system is attached to the formation. Then we get a steady flow pattern which is identical to the pattern observed in a wind tunnel when the formation is standing still and air is blown past it. From the point of view of a coordinate system attached to the formation, the formation *is* standing still and the air *is* blowing past it at terminal velocity. This follows from the Newtonian principle of relativity.

Because of the validity of the Newtonian principle, Bernouilli's law furnishes a very useful first approximation in the computation of forces on the surface of the formation:

Or, $P_1 + \frac{1}{2}pv_{2/1} + pgZ_1 = P_2 + \frac{1}{2}pv_{2/2} + pgZ_2$

Now, we propose that 28 color-coded divers strap a skateboard to their chests and build a 28-man wedge. The Point and Tip men should have *good* control. After formation of the 28-man wedge, the entire formation does a normal 180° turn-approach to the runway and lands at 117.8 MPH.

Pat Works, RWu, June 1975

Putting Skydives Together

"What are we doing?"

"I don't know... Are you having fun?"

"Yeah..."

"That's what we are doing..."

The way you organize a dive depends on why you are doing it. Is it a dive you made up and are looking for people to do it? Or do you have a load of people and you're looking for something to do?

Perhaps it is a demo jump. Or maybe you have some students who want to try their first backins.

You can do a sequence one way for competition and a completely different way for the camera... and even a third way just for fun. You have to read the mood of the moment. Every situation is unique. The hottest dive in the world is worthless if the people on it don't like it.

Organization is an extremely complex activity. There are no final answers — only tradeoffs and choices.

"The first secret to the inner mysteries of super sequential skydiving is that...

In a neutral frog everybody falls at the same speed. Several jumpsuits? No. One. Adjustable... Because with everybody calibrated we will also know that if you are going last on a 42 man floating razzle dazzle, your ordinary size three wings ain't gonna cut it. That's a size five job. While if you are one of the leaders, you won't wear any wings at all... And you better be able to track..."

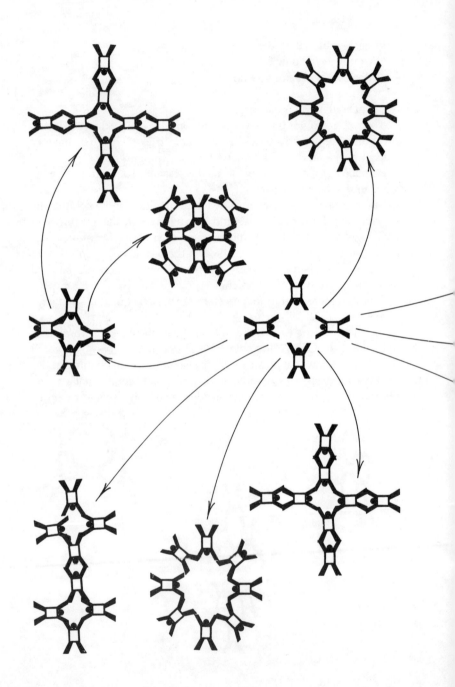

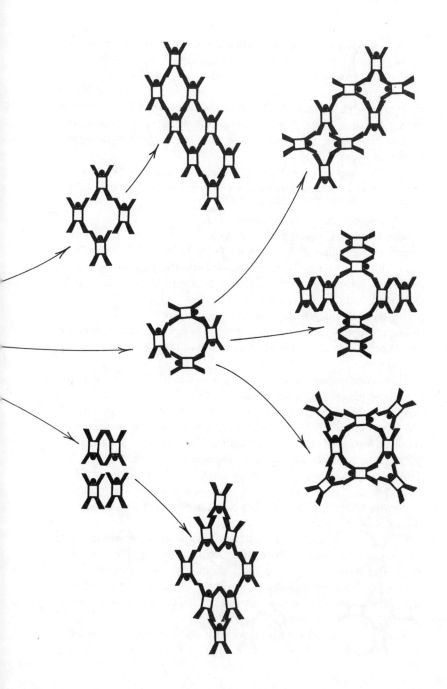

The key is in the transitions. When you let go to move from one to the next, the group stays together. No unwanted vertical separation. The neutral frog is in the center of your maneuverability.

The structural properties of hookups can be analyzed just like bridges and buildings and other physical structures. Visualize the formation falling in steady state equilibrium. What happens when you push it here and pull it there? Notice how the forces propagate and where the weak points are.

You soon see that some disturbances are much more destructive than others. And some formations are much better connected than others.

"Fly into position and then grab hold."

Sometimes it is possible to purposely exert a helpful force when entering a formation, but it is usually better to let it settle on its own.

Thinking about these technical details helps the organizer anticipate problems, estimate probabilities, and determine the distribution of experience, administrative ability, etc.

But there is much more to organizing than that.

The current fascination with geometric patterns is a passing phase, just as stars once were. What is important is all the flying that goes on in between.

That is one reason no-contact work is so much fun — you get to fly the whole jump. You never have to hang on.

With small numbers like eight and four you can make an efficient exit from almost any plane — just ease up slightly from the killer exit required for speed stars. The concept of a base man — a person who goes out first and is the target for the rest of the load — is obsolete. Today we think in terms of leaders — one who is leading the formation at any particular moment.

Always have someone with lots of experience near the door, and in the front of the load.

Falling through clouds is more fun than just about anything... It is also dangerous, exciting, distracting, exhilarating and against the rules. But rules are only rules and it's the mountains inside those clouds that we must think about. If you are not absolutely certain that the whole load will land in a safe place, then don't lead them out the door.

Think twice about clouds at breakup and opening altitude too. People become unrelated and unrelated people are dangerous...

Cultivate the habit of looking down...People who get below sometimes pull high...and sometimes chutes open accidentally. Watch for the stray glider passing through...the bad spot and unexpected freefall drift...and for the altimeters that don't work.

Look at the ground. Study it. Learn it. The first step is to be able to tell whether you are safe or not. The second step is to be able to estimate how much more can be done on this jump. Look at the ground first and then at your altimeter...If you are down where fractions of a second count, it will be obvious. Pull the first ripcord you come to. Don't waste those fractions trying to figure out which one.

Knowing when to breakup is probably the hardest single thing in all of jumping. You have to work at it. It doesn't just come. It is a well developed sense of when to have fun and when to "SAVE YOURSELF!!"

Planned breakups are part of the organization of every dive. Everybody is responsible. It is much too important to leave up to anybody other than yourself. If you see it is time, give people a wave-off before you leave. If you are hanging on to somebody, give them a shake. Help each other...you might need it yourself someday.

"Why do I always have to sit in the cold seat?" In one sense figuring out the exit order is easy. You just choose a suitable development (logical, efficient, artistic, experimental or whatever) for the first part of the dive and divide the load into groups accordingly. The last group to enter the formation will be last out of the plane — and so on down to the initial leaders who will be in the first group. Within each group the people who have the furtherest to go should go first. That is the basic idea.

Floaters are fun and efficient. With multiple planes timing is a factor, but avoiding cross traffic is more important.

A smooth start is half the secret on all these dives. Going through the door is just a detail. The whole load should by flying together before it ever leaves the plane.

ESP...Ecstasy Sensory Perception...Do you dive out the door with your ecstasy sensors extended?

Creation, Recreation, Exploration. We are mapping out a whole new area of human experience. To fly is one of man's oldest dreams. Skydivers are the first people in history to have more than a few seconds direct experience. It is freedom and expression and open-ended — and doing it in a closed framework is unharmonious and wastes a lot of energy.

Skydiving is easy...Belief is what's hard.

The most difficult organizing is when there are one to three loads available. Some people have more money and some have to leave early and it is hard to make things mesh. With fewer it is easy because you just take everybody in sight. And with more it is easier because there are enough combinations available for everybody to get more or less whatever kind of jumping they want.

Work with your students on the most important four-man maneuvers...the diamond, donut, star, bi-pole. And on the basic skills of coming in forwards, sideways, and backwards...the main thing about going backwards is looking where you are going. That open star to vee or stairstep with backins is good. Develop their body awareness...Try flying with your hands closed into fists...or on your helmet. Tell them about airflow. Inspire them with camera jumps.

Skydiving is easy...Inspiration is what's hard. The most important thing about organizing is that we are dealing with human experience. It is not drawings on paper. It is the way people feel when they go up there and skydive.

-Skratch Garrison, excerpted from a letter to a group of Swedish jumpers

Part IV: Sequential history...where we've been

10-Man Star Competition — Floaters (1973). Some competition teams "float" one or two people. The best subterminal RWers are picked for this — they're usually light and lanky. They exit in front of the Base — the idea is to get the Base *closer* to the last men out of the door for faster times.

I jumped this position at the Zephyrhills meet. It's a neat position in that it's all subterminal and you get to see the exit and most of the star building — it's a heavy visual trip.

Prior to Z-Hills I had zero experience at exiting first and tended to get too far from the Base on the horizontal plane in the beginning. I found that by concentrating on keeping the distance between the Base & I as short as possible, the vertical would handle itself. The base should fall faster than a floater.

If you'd like to try it, I suggest you get your Base-man to show you how to exit. I exited first and was able to enter fourth. The second floater can get in third staying on the back side of the star (away from the aircraft) to lessen traffic.

Dan Poynter floats second and Helen Tyson floats first for the "Pieces of Eight" team. They hit right after the pin is made and have found that "when you do it right" it's a fast 4-man. "It's easy," says Dan.

Whether floating will work for your team probably depends on the relative size/weight ratio of team members, the adaptability of the base-pin to exiting third and fourth, and finally, the concentration of the entire team on RW and not the exit order — (and it don't mean a thing if you don't pull the string!)

Pat Works, RWu, June 1973

More Fun for Your $$$ (1973). More learnin' for free. Twice the practice and half the cost. Add a little challenge and variety to your 10-man practice with large star sequential relative work.

Ten-man sequential relative work may be a long time comin' in some competition meets but it is lotsa fun for team practice. As a plus, it gives everybody on the team a chance to "fly" their ass off on every jump and not just "do" their assigned slot. A real competition-oriented advantage is the fact that it gives a chance at a *second entry* and helps teach you to handle a tough problem in any fast star — traffic jams. Importantly, it requires you to think, an area in which we often think our teammates need lotsa help.

How's it work? Simple sounding enough...go make a ten-man star. OK? Now, instead of waiting for break-off time to come, use whatever altitude you might have left to do more relative work.

We'll discuss a sequential formation used by "Jerry Bird's All-Stars," the "James Gang" and the "Get It Together" team from Stormville, N.Y. — the 10-man star, to a line, to two 5-man stars, to another 10-man star. It's very popular and gives everyone on the team a maximum amount of RW flying and competition star-building practice.

First, make a 10-man star; then have the captain or someone drop a grip so you end up with an open 10-man horseshoe. Straighten the horseshoe into a line without wasting any time. This gives everyone a bit of flying experience that'll help if you ever drop a grip in competition. Also it's neat to look down a long line in freefall.

After a jump or two you'll then have time to break the 10-man line in two. You gotta think here. It requires the ability to count five people while in freefall. Immediately close the two 5-man lines into two 5-man stars. This gives *excellent* practice at closing a star or putting a mess back together. Mainly, it's beautiful to fly two 5-mans 20 feet apart.

Now, as soon as you get your 5-man star closed, one of them will have been designated to either tuck up or flare way out so that one 5-man is 10 to 50 feet below the other. This takes 3 to 5 seconds. Now the guys in the high 5-man split and boogie their ass off, entering the lower 5-man to make the *2-second* 10-man. It's simply amazing how fast you'll move if you're gettin' close to breakoff time. SWOOOOOOP!

Don't expect to be able to accomplish any of the above unless you run through it about 20 times on the ground and each member of your team has the ability to count to five. Ground practice is a lot cheaper than a jump and sorts out all kinds of problems of traffic and timing.

When you start trying it for real, remember it's gonna take about 10 jumps before there appears to be any hope. You're gonna think you're a bunch of turkeys for sure. But nothing that requires skill is easy at first, and a lot of your team members probably have never done much more RW than exit, dive, swoop, flare, shake-&-break, and smile. ·

Ten-man stars are fun, Doing two ten-man stars on one jump and involving your entire mind, body and soul in precision freefall relative work with your mates is something more than fun . . . it's exhilarating. (And it's sure to improve your times — this could help you win your next 10-man star meet.)

R Wu, March 1973

New Exit Theories (1974). *R Wu* has had reports of "hard core" competitive 10-man teams who, in their continuing quest for the fastest way to build a star, are experimenting with some unusual techniques. All center around the theory that you "build an exit, not a star."

The "Slots Are For Tots" team, for example, pack themselves carefully in the door and, we understand, exit in such a way that a little grab-ass out the door (in other words, trying to get your hands on somebody immediately) results in an instant three- or four-man, which is *then* stabled out for entry by the others. There are no assigned slots and no specific floaters on their team — just whoever can get a handhold on whoever else right away.

It must work, as "Slots Are For Tots" took first place (out of 52 teams) at the Z-Hills 10-man Meet. *RWu* hasn't seen the official meet scores to know whether or not they are consistent in their times, but their fastest was reported to us as 16.7 seconds.

Some teams are experimenting with using lots of floaters — up to four — and are very successful. Several championship teams manage reasonably consistent times with this technique.

RWu, December 1974

The United States Freefall Exhibition Team. In 1975, B.J. Worth had an idea — a new way to promote skydiving while exploring a whole new world of relative work — the United States Freefall Exhibition Team.

Twenty hand-picked skydivers spent many weekends at Casa Grande, Arizona. Their sequential dives — amazing patterns of lines and forms, emphasized with color-coded jumpsuits and maneuvers, each more complex, more beautiful and more amazing than the last — were recorded on film by freefall photographers Rande Deluca and Ray Cottingham. Those dives have become the movie *Wings.*

B.J. won support from U.S.P.A. for his team, and the U.S. Freefall Exhibition Team was invited to demonstrate their art at the Relative Work World Meet in Warendorf, Germany. Here is how B.J. explained his purpose for the U.S.F.E.T. in the proposal he presented to U.S.P.A.:

"Our goals are to promote skydiving as a national sport in the eyes of the public; to promote the expansion of skydiving among all members of our sport; and to learn as much as possible about the actual skydiving.

"...We are concentrating on the expansion of progressive relative work through all possibilities of sequential maneuvers in freefall. We feel very sure that sequential maneuvers will play a substantial role in the future of relative work around the world. However, we are in no way trying to exclude round stars from our repertoire of regular weekend jumping, as they are one of the infinite number of maneuvers encompassing the total realm of relative work."

Introduction: Skratch Garrison, SCR-16, was one of the members of the U.S.F.E.T. The following is excerpted from a letter Skratch wrote to Eilif Ness, a member of the international CIP Committee on relative work, prior to the team's demonstration jumps at Warendorf in 1975.

Tuesday, July 15, 1975

"Some of the hottest skydives that have ever been made were made here today, and I'm in a festive mood. You can tell them that I ain't coming." That's Jerry Bird standing outside the Friendship Saloon at Tahlequah at the end of the Nationals telling someone why he isn't at the team captain's meeting now in progress.

Only a couple hours ago, people were standing there looking up at a 25-man diamond. And just before that Captain Hook's team went up and made a 12.8 second star. And before that there was a clean, round 32-man for people to look at. Hot skydives, indeed.

For USFET, the Nationals was many things. A place to learn about demo jumps; a trial run for Europe. At Casa Grande we were jumping for the camera. Now we are doing it for the ground effect. The organization is different. Know where people are sleeping, be on time, walk through the jumps the night before, have alternate plans...we learn a lot.

It is also a place to meet people, see what they are doing, and turn them on to what we are doing. To exchange technical knowledge about how to do this or that. To wonder where it is all going. To be brothers together once more before we all scatter to the winds and collect somewhere else.

And, of course, it is a chance to get out on the edge one more time. To try things that we have never done or even thought of before. That edge keeps moving outwards, and if you don't move with it, you get left behind. Sometimes, when you go too far, you fall off. We blow a few jumps. But we pull off some hot good skydives, too. Some of them we did for the first time ever as demo jumps.

We have only a few jumps left as a team now. Some practice jumps at the Scrambles in Elsinore, and whatever we do in Europe. Most of the people have 100 to 150 team jumps now, and we are just starting to mesh and fly together. The momentum is there and I think we should take it as far as we can in the jumps we have left. If we blow a third of our jumps, I'll be satisfied.

You are right when you say we "have reached the point where technical proficiency has become a tool to do what your fantasy impels you to." We have only scratched the surface of the technical knowledge we will have ten years from now. But for the first time, the artistry of the jump has become a major factor. That "brick wall"...the limits set by the laws of physics... is out there all right. Although I don't think we need fear running into it for a while yet. But more importantly, it doesn't matter, because there are no limits to imagination.

We started jumping Thursday at Wagoner, a little town about a half hour from Tahlequah. We ended up spending a lot of time going back and forth between Tahlequah — for the morning and evening demos — and Wagoner — for whatever other jumps we could fit in.

Thursday was the first day of practice, but for me the Nationals started Wednesday night at BJ's parents' house. All these people — most of them strangers only a few months before — and now some of my closest friends. The energy of the team trip is like a whirlwind and the whole house is alive with interconnected conversation and good vibes... "what jumps are we gonna do?... I dunno. Do you think that long layoff has hurt us?... What time do we have to get up in the morning?... tracking wedges or diamonds apart with smoke would look good at breakup... who stole my beer?... here's 20 smoke brackets that Dick Gernand made for us... show the movies... we can't do that because the movements wouldn't show from the ground... what planes are we gonna use?... yeah, I spent three daze there one night... I think we ought to jump with other people as much as we can... so do I, but first we have to get our own act straightened out..." The team is together for one more boogie — the Nationals — and it's a good feeling.

Oklahoma is hot, humid and windy. The Casa Grande Beech is at Wagoner and we make three practice jumps. A five-point donut-flake, which breaks into five cats that track off, and then the tail pulls off, and then the leaders dump. We also did a diamond dock... build a nine-diamond, back the small diamond out, do a 360, and redock. And we tried a rotating donuts jump with five-man donuts. The fifth person in each donut added a noticeable amount of inertia.

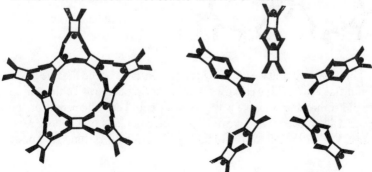

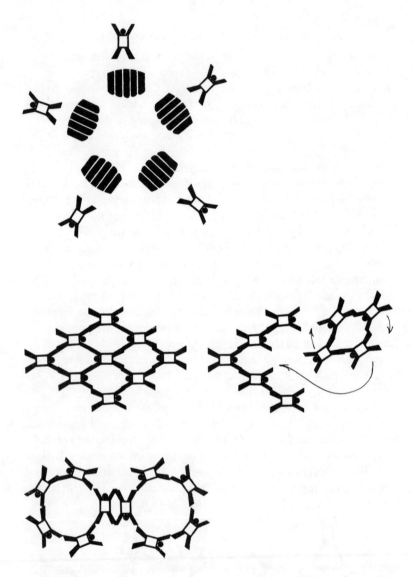

Thursday evening we jumped in at Tahlequah and did the five-point donut-flake to tracking cats dive. It was our first demo at Tahlequah so we did something we were pretty sure we could do. The people on the ground all enjoyed it and we did, too. You can really make those cats move. We were glad to see we hadn't forgotten everything we knew.

Friday we jumped into Wagoner from Tahlequah and built a 15-cluster, broke it into five wedges, and reformed the cluster. On the next jump we started with a 16-diamond. But one person got low so we didn't break into four small diamonds and try to dock them, which was the plan.

Next we tried the quadra-bipole jump but had some trouble with one of the four backwards shots, so we didn't finish that either. We did track the wedges off. Breaking up in wedges and diamonds will probably be in a lot of our jumps in Europe.

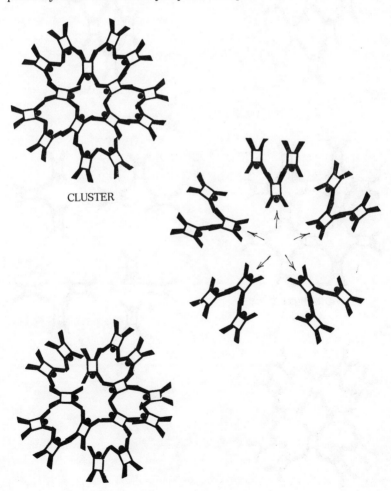

CLUSTER

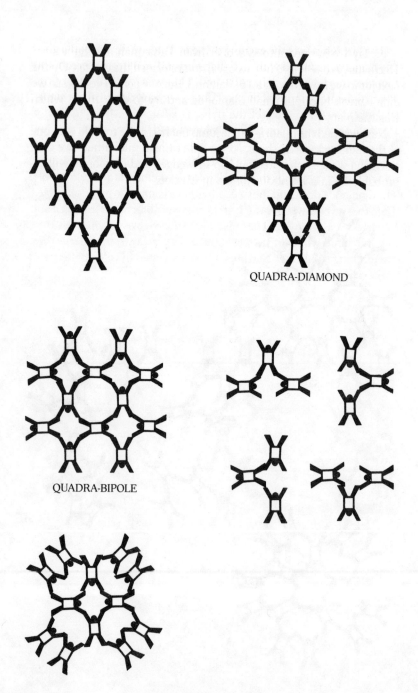

QUADRA-DIAMOND

QUADRA-BIPOLE

The last jump was the evening demo in Tahlequah. We had a good one planned. It started with a 16-diamond and went from there, but we funneled the diamond right at the end. That was really discouraging. That 16-diamond is one of our best dives. We have done it six or eight times before...and most of the flying is straight in. It's like Jim Heydorn once said: "You take your lumps and keep on truckin'." And that's what we did.

Saturday was the first day of the ten-man competition. We started it off with triple diamonds that break into two diamonds and two people. The diamonds dock and the two individuals come in to make an eagle. Then two reverse wedges track off in opposite directions, leaving a star falling down the middle. The tails pull off the wedges and the pairs fan out and dump while the people in the star open down the middle. We are jumping solid color Starlites, so we can open in color patterns. It still needs a little work.

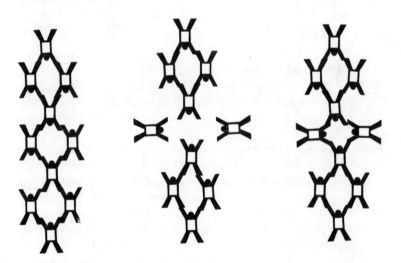

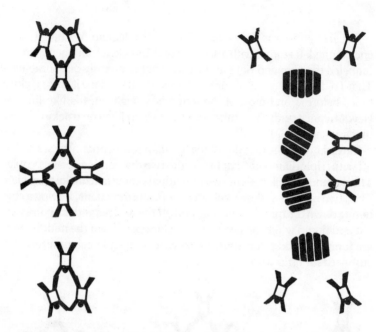

The competition was finished in one day. The whole day felt unreal. We had been jumping and partying for two and a half days. The ten-man event was going so fast you could hardly keep up with it, and all of a sudden it was over. Captain Hook won with six stars in the 15's.

We went up for the evening demo and did a 16-diamond with smoke on the corners. We held it down to 5000 ft and then broke into red, yellow, blue and green sub diamonds. The red and yellow ones tracked off and the blue and green ones docked and then tracked off. The tails pull out of the diamonds and the wedges fan out and dump to leave four columns of canopies...red, yellow, blue and green. It was perfect! One of the hottest skydives I've ever been on. There would be more of those in the next few days, but I don't think we could have felt any better about that one than we already did.

Sunday morning at 6 o'clock we sleepwalk through our morning demo for the four-man event. I overhear Taylor saying "We didn't get loose last night but we stayed up till 5 o'clock trying." Our morning organization breaks down in a couple places and we get off to a late start and have to cut the jump in half. We did an 11 man hourglass, but ran out of time and one corner didn't get on.

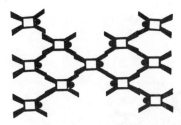

That diamond jump the day before had led to a discussion in the wee hours of the morning about whether the red diamond had out-tracked the yellow one. So we got in the Beech and jumped into Wagoner. The plan was to form the diamonds nose-to-nose and then turn and track side-by-side. We got in such a hurry to get the diamonds formed that we funneled it and ended up tracking a couple pieces and several individuals.

Next we made a jump with half Texas and half USFET people. We built a quadra-diamond and then broke and tried to fly the four diamonds into a 16-diamond. It went pretty well. We got through the quadra-diamond and into the breakup. Then the base diamond sank down a little and slid under the others. It ended up as one diamond with a couple people hanging on and two diamonds flying around trying to get in. We haven't worked out signals for the leader to tell the others where he wants to go yet.

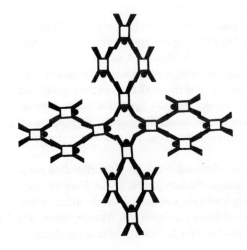

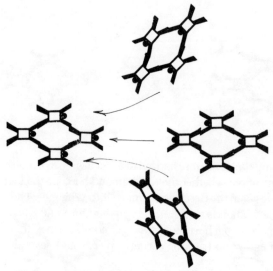

Our next jump was the evening demo at Tahlequah. The plan was an eight point donut-flake. The base started to turn when Matt Farmer's reserve tiedown came loose and his reserve started beating him in the face and knocked his ripcord out and other hassles. Contrary to policy people came in anyway with out letting it settle down. It was a great chase but not much of a demo.

Monday was our last day. It is just as well. We have been on a full-tilt boogie since Wednesday night and people are starting to burn out. Yet Monday saw some of the hottest skydives that have ever been made.

We started it out with the morning demo out of a large door Beech. It is cold at that time of day at 14,000 ft. There are patchy clouds in a thin layer at 8000 ft. We are doing a 9-man diamond dock sequence. They saw us leave the plane and start to form; then we went behind a cloud. We had the diamond clean and stable by 10,000 ft. and we got to just lay there and fly it and watch the clouds come up. It is only one second thick, just a flash and we are out in the open. They say that diamond popping out of the clouds with a smoke on each end looked pretty good from the ground.

We backed the small diamond out and back in. Then BJ pulled out of the center and we flew the hollow diamond for a while. Then the two ends came in and broke wrists and the two people on the sides of the original diamond de-donutized into a nine man star. We ran out of time and one person didn't get de-donutized, but it was a great demo.

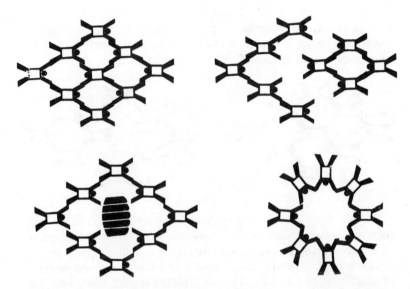

Monday was the day for the ten-man star-BL-snowflake event. The Wings of Orange team almost did the sequence twice from 10,500 ft. which really looked good. Very quickly it was all over and time to try a few record attempts. Bird organized a 32-man load from the first four teams. The first time it built to 31, and the second time to a clean round 32-man. Peter Böttgenbach set up above it and framed the airport with the star. Then Captain Hook went up and smoked out a 12.8 sec star.

Our evening demo was next but these were hard acts to follow. So BJ organized a 25-diamond. You just take a 9-diamond and add four to each side. I'm not sure what to say about a jump like that. I haven't quite taken it all in yet myself. I'm running out of superlatives, but these jumps just boggle my mind.

I don't know where it's all going. I sometimes get the feeling the creation is outrunning its creators.

Skratch Garrison

Patterns In The Sky (1975). "You can't make them any rounder than that." That's what I thought when I saw the pictures shot by Rande Deluca last weekend over Casa Grande. Some places make them big — and some do it fast. But at Casa Grande they make them round — and perfect — and smooth. Which is typical of the way they jump here.

Their (Lockheed) Lodestar carries 24 people. On this jump I am in the second group. The plan is to build a diamond, back the small diamond out, and fly it back in — a diamond dock.

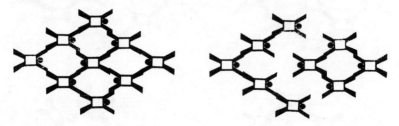

The other two groups are doing something equally interesting. But then, somewhere toward the end of the ride up, the guy whose legs I'm sitting between tells me that something is wrong with the plane and we have to get out. We will make one pass for the first group, and the rest of us will go out on the second pass and build a star. So that's what we did — 17 out of 17 — smooth, round, and high. And Rande was right there to take a picture of it.

That was my first jump with most of these people. The next one was two four-man donuts rotating around each other like gears. You start with two diamonds, hooked together like a compressed accordion. When everybody is on, four people "donutize," and the donuts start rotating around each other.

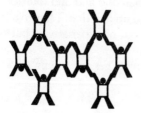 

A mobile! Does it fill your head with ideas? It did mine. You know, I've always thought of mobiles in terms of flying unhooked up. Like a jump Clarice and I and Willy Manbo did once where we kept changing positions in a three-man V, repeating the basic pattern: right wing moves forward and the other two fall in behind. So that from the ground it would look like three smoke trails braided together.

And I had even seen Ray Cottingham's movies of the Seattle people grip-shifting from one incredible hookup to another. But I always considered those discrete, while a mobile was something with continuous flow. So as soon as they showed me this jump I had visions of a string of four or five all going at once, and maybe a big one with a couple little ones going around it, and other Rube Goldberg machines with levers going back and forth and...

Later that night, out in the parking lot, I was talking to Ron Luginbill about this. He stood there and listened to it all, and then he said "Yeah — and you can do funny stuff, too. Like start with a wedge and someone out in front — in white — and here comes a four-man caterpillar with smoke on the last guy." And Pow! He hits his palm with his fist. I had to laugh. The jump was funny — it was Saturday night — and it felt good to be around such people.

Right! So we are going to do rotating donuts on this jump. "Rotating Donuts!" The language really cracks me up. I can just see one of my early impressions of B.J. (Worth) standing there in his cutoffs with a serious look on his face. "...so on this dive we're gonna start with a frisbee-figbar-flake with red bipoles here, here, and here. Okay? Then the blue jumpsuits will come in and donutize. Only this time we're gonna have double flakes so that you guys in the yellow will have to wait until..." The words start rolling over me like a fog and I stand there thinking, "Jesus — I hope I can remember what color my jumpsuit is."

But it is harder to describe than do. We put on our jumpsuits and go through it from exit to breakup until everybody is clear about what they are supposed to do. Then we go through it a couple more times at the plane with our gear on. Then we go up and do it in the air. And the rotation — so awkward on the ground — is surprisingly smooth.

Actually there is another version of this using in-outs:

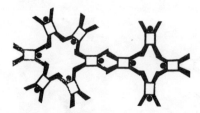

But these people are not just doing it, they are making a movie of it. The movie and the team activity naturally influence what the other people on the drop zone do.

Sunday morning Clarice and I get on a filler load. There are eight of us — with mixed experience. So we tried the simplest of diamond docks. Build them hooked up. Let go (don't push off — just let go — they will separate by themselves). And bring them back together again.

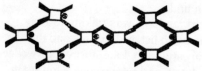

The two points were lightweights with big fluffy jumpsuits — which I want to talk about later — and when they hooked up they spread out and started turning — which made it difficult for the rest of us. I was one of the slot people, and when it was my turn to come in, all I could do was grab some air and let it come up to me. The other slot never got in. No one person at fault — a combination of many things. But the point is — this was a filler load. This is the type of skydive that students around here try to make. These people grow up taking for granted such ideas as assigned positions and diamond docks.

Seattle had called Saturday night to tell us they had made a 21-man wedge — an extremely difficult maneuver because it floats so much. They had had a break in their winter rain and fog and had gotten together and done it. There is already some rivalry between Seattle and Casa Grande — as well as a healthy cross-fertilization of people who follow the seasons and oscillate between the two.

So on the last jump Sunday, B.J. decided there were enough people around to try a 24-man sunburst-flake. We made it smooth and high, with only a couple of small vertical warps about halfway through. And Rande got some nice shots of it.

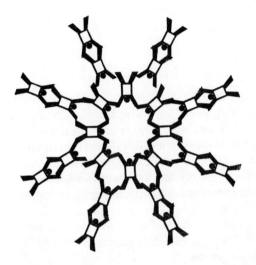

That was a good jump, and I enjoyed it. It makes a nice picture. And it is nice being in a first or in a record of some kind once in a while. But I had more fun on that gear dive. Dynamic jumps, mobiles, flying pieces around, or flying unhooked up are the jumps I like best. They have more possibilities— they are logistically easier—and they are more fun. It's always more fun when you get to fly around on a jump.

They look better in movies, too. Movies, of course, are the best thing that ever happened to skydiving. They do more even than inter-drop zone rivalry to stimulate imaginations and enthusiasm. Bob Buquor at Arvin, Carl Boenish at Elsinore, Rande Deluca and Ray Cottingham at Casa Grande—there is always a cameraman involved when our knowledge of skydiving makes a quantum jump. You can see what really happened, and watch the movies over and over and study them until you can see and understand both the individual actions and the flow of the jump as a whole.

It was our first weekend at Casa Grande. As you might expect, after a weekend like that we were back the next weekend to do it some more.

Seven of us made the first filler load on Saturday. We built a spider, and then the last two people came in and closed it. Nice and clean and high. Then we flew it, and dug it.

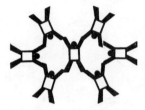

You might be thinking that's pretty hot flying for a bunch of students. But it's not really. For one thing, the filler loads are not pure student loads. They are a mixture — with a wide range of experience. Team members go on them, too; they are one place where people learn.

Beginning students are another story. But if you work with them, it doesn't take that long to get them good enough to start jumping on filler loads. When a person can handle a 30 — when he can pack his chute — and pincheck it — and spot (somewhat) — and dive out the door and feel comfortable doing individual maneuvers — then he is ready to be in the air with other people.

Teach him how to track and stay clear under the canopy. Teach him how to look at the ground and tell whether he is safe or not. Take him out and fly formation (un-hooked up) with him and show him how to move around and side-slide and slow fall and use his legs. Make use of simple jumps such as flying a star unhooked up and passing a baton around, or hookups and backloops to integrate his knowledge — to teach him *when* as well as *how*.

Teach him about flying a hookup. That it is being a damper for the tension waves as they pass through you, absorbing the energies and momentums that are trying to distort the hookup, going with the flow of the motion, smoothing things out. It is flying so smooth that everybody could let go at once and nothing would change.

And before you know it he will be showing you something. The only cure for turkeys is prevention; we all know that.

On our last jump Saturday, the plan was to start with a wedge, hold it a few seconds, have the right rear corner pull out of it, and the left rear corner move around to make it a diamond, hold that a few seconds, have the right rear corner pull out of it, and the left rear corner move around to make a diamond, hold that a few seconds, and have the center pull out leaving a hollow diamond with everybody keeping their headings.

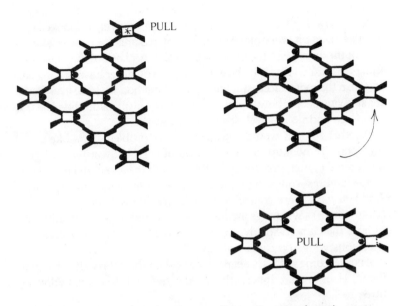

I don't care too much for these pullouts. I guess there is some question in my mind about how well a chute opens in all that turbulence and wash above a hookup. And there is the sudden relative difference in speeds. Everybody is moving along together at 120 mph, and suddenly somebody stops. I've done it before. I was even KAP-3'ed out of a star once at 4,000 feet for a TV commercial that Clarice was on and Bob Sinclair was filming. But I don't like it. We can't ever forget what it is that we are really doing up there.

This jump didn't go as planned anyway. About the time the spider was formed, we saw that the guy marked "low" had gotten under us. We tucked up but it didn't do any good. These hookups that are a solid mass of people really float. Their porosity is too low. The rest of the people came in and we were flying it and tucking up when I looked off to my left and there was Jim Captain — one of the Kansas people and the guy who was supposed to move around to make it a diamond. There was Jim, with this matter-of-fact look on his face, flying his position on the corner like it didn't matter to him if he were hooked up or not. That's where he was supposed to be and that's where he was. I was really impressed. People are getting good when they can fly these hookups with parts missing and never know the difference. And it looked good on film too.

You know, I talk a lot about formation flying — flying unhooked up. That's because it is one of the great unexplored areas of relative work. One of the areas with the greatest potential. And one of the most fun things to do. You get to fly the whole jump. You never have to hang on. It is also the most successful and efficient method we have ever found for showing people how to slow-fall and fast-fall and side-slide and use their legs and do other close-in relative work.

Another thing it would solve is the float problem. It is like a high-porosity hookup. So that instead of everybody striving to get lighter and lighter, everybody is trying to fall the same. Relative work is cooperation — not competition. Cooperate means jointly operate. And you have more control when you are falling faster. Ray (Cottingham) says things are falling so slow that it is getting difficult to hold the camera steady, flying all spread out. And he wears enormous wings on camera jumps.

Another thing it does is open up the possibility of three-dimensional flying. Hookups are inherently two-dimensional, but we skydive in three.

Think of the possibilities! I have. I don't know why it hasn't caught on more than it has. Richard Economy showed it to Clarice one day at Lancaster in April, 1965. And I know that the Army team has been flying their diamonds at demo jumps since 1961 or so. Maybe some of the Casa Grande people will get into it after the movie is finished. I hope so — it would be exciting.

The next jump was unusual. We did it from 10,500 feet out of the Beech. I am in the point of the blue diamond on this one. We get the cut. The floaters climb out. The countdown starts, and we are through the door and into the prop blast.

I keep my eye on the floaters as I turn to watch Bob Taylor, the red point, dropping in on me. Slow and easy — there is no need for an instant pin. In fact a lot of positioning goes on before we hook up and turn on heading with the sun. The wing men, Capain Smooth and Ruben, come in on my knees as the red diamond builds behind Bob. He shakes his head "yes" that the blue diamond has formed, but the red slot man is still a couple feet out so I shake my head "no." Communication is as preplanned as the rest of the jump. Eye contact, nods, and shakes.

Now the red slot man is in so I nod and we let go. Bank to the left — gently — too much will distort the diamond and cause it to move around. The slot man has a lot of control on turns. The wing men go with the flow. We stop the turn early but overshoot a few degrees anyway. Now we wait, for all the action is behind us.

Finally I get the shake from the wing men that the red diamond has docked. We start our turn to the left and there is the red diamond right beside us, 15 or 20 feet away, making their turn, and it is a beautiful sight. I hate to quit now but the sage brush is coming up and there is no choice. I wish we had gone to 12,500.

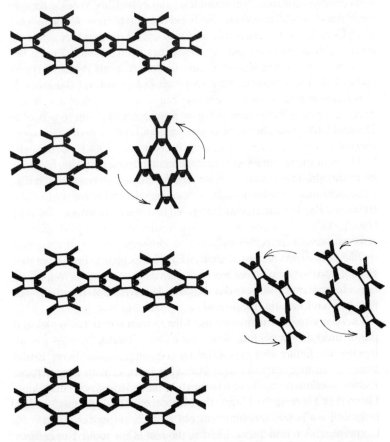

While I'm hanging there under the canopy I think how much fun it would be to fly two diamonds side by side and track with them. (Two weeks later a filler load completed the first half of this — from 10,500.

Everybody on the whole drop zone is getting into it.)

The rest of the day is devoted to documenting certain jumps and parts of jumps — like a point of view of Fiegel backing into a slot. For one reason or another the usable footage to date is not what Carl (Boenish) thinks it should be. You know how camera jumps are. The lighting is wrong or the jumpers screw up or the camera doesn't work or something. There is always something.

B.J. is totally into the juggling act necessary to keep all the ingredients organized long enough to make the film. Weekly trips to Los Angeles — 450 miles one way to get the film processed and talk to Carl. Deciding what jumps and who and what's next and coordinating and on and on and on. And the time pressure. The filming must be done by June, because after that Casa Grande is so hot that if you pull above 1,000 feet, your canopy will melt before you hit the ground.

B.J. was in a 12-man one night over Sheridan, Oregon, at a style and accuracy meet. At the time, he was jumping and going to school in Missoula, Montana. Some Seattle people had come down to the meet, and they all got together and made it, nice and clean, and high enough to let it rotate three times while they watched the moon go by. Elsinore had the night record with 16, but that 12-man was so smooth that B.J. was convinced they could add 5 more people and break it. So he contacted Ray Cottingham, who agreed to come up to Snohomish and film it.

While he was there, they naturally made some camera jumps during the day, too. That was in March 1973. The Seattle people were just getting into it. By the Scrambles in September there was a group of 15 or so doing it every Wednesday evening. B.J. went down to the Gulch for the Thanksgiving boogie and came back again in January 1974, when he started jumping with the Allsnoids, a speed-star team, and they would do some kind of maneuver after each star.

After the Chute Out in '74, he started jumping with Jerry Bird's Wings of Orange team. A good place to learn about team organization.

Meanwhile, the movies and things had turned a few people on. Matt Farmer, Jim Baker, Pat Melroy, Jim Captain — all from Kansas — Ron Luginbill — a Texas transplant and one of the first Casa Grande people to get into this — and Rande Deluca, who later got hooked on camera jumping after buying a motor for his Nikon.

While the Allsnoids were doing their thing, these people were going up and working on wedges and diamonds and such. But they had a hard time of it because most people were interested in speed stars. They would go up and make the beginning of something and get two or three people to go along and try to finish it.

They teamed up with four guys from Seattle and entered the Chute Out, and then ignored the competition and did maneuvers instead of stars on their jumps. Interest continued to grow and by the time B.J. got back from Africa, there was a group of 10 or 12 doing it on a regular basis.

Actions and reactions, feedback and momentums. Ray Cottingham naturally had a lot of ideas on movies and camera jumps. B.J. had talked to him about filming some more jumps at Casa Grande for an article he wanted to write. When Ray went to Orange, they talked some more — about solid color jumpsuits and movies and many things. B.J. hadn't written the article yet, but they decided that when he got back from Africa, Ray would go to Casa Grande every three weeks and get some film and see what happened.

In Africa and Europe they showed the movies, and they saw the people's reactions. Somewhere in France it all fell into place. Now is the time, and the way to do it is to form a demonstration team and make a movie and travel around and present it all at the world meet in Germany. He spread the word that there would be some good jumping in Casa Grande this winter. But he kept the team and the movie idea to himself until he could talk to Ray, which he did between November, when he got back, and the Rumbleseat meet (the 1974 edition of the original 10-man star meet held at Taft in 1967).

Ray had just bought a house and couldn't afford to do it by himself, so B.J. started looking around for money, sponsors, whatever he could find. He was over at Carl Boenish's house one night looking for leads and contacts. Ted Webster was there. He and Carl have been working on a movie of their own for a couple years now.

It was okay with Ted if he used the name USFET — United States Freefall Exhibition Team, the name of the team that went to Bled, Yugoslavia with such good results. And it turned out that Carl was willing to furnish the film and produce the movie. Wham! Back to Casa Grande the next day — a team meeting — start with 16 people — leave two slots open for expansion — and Rande and Ray, the cameramen, make 20. They got solid color jumpsuits from Joe Garcia and started jumping on January 11, 1975.

B.J. told us about all this when he stopped by our place one day in the first part of February on one of his weekly trips to L.A. Remember how much fun it was when we were first learning, and there was something new on every jump? Well, it is like that over there now. It has been a long time since I have been around people who can point out each other's mistakes and be thanked for it. And I dig it. The movie atmosphere is unmistakable. Counting the drive by Elsinore to pick up Max Kelly, it is 500 miles — one way — to the Grimy Gulch. But this is one of the key periods in the evolution of relative work, and I wouldn't miss it for anything.

What better communication between skydivers than movies? Let's have a running competition between drop zones all over the world — by movie — one big continuous meet with subgatherings like the Scrambles to revive the spirit. And we'll see who can boggle each other's minds with incredible flying.

Making movies creates an atmosphere that is as important as the movies themselves. And we'll have demo gatherings that start where today's meets end... with the fun jumping. Completely freeform — no rules. Hinckley started it a long time ago at Zephyrhills when they did the first 10-star — backloop — 10-star. Those guys had a lot of class; they helped set the tone of the Z'hills meet.

Another place jumping is going is formation flying... flying pieces around, flying unhooked up, mobiles, dynamic jumps. Just building things is okay, but flying them around and doing things with them is more fun and has more possibilities. Pieces that move around and change and exchange members...

Another place is three-dimensional work. Open your movie with six guys in a three-dimensional diamond — at 15,000 feet — going by some nice looking cumulus clouds — with the sun glinting off the convex mirrors people are wearing so they can see what is happening above them — making nice flashes in your star filter... and just when the audience has kicked back to groove on this, it starts to move and flow, like a three-dimensional dance...

I started this last Sunday on the way home, but we have been back over there again since then...

Yesterday was weathered out; today was perfect. On the first jump we started with a cluster made of three wedges — red, white and blue.

The plan was to build the cluster, separate into three wedges, do 360's, reform the cluster, hold it, then do 180's with the wedges and track them off for breakup. We took too long building the cluster and only got two of the wedges back together.

But the interesting thing about this jump is the planned breakup. Some of these jumps, especially the big ones, can get a little crowded at opening time. That's one nice thing about a star — when you do a 180 and track, you don't have two or three layers of people out in front of you. Eco, the guy who showed us the formation flying, said, "I just dive down to a grand or 600 feet and pull there." And he did. But that was a long time ago. Bob Federman once said, "Going low is a rush, but it's not practical." Succinct, and accurate.

Planned breakups are the obvious answer. They fit right in with this type of jumping. And they look good in movies and on demo jumps too. Like in Europe. The team is going. The meet director has OK'ed it. There are always a few problems — like money — but some version of the current team will be at the World Meet. Their main concern in Germany is that there be no interference with the meet. That's understandable. They can't guarantee any jumps — during the meet anyway. But I'm optimistic.

There is one jump that I want to tell you about — the way I saw it, if I can. We are on jump run in the Lodestar. Schafer gives the cut and three floaters — red and blue — climb out. The fourth is coiled low in the door. Dugan, the red point, is high in the door. I am hair-triggered up against his backpack and Schafer, the blue point is behind me. Ron Luginbill, the yellow point, is next with the remaining wing and slot people behind him as we compact ourselves into the pre-exit mass which, hopefully, will fire out the door with good flow and no gaps. The wing-mounted camera tells the whole story, and if you don't look sharp, it really stands out.

Dugan starts the (accelerated) count, using his fingers for the floaters outside the plane. "Ready! Ready! Threetwoone-GO!" Through the door and into the prop blast, flying formation off of Dugan's left wing as he goes straight out and then makes a swooping 180 left to take up his heading and position.

I am the left wing of the red diamond and I see Robin, one of the floaters on this jump and our right wing, is already flying loose formation on Dugan, waiting for me to move in. There are blue jumpsuits converging out in front and yellow ones off to my left in my peripheral vision, but mostly I am focused on Dugan...to hook up with the jumpsuit on the inside of his left knee, on his heading, without moving him even a tiny bit. Smooth — easy — fingertip relative work — fly into position and then grab hold — whoops! — last minute bobble — Aarrgghhh! — God dammit — unsmooth — unsmooth — and on film, too. But it doesn't do any damage and Robin is in a second later.

Glance at the blue diamond forming out in front and see that it has floated up about 30 degrees. Flash a look at the yellow diamond off to the left which looks about the same altitude and a little further out. Dig in with my right knee and concentrate on staying on heading with Dugan. Moments later Zinger, the red slot man, comes in. Then I really start to over-amp as I watch the blue diamond settle in — four guys — four times the momentum — all working together, and we dock with only a small warp. Look across at Tony DeRosa in the blue diamond.

Then I am completely blown away as the yellow diamond comes swooping in, like a big manta ray, so clean and nice. There is Hod, their right wing, only a couple feet away. He looks at me with about 6 yards of teeth-to-teeth looking in all directions at once — and luxuriating in that moment when you can read everybody's thoughts on the whole jump. Off to the right I spot Rande about 60 degrees up, shooting away. Then he drops down and shoots from underneath. We still have a few seconds left, so I lie there and try to take it all in. At 4,000 feet the diamonds do 180 right turns and track off.

I think that was a first, a record. I don't know. I don't care. I couldn't possibly feel any better about the jump than I already do. Anyway, B.J. is keeping a record of every jump — who went where and what happened. I'm just having fun making skydives with a very professional group of people — The United States Freefall Exhibition

Team. We were talking about it all one night after studying the films and B.J. said, "It's gonna spread like wildfire."

I think he is right. It sure gives me an airgasm.

Skratch Garrison, SCR-16, Parachutist, July 1975.

More Patterns in the Sky. If you dug Skratch's "Patterns In The Sky" thing (July *Parachutist*), then here's some more to whet your whistle. Skratch is a member of the U.S. Freefall Exhibition Team. He drove from Los Angeles to Casa Grande, Arizona to practice with the team every weekend throughout the spring. "When I think of the implications of what we're doing," he says, "it gets so interesting and complicated that I can't even keep track of it. Any size load and anything you can figure out how to do...it's a healthy development. The natural evolution from competition to cooperation. Speed stars taught us about exits. Now we have time to learn something about skydiving. *That* is exciting."

Here's Skratch's description of a *Venus Flytrap:* "It starts as a six-man star flying in front of a four-man diamond. The star opens into a line — the line and the diamond fly together — the line closes on the wings of the diamond — and the point of the diamond pulls out of it. What an interesting jump!"

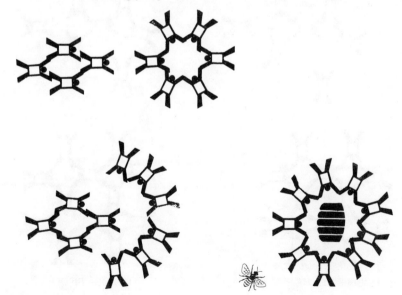

Skratch describes a *quadra-bipole:* "It starts as a four point donut-flake. The next four can come in like the first flakes did and make it a donut-double-flake. Or they can fly into the same slot backwards and form a quadra-bipole. It really changes the character of the jump. On all of these jumps each group or wave is supposed to fly in as a unit — all at the same time. It looks good when we do it right...

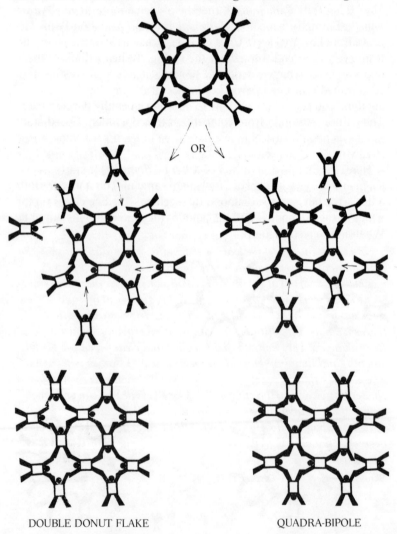

DOUBLE DONUT FLAKE   QUADRA-BIPOLE

"*Take a size 8, red donut-flake some Sunday afternoon and have four people in yellow fly in backwards to form a quadra-bipole...*

"*Schafer gives the cut. Rande backs out and swings to the rear, being careful not to bump his camera. Amazing. Constantly amazing. Camera jumpers are a breed apart from us ordinary skydivers.*

"*Grab ahold and start oozing around the door frame to the front. Urk! Strain! It's really windy out here, being forward floater. Zinger squeezes out between us. Twist down, looking under his left armpit–Melroy's face, counting: three-two-one-GO!! It's a neat position, forward floater, almost like coming from another airplane. The base dropping away and the rest of the load stringing up in a perfect curve leading right to the door.*

"*Start side-sliding down, and to the right–relativizing with the center of momentum of the initial diamond that is already starting to form. Settling in as they donutize, fine tuning with the flow of the donut. It's a good swoop–everything feels right. Grab the jumpsuit right where it's flapping on Melroy's left knee, right hand reaching for Zinger's left. Look up to see the happy, bearded smile. TAYLOR?!?!??? YAAGGGHHH!!!! I've spaced out and flaked the wrong slot. Let go like a hot potato and track-slide-hurry around to the right one! The jump continues, but we run out of time and don't finish it.*

"*Every time we try it we learn a little more. Yesterday–through the quadra-bipole into the breakup–through the grip switch into wedges–coming out of the turn and catch sight of the other three–and that's when you know. Off to the left...a little low–out in front...even with us–to the right...a little low. The electric realization! It's there–we have the altitude–we can do it–everybody knows it. Everything got very smooth and synched and clear–even the air felt smooth–and the jump started happening at 200 frames per second. The wedges flowed together–nearly a simultaneous dock–the last cluster grip closed on the other side–WE DID IT!!! You can yell much louder than you can type. They heard us on the ground.*

"*That's about as closely synched with 11 other people as I have ever been. We are clearly skydiving at the edge of our ability, and it is wonderful.*"

Skratch Garrison. RWu. October 1975

RW Game, by Tony DeRosa of Arizona:
Relay Relative Work
✱= a passable item
#1 has passable item on exit.
#2 takes passable item from #1 in freefall & faces out (right) from plane heading.
#3 coming from outside takes passable item from #2 & is facing left from plane heading.
#4 coming from inside takes passable item from #3 & is facing right from plane heading.
#1 pins #4 from outside, #2 takes near side; #3 around back.
"Optional, for hot dogs only" says Tony. "Do a backloop when you get the item (#1 does his backloop out of the plane). Do a 360° turn after you give it away, but still make a 4-man star by 2500 ft. Keep the deck in sight!"

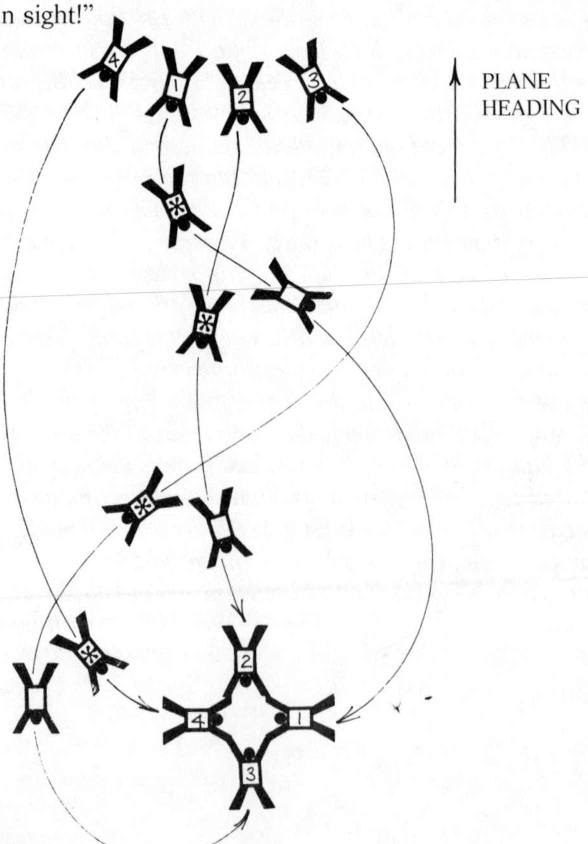

Double Diamond Dock, performed by jumpers from Seattle, Kansas and Arizona over Casa Grande recently. As described by Matt Farmer, "The diamonds flew about 30 ft. to a clean double dock...

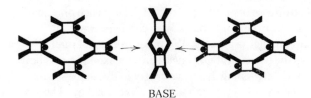

BASE

"Other-than-star-flying is not difficult, but there are some new flying positions and, of course, some new ideas. The symbolism used to draw out the dives is sometimes confusing but if you get four people standing around trying to hold on to each other like the drawing shows, it becomes a lot easier to see.

"Formations have really turned me back to where RW was at when we were all learning. On a formation jump the question is not how fast can we make this happen, but can I and all these other people pull it off, make it happen at all. Formations also make exit orders less important — with more happening up there, the base man might at some time during the jump be doing *a lot* of flying, and the last man can end up base.

"Maneuvers foster group consciousness — you have to know your place and everyone else's. On most maneuvers, your slot isn't even there until the people in front of you are in. In formations that are built by flying units together (as in the double dock), you must do RW as a group — and that's a unique, interpersonal experience at least!," says Matt.

RWu, June 1974

Sequential RW as Done by the Seattle-area People (1973). "It's more fun than all the jumps you have to make to be good at 10-man speed stars," says Craig Fronk of the "Clear Eye Express" 10-man team and the 4-man team of Bunky-Rocky-Herman-Frank which won the *RWu* Combined Championship RW Trophy at the '73 Nationals.

According to Craig, sequential requires more from all the people on the formation team. Mistakes on sequential make for a crash formation. No one can be late or get low because there are other people waiting for him to fill his position. Every man is assigned a particular slot and plays are run as in football. They use a playbook created by team member Ken (Gruber) Gorman.

"The 'plays' our formation team fly are hard to visualize, even on paper. We have to do a lot of ground practice. We start each play small and build up. A lot of the stuff that seems complex is simply constructed from smaller segments. We practice these 4-man segments to learn the basics of flying backward, for example, and how to switch grips. Grip switching gives symmetry in the sequence from maneuver to maneuver. The 'switch signal' system is key. The last man in shakes and it telegraphs up front. The key men drop or switch grips and the flyers run their pattern until the next maneuver is completed. We've found that loads of either 4, 10 or 16 give the best plays and sequence."

The "Clear Eye Express" is a competition 10-man team. "We do speed stars because that's the recognized form of large-star competition," explains Craig. (They placed 5th at the '73 Nationals). "We started out doing 4-man RW, then we had two 4-man teams. We added two and did 10-man RW. Then we just kept on jumping. We try to train people to do RW because it takes a lot of good flyers for our sequential. The only way to get them is to help them learn."

When they want to do a 16-man play they simply call everyone from all over the NW Conference. "It helps keep us together," says Craig. "It's probably the best warm-up jumping you can do for a 20-man attempt, too. It puts everyone's head in the right place for working together and flying properly. It eases the big-star jitters and generally mellows things out into lots of grins.

"Try it, you'll like it."

RWu, December 1973

MAIL ORDER
Enjoy these freefall goodies.....

1. "The Art of Freefall Relative Work," called the Bible of RW, considered the standard reference text, newly revised. Explains the technique of perfect flight utilizing the attitude of joy. (ISBN 0-930438-01-9) $7.95

2. "United We Fall," a collection of articles and short stories about skydiving. Includes fiction, jump stories and factual how-to's on every aspect of relative work. Exciting original illustrations. (ISBN 0-930438-02-7) $11.95

3. Skydiving Art Prints...prints of the original illustrations from the book "United We Fall." Lithographed on high quality paper, suitable for framing, signed limited edition of 11 drawings. Suite of 11: $20.00
(Includes the silver-foil "Art of Freefall" poster—sold separately—ask for #4, below—$3.00 each)

4. "Art of Freefall" poster, silver-foil reproduction, suitable for framing. $3.00

Available from book stores, parachute equipment dealers, or by mail.

How To Order:	quantity	amt. $
1. "The Art of Freefall Relative Work"	_____	_____
2. "United We Fall"	_____	_____
3. Skydiving art prints (suite of 11)	_____	_____
4. Silver-foil "Art of Freefall" poster	_____	_____
Additional for packing & shipping ($.80 per order)		_____
Sales tax, if any		_____
TOTAL ENCLOSED		$ _____

Normal delivery time is 2-4 weeks. California residents, please add 6% sales tax. Overseas orders, please add $4 per book or set of prints for airmail shipping.

Name _____

Address _____

State _____ Zip _____

Country _____

Send your name, address, zip code along with your check or money order (be sure to mention items desired!) to:

RW Underground Publications
1656 Beechwood Avenue
Fullerton, Calif. 92635

GIFTS! Send gifts to your friends. Select items above, and mention with your order:

"Gift from _____ to _____
              (your name)   (name of recipient)

_____ .
                    (address of recipient)

We'll include a handwritten note with the gift.